the
parent
survival guide

the
parent
survival guide

Positive Solutions to 41 Common Kid Problems

dr. todd cartmell

ZondervanPublishingHouse
Grand Rapids, Michigan

A Division of HarperCollinsPublishers

The Parent Survival Guide
Copyright © 2001 by Todd Cartmell
Requests for information should be addressed to:

ZondervanPublishingHouse

Grand Rapids, Michigan 49530

Library of Congress Cataloging-in-Publication Data
Cartmell, Todd, 1962– .
    Parent survival guide : positive solutions to 41 common kid problems / Todd
Cartmell.
        p.   cm.
    ISBN 0-310-23654-1
    1. Child rearing.   2. Parenting.   3. Parenting—Religious aspects—Christianity.
4. Discipline of children.   5. Behavior modification.   6. Parent and child.   I. Title.
HQ769.C34147   2001
649'.1—dc21   00-068670
                                                                              CIP

This book is not intended as a substitution for professional evaluation and treatment. If your child is experiencing significant behavioral or emotional problems, please consult a mental health professional.

The vignettes in this book are based on the author's personal and professional experiences. The names used are entirely fictional and any similarity to living persons is unintended.

All Scripture quotations, unless otherwise indicated, are taken from the *Holy Bible: New International Version®*. NIV®. Copyright © 1973, 1978, 1984 by International Bible Society. Used by permission of Zondervan Publishing House. All rights reserved.

Interior design by Melissa Elenbaas
Printed in the United States of America

---

01 02 03 04 05 06 /❖ DC/ 10 9 8 7 6 5 4 3 2

This book is dedicated to all of the children
and families with whom I have
had the privilege of working and from
whom I have learned so much.

Table of Contents

Introduction

"Can I have a snack?"

It all began with an innocent question from a three-year-old boy with a penchant for fish crackers. His dad, looking up from the kitchen table and considering that lunch concluded less than an hour ago, answered with a smile, "No, not right now, buddy."

What a cute little boy, the dad mused to himself as he turned his thoughts back to his work.

The father, however, had seriously underestimated the situation. Young Luke was skilled beyond his years in negotiating and was not about to throw in the towel. Undaunted, Luke walked over to the pantry where the snacks were kept, picked up a chocolate pudding and asked, "Can I have a pudding?"

Looking up again from his work, the dad felt his first tinge of annoyance. With a little stronger tone this time, Dad reiterated his initial verdict, "Buddy, we're not having snacks right now." *There, that should do it. After all, my little boy is really a very good listener*, the father thought.

Out of the corner of his eye, he saw Luke accept the pudding judgment and turn to put the package back on the shelf. Another parenting victory.

About ten seconds later, he felt a tap on his shoulder. "Can I have some goldfish?" Evidently, Luke felt the need to get a clear answer on every specific type of snack available in the pantry.

Fighting the temptation to snap back with, "Which part of no did you *not* understand?" the dad pushed his chair back, looked at Luke directly in the eyes, and said, emphasizing each and every syllable, "You're not having a snack right now!"

Aware that he was now feeling irritated by the intrusions, Dad assured himself that this episode had come to an end and returned to his work, trying to remember where he had left off.

"Can I have a fruit roll-up?"

Something snapped. Enough was enough. The father got out of his chair, walked over to his son, standing there with a fruit roll-up in his hand, and shouted with a voice that was probably heard in China, "You're not having any snacks right now!" The dad grabbed the fruit roll-up from his son's hands and slammed it back into the snack basket in the pantry.

Immediately, he knew that he was out of line, but he was too angry to even care or try to redirect himself. As Dad stood there and glared at Luke with a steely, angry gaze, he saw his young son's eyes slowly well up with tears.

That was the turning point.

Luke's lip-quivering face hit that father right between the eyes with the power of a freight train. Instinctively, he knew that his son's tears were not from being denied a snack. They were from a little heart that had been hurt by the one who is supposed to protect it. The dad had damaged his most prized possession over a square of sugary candy. He knew right then that he had blown it.

That dad was me. And the fact that I am a child psychologist did not matter to me at that moment. I knew that I had hurt my son and that my reaction had been wrong. I didn't have to ask myself what God thought about my behavior; the conviction in my heart was evidence enough.

Luckily, I was able to regain enough composure to kneel down, take my son by the hand, and apologize for my outburst. Even more luckily, Luke was gracious and quick to forgive his old dad for yet another blunder. "That's okay, Dad," he said, patting me on the back.

A three-year-old forgiving his thirty-five-year-old father. That's a picture for the memory book. We hugged, and I reminded him that he needed to listen when Daddy said, "No" and assured him that he could have a snack in a little while.

Luke simply said, "Okay" and went off to play with his blocks. The situation was over. But not for me.

I sat down and wondered how I had let myself get so out of control. I knew better than that. Where were all my years of training when I had needed them the most? Why didn't I just give him the option of accepting my decision about the snack or losing the chance of getting a snack altogether?

It sounded so obvious from the Monday morning quarterback chair. But somehow, the combination of my work demands, my own lack of control, and my son's persistence in his quest for a snack had been enough to tip my canoe completely over. I asked God again to forgive me for shouting at my son and failing to keep things in perspective. How could I be so quick to damage the things that are so priceless to me? I still had much to learn about handling the challenges of parenting.

That experience three years ago helped lay the groundwork for my writing this book. I know that as a typical parent, if I struggle with the everyday challenges of parenting, then many of you do as well. And although I love my two boys more than I can possibly describe, there have been moments when my frustration with their behavior has gone from one to ten in a split second—so much so that I have actually scared myself with how angry I felt. And this from a guy whose feathers are pretty hard to ruffle.

And what brought on these surges of anger?

- Muddy footprints on the carpet.
- Getting out of bed for the fifteenth time that night.
- Being untruthful to avoid getting into trouble.

That is, the regular, everyday stuff of parenting.

We all have to deal with many situations and behaviors that bewilder and frustrate even the best of us. Tantrums at the grocery store, arguments at bedtime, and squabbles with siblings are among the hundreds of challenges parents face every day. Sometimes we handle them well and feel a sense of pride, secretly wishing a TV crew had caught our parenting brilliance on tape for the next edition of *Oprah*. Other times, we know that we could have handled it better, perhaps much better. We feel ashamed our children have to bear the brunt of our inadequacy. But we don't know how to change. We're not sure exactly where we went wrong, or more importantly, where we could have gone right.

This book is designed to help you on that quest. God intends for you to be a wonderful parent. He did not design you to be a bad parent. He has entrusted his most prized possessions into your care and wants to walk alongside you as you love and raise and teach the children he has shared with you. And whatever it is that you may be lacking, he has in full supply.

These are not only kind and reassuring words; they are absolutely true. In Philippians 1:6, Paul reminds us that God, who started a good work in us, has the power to complete the job. In Ephesians 3:20, Paul stretches our minds to understand that God is able to do immeasurably more than all we ask or imagine, through his power that is at work in us. And Paul puts an exclamation mark on his point by declaring that we can do everything that God asks us to do when we rely on his strength (Philippians 4:13).

Do you think that part of God's plan for you is to have a godly and defining influence on the priceless children he has entrusted into your care? I believe it is. And he has allowed you a peek at the end of the book—you *can* become the parent that he has designed you to be! As he spoke to Jeremiah at the potter's wheel (Jeremiah 18), he is able to do wonderful things, even with a marred piece of clay, if that piece of clay will allow itself to be molded in the potter's hands.

Part of that molding process is learning. This book is designed to help you learn how to handle those "hard-to-handle" situations that perplex us all. During the last ten years, as I have worked at different locations while earning my doctorate from Fuller Theological Seminary, at the Children's Hospital of Columbus, Ohio, and in my current practice in Wheaton, Illinois, I have had the opportunity to see family after family where the parents felt stuck and didn't know how to respond to difficult childhood behavior.

We examined their previous attempts to solve the problems and experimented with new ways of handling things. Over the years, I have seen certain approaches meet with success and other approaches meet with failure. When certain approaches bring positive results a large majority of the time, you begin to take notice.

Of all the approaches I have seen parents use, the most effective can be summarized in the following list:

1. Creatively preventing the problem
2. Building and maintaining strong family relationships
3. Setting a healthy example for your children to follow
4. Teaching your children how to handle difficult situations
5. Making them glad that they did it right
6. Allowing them to experience that negative behavior never pays off

While this list may sound simple, we all know that it is not simple to do.

How can you creatively prevent Shawna from resisting bedtime each night? How do you build a strong relationship with Jason, a difficult and angry child? How can you set an example that makes a difference in Peggy's play behavior? How do you teach Tom to respond positively to sibling aggravation? How do you make Jessica glad that she told the truth when telling the truth got her in trouble? How do you help Andrew learn that arguing never pays off?

This book will help you find the answers to these questions. Focusing on children ages three through twelve, you will find many examples of how to prevent problems, strengthen relationships, model positive behavior, teach your children how to handle difficult situations, reinforce positive behavior, and provide effective negative consequences for many of the common "kid" problems that you face every day.

Not surprisingly, the basis for these parenting approaches can be found within the pages of Scripture. In Deuteronomy 6, one of the most powerful biblical passages on parenting, Moses instructs the Israelite parents to give their children a living example of what it means to genuinely love and obey God. Moses commands them to love the Lord with all their strength and to keep his commands fresh on their own hearts. He then exhorts them to teach God's commands to their children by discussing them and living them together through the ins and outs of everyday life.

At the heart of this process lies the continual effort to build strong family relationships that honor God and reflect his character.

We are to walk through life with our children, showing them by our own example how loving and obeying God guides, enriches, and fulfills every area of life.

The book of Proverbs, using the language of a father passionately preparing his son for life (see Proverbs 1–4), makes it clear that we are to teach our children how to make wise choices, help them learn that wise choices really do pay off (short-term and long-term), and allow them to experience the reality of the consequences that result from poor choices (check Proverbs 6:23; 19:18).

Some children exhibit behavior that is difficult to handle, resistant to change, and, if left untreated, can have a detrimental effect on their emotional and social development. As a result, some of you may need to consult with your pediatrician or with a qualified child therapist about your children's behavior if they pose a danger to themselves or others, if their behavior is having a significantly negative impact on their emotional, social, family, or school functioning, or if the problem persists despite your best efforts to resolve it.

The Bible identifies Solomon as one to whom God granted an extra portion of wisdom: "I will give you a wise and discerning heart, so that there will never have been anyone like you, nor will there ever be" (1 Kings 3:12). The words of this wise teacher, which were echoed years later by the apostle Paul (see Ephesians 6:4), are that we need to train our children in "the way [they] should go" (Proverbs 22:6).

You are the teacher that God has placed in your children's lives. As you present yourself to him as a humble and moldable vessel, he will shape you into the exact teacher your children need. It is my prayer that you will find this book to be a helpful and practical "hands-on" resource that will restock your shelves with effective teaching ideas and tools that will help your children handle the challenges that life will bring.

So, dust off your box of chalk, because the classroom bell has just rung and your students are waiting.

Glossary of Parenting Tools

The following are definitions for several of the terms that are used throughout this book. (More detailed explanations of these tools and approaches can be found in my *The Parent Lifesaver* [Grand Rapids: Baker, 1998].) All of these tools are extremely effective in teaching your child powerful and positive lessons about his or her behavior and helping your child learn to make better choices.

Detour Method

Proverbs 22:6 tells us to "train a child in the way he should go, and when he is old he will not turn from it." One of the most effective ways to stop a negative behavior is to teach your child a positive behavior to take its place. As the name implies, your goal is to help your child find a "detour" around the negative behavior by learning a better way of responding to a difficult situation. The Detour Method is most effectively used with children ages three through eight and has three steps:

D—Decide
E
T—Teach
O
U
R—Review

Decide. In the first step, you identify exactly what you would like your child to think, say, or do instead of the negative behavior. It often helps to break this into a three- or four-step plan. Younger children will do better with a simple one- or two-step plan. For example, a plan for picking up toys might be: (1) Say, "Okay, Mom" (when asked to pick up the toys); (2) start picking up the toys.

Teach. Explain this plan to your child (with older children, you can actually develop the plan together) and then practice it together during a positive time. Role play the positive behavior in situations where your child might typically misbehave. To increase their effectiveness, make these rehearsals brief, fun, and enjoyable for your child. Let your child know that he or she is doing a great job!

Review. Finally, review and rehearse the plan as needed, several times a week at first. Frequent rehearsal will help your child memorize the plan and will improve skill at using it in real-life situations. The more you practice the positive behavior together, the better chance that the plan will become more "automatic" for your child and that he or she will use this new skill when it really counts.

Fork-in-the-Road

When your child begins to misbehave, it is important for you to respond in a manner that will either redirect the misbehavior or allow your child to experience the appropriate negative consequences immediately. Giving your child a Fork-in-the-Road is a great way to accomplish these goals. A Fork-in-the-Road includes the following components:

1. A specific description of the behavior you want your child to do
2. A specific description of the negative consequence that will happen if your child does not do the desired behavior

The Fork-in-the-Road can be diagramed as follows:

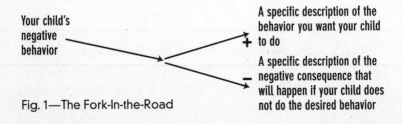

Your child's negative behavior

+ A specific description of the behavior you want your child to do

– A specific description of the negative consequence that will happen if your child does not do the desired behavior

Fig. 1—The Fork-In-the-Road

For example, if your child is ignoring your command to turn off the television and get ready for bed, you would immediately respond with a Fork-in-the-Road by saying, "Johnny, you need to get up, turn the TV off and get your pajamas on OR I will turn the TV off and you will go directly to Time-Out."

Once you have given your child a Fork-in-the-Road, allow between five to eight seconds for him to respond. You are looking for a verbal or physical response that indicates that he is listening and doing what you have asked. When your child listens, make sure to use the Pour-It-On technique to make him glad that he listened.

Remember, he was on the road of noncompliance and with a single reminder from you, decided to get back on the right road. Make him glad he did it!

If your child does not respond appropriately, then immediately administer the negative consequence, which may consist of a Logical or Natural Consequence, Response/Cost, or a Time-Out.

Regularly giving your child a Fork-in-the-Road when he begins to argue or display negative behavior will do several positive things. First, by giving the Fork-in-the-Road quickly, you will be able to either redirect the situation or administer the negative consequence (if needed) in a much calmer and more controlled way than if you had let the negative behavior continue indefinitely. It's pretty tough to stay calm and handle things right when you've been going back and forth with your child for five or ten minutes. With the Fork-in-the-Road, the situation is often brought to an end very quickly, which makes it much easier for you to administer the negative consequence in a respectful and effective manner.

Second, if you consistently give the Fork-in-the-Road immediately following your child's decision to behave negatively, you will help your child learn that negative behavior goes nowhere fast. In fact, just hearing a Fork-in-the-Road will eventually serve as a cue for your child, indicating that the arguing or not-listening game is over before it even had a chance to begin.

Third, by specifically describing the positive behavior you would like your child to do, you are literally increasing the chances that he may actually change behavior and avoid the negative consequence. When your child is arguing or not listening, he is not at his thinking best. He is choosing a negative solution to solve the problem. If there is a positive solution in his brain somewhere, it is packed up in a box in the basement and he is not likely to spontaneously find it on his own at that moment. When you use a Fork-in-the-Road, you are helping him by locating and unpacking that positive solution and putting it right on his front porch. This won't force him to choose it, but now he has a better chance. You have shown him the way out of the maze, you've lit up a neon EXIT sign before he has gone too far. And you'll be surprised at how often he'll take the hint.

Logical Consequences

Along with Time-Out, Logical Consequences will be one of your most frequently used discipline tools. The idea here is to make the negative consequence "logically" fit the misbehavior.

   The benefit of a Logical Consequence is that your child will learn a logical social lesson that can be more effective and can generalize to more situations than a punitive response, such as shouting or spanking. For example, losing television privileges for the day as the result of refusing to turn the television off is a Logical Consequence. Similarly, going to Time-Out after hitting a sibling is a Logical Consequence, as the privilege of free time is earned by treating other people respectfully.

Natural Consequences

A Natural Consequence is a negative consequence that is already "built-in" to the situation. Of course, it should be used only in a way that is safe for the child.

   For instance, if your child refuses to eat dinner or displays several instances of inappropriate mealtime behavior, a Natural Consequence would be the removing of his plate for several minutes, and he consequently will have to eat a somewhat colder or soggier meal. The Natural Consequence of lingering in the morning before school could be to be late for school and then experience the consequences that come from too many unexcused tardies.

Natural Rewards

Natural rewards are the activities that your child likes to do that are a natural part of her everyday life. Playing with friends, watching television, special snacks, fun toys—all of these are rewarding activities that your child regularly experiences. However, your child may not realize that these activities are actually the natural rewards of making positive choices.

One way to strengthen your child's positive behavior is to help her learn that there is a connection between her positive choices and these rewarding activities. You can easily do this by commenting on the connection when your child is about to participate in a natural reward.

For example, "Sure, you can turn on the TV, since you did such a nice job on your homework." Or, "Since you have listened so well today, I'd be happy to let you go to Julie's house to play."

Negative Thinking Traps

Scripture has much to say about the importance of our thoughts. Paul writes that we are being transformed by the "renewing of our minds." He continues, "Do not think of yourself more highly than you ought, but rather think of yourself with sober judgment, in accordance with the measure of faith God has given you" (Romans 12:2–3). Elsewhere he writes, "Whatever is true, whatever is noble, whatever is right, whatever is pure, whatever is lovely, whatever is admirable—if anything is excellent or praiseworthy—think about such things" (Philippians 4:8).

The quality of our thoughts is so important to God because they have such a powerful influence on our lives. If you control the rudder, you can steer the ship. Our thoughts are our rudders and God wants our rudders to be fully in line with his Word.

A negative thinking trap is a thought or belief that is distorted or untrue, either biblically, logically, or factually. These thoughts may be about yourself, another person, a certain situation, the past, or the future.

When a person falls into a negative thinking trap, one's perception becomes distorted and one's feelings and actions are likewise thrown off balance. We want your child to learn to think "true thoughts"—thoughts that are biblically, logically, and factually true.

Here are a few common negative thinking traps that children (and adults) fall into:

Overgeneralization: Arriving at a conclusion that is based on a single experience or piece of evidence and thinking that this signals a never-ending pattern. Following a poor math grade by thinking, "I'm no good at school!"

Magnification: Exaggerating mistakes and imperfections and "magnifying" them to be much more significant than they really are. Following an accidental burp in public by thinking, "That was the most embarrassing thing that could have ever happened to me!"

All or nothing thinking: Seeing things in black or white categories and leaving no room for mistakes. You either do it right or you do it wrong. If you don't do it perfectly, then you have failed. Following a missed attempt at a soccer goal by thinking, "I'm a lousy soccer player."

Mind reading: Assuming that you know why someone else did something or what another person was thinking. Following a presentation in front of the class by thinking, "They all think I did a terrible job!"

Disqualifying the positive: Insisting that positive experiences or successes don't count and focusing only on the negative experiences. Following an argument with a sibling (even though you often get along well) by thinking, "He is always bugging me!"

Personalization: Assuming that a situation or another person's behavior reflects negatively on you. Following the realization that a friend is talking to someone else during recess by thinking, "I guess he doesn't want to be my friend anymore."

When you suspect that your children may have fallen into a negative thinking trap, spend some time talking together about what they are thinking and feeling. Then, gently help them examine their thoughts by asking the following questions:

Where is the evidence for this thought?
What are the facts?
What does God say about this situation?
Does this thought fall into a negative thinking trap?
Is there a different way of looking at this situation?
What is the best way for me to handle this situation?

Without running roughshod over your children's feelings, help them develop a way of thinking that acknowledges the difficult experiences and emotions of life without leaving them stuck in the gutter without a ladder. While a situation may be difficult and your children may feel hurt or angry, true thinking does not stop there.

True thinking reminds us that God will walk with your children through every situation and give them the strength to handle it. There is always a way to cope with a situation, get support, or begin to put together a solution. A true thought in a difficult situation might be, "I feel sad that Alex is moving and I'll miss him a lot. But we'll always be special friends and we'll figure out a way to stay in touch." Or, "Math is hard for me this year, but lots of kids have a hard subject. God will help me to do my best and I'll get better if I keep on trying."

Pour-It-On Technique

Ecclesiastes 10:12 says, "Words from a wise man's mouth are gracious" and Proverbs 15:23 reminds us, "A man finds joy in giving an apt reply—and how good is a timely word!" The Pour-It-On Technique is a wonderful way for you to use your words to strengthen your child's positive behavior and to help your child conclude that obeying God and making good choices really pays off!

There are three steps:

1. Identify the behavior you want to strengthen.
2. Watch carefully for that behavior to happen.
3. Immediately give your child a specific, verbal reward when you see the behavior.

A specific, verbal reward tells your child that you are very happy with her behavior and lets her know *exactly* what she did that you are so happy about. You specifically tell your child what she just did or said, how quickly it was done, and the tone of voice that you so appreciated. For example:

"Susan, I love it that you just put on your coat when I asked you the first time!"

"Johnny, I just saw you do a great job of sharing with your sister! Way to go!"

"Hey Brandon, that was super listening to your mom and zipping up the stairs to get your pajamas on right when she asked you. What a good listener!"

The power of a specific verbal reward lies in the combination of parental attention (which is very rewarding) and a specific description of your child's positive behavior. If given every time your child displays a positive behavior that you are trying to strengthen (such as listening the first or second time), the Pour-It-On Technique will help your child conclude that positive behavior, even when it is takes a little work, is worth it.

Problem-Solving Steps

One way of viewing misbehavior is that your child has made a bad choice in the face of a difficult situation. You can help correct this problem by teaching your child to handle this situation more effectively. Best used with children eight years and older, here are the problem-solving steps that will help your child learn this important skill:

S—State the problem
T—Think of solutions
E—Evaluate the solutions
P—Pick a solution
S—See if it worked

First, help your child state what the problem is from his point of view. Then, he needs to identify at least three different solutions, or ways he can solve this problem. Next, he needs to evaluate each solution, identifying it as a positive or negative solution. If he has done these steps properly, he should be able to pick one or more solutions that will help him handle the situation in a positive way. Finally, he should pay attention to how his solution(s) worked out, so that he can learn from his experience.

You will need to help your child through the problem-solving steps a few times, until he gets the hang of it. Then, review them together when your child is faced with tough problems. Eventually, these steps can become a regular part of his decision-making process. See the section on "Solving Problems" for more detail.

Response/Cost

Response/Cost is a discipline or behavior-weakening tool. The idea is that every inappropriate response costs your child some portion of a privilege. For instance, if the daily privileges of television and video games have been divided into thirty-minute time segments, each instance of clearly defined disrespectful behavior can cost your child one thirty-minute segment of these activities, in addition to a possible Time-Out.

Response/Cost can also be used in conjunction with a simple contract where a certain number of daily points (for instance, five) are given at the beginning of each day and can be lost, one at a time, for instances of inappropriate behavior. The points that are left at the end of the day are kept and can be used to purchase privileges from your child's reward menu.

Simple Contract

A Simple Contract is a way of providing your child with powerful positive reinforcement for positive behavior. Often referred to as a point- or token-system, your child earns either tabulated points or tangible tokens that are kept in a token-bank. The points are earned for specific positive behaviors (chores, homework completion, respectful behavior) and can be used to purchase items or privileges from a reward menu that you and your child create together.

A reward menu might include special privileges such as playing a game, baking with Mom, going to the park, a special outing with Dad, staying up thirty minutes later, hosting a sleepover, renting a movie or video game, or a special family outing. Each item on the menu is worth a predefined number of points (for example: baking with Mom = 10 points, fishing with Dad = 25 points, and so on).

The points can be given immediately following positive behavior or they can be given ahead of time and then removed for instances of negative behavior, as in a Response/Cost program. It is also possible to include various negative consequences in a Simple Contract in a systematic way, by having certain privileges lost as the result of losing a predefined number of points.

For example, if your child has a Response/Cost contract where he begins each day with five points, then he can lose television privileges for the day if he gets down to two points. At one point, he loses television for the day and earns thirty minutes of early bedtime. If he loses all his points, he loses television and earns sixty minutes of early bed.

While Simple Contracts are an extremely fun and effective way to strengthen positive behavior, it is important to set them up carefully to achieve maximum effect. If you feel like you need a hand, an experienced child therapist can help you effectively design and administer a Simple Contract.

Time-Out

When used correctly, Time-Out is an effective discipline tool for children between the ages of two to twelve. Its effectiveness lies in pairing negative behavior with the immediate removal of all sources of positive reinforcement for a set period of time. For this reason, the actual Time-Out spot is very important, as it needs to be a location that is very *un*reinforcing for your child. This is why a bedroom is often an ineffective Time-Out spot, as there are so many positively reinforcing items that your child can look at or play with.

Three criteria for a good Time-Out spot are that it should be boring, safe, and easy for you to monitor. Once your child has chosen a Time-Out, administer the Time-Out in a calm and mat-ter-of-fact manner. I recommend starting with three minutes of Time-Out and adding one additional minute for each instance of inappropriate Time-Out behavior. For children two and three years of age, you can reduce the time segments slightly. If Time-Out lasts beyond thirty minutes (due to inappropriate Time-Out behavior), then bring Time-Out to an end by informing your child that Time-Out is over and that she has earned the loss of a daily privilege for not appropriately completing her Time-Out.

If you are away from home and an effective Time-Out spot is not immediately apparent, you can give your child a "Time-Out ticket," which signals that a Time-Out will be served immediately upon returning home. An effective Time-Out spot, consistency, and administering the Time-Out in a matter-of-fact way are the keys to making this an effective learning experience for your child. See the section on "Time-Out Troubles" for more detail.

Part 1

Common Home Problems

During our childhood years, we spend a great deal of our time in one place: home. We sleep there, eat there, play there, cry there, get mad there, and grow up there. You can think of your home as a schoolhouse, because the home is where the crucial first lessons of life are learned.

Your children learn many lessons at home. Lessons about relationships, honesty, and sharing. Lessons about how to handle it when they don't get their way. Lessons about working hard and being flexible when plans change. Lessons about what happens when they make the extra effort to deal with a difficult situation the right way and lessons about what happens when they succumb to the temptation to handle it the wrong way.

Your children also develop many habits at home. It has been said that our consistent behaviors turn into habits and our habits shape our character. We all have habits. Habits we are proud of and habits we wouldn't want anyone to know about. Habits of how we think, words we say, and actions we take. Your children are no different. You have a profound influence on the mental, spiritual, and physical habits your children develop, and as a result, on the formation of their character.

In this section, you will find ideas for how to teach your children to handle daily home situations in a way that honors God and respects others. You will help them learn to express their feelings respectfully, to examine their thoughts in light of their developing Christian worldview, to develop self-control, to learn positive coping strategies, and to learn from the positive or negative results of their choices. By so doing, you will be shaping their habits and, by logical extension, building their character and allowing them to experience the truth of God's loving commands.

At times, you will find comments indicating how an approach can be tailored for a younger or an older child. As a rule of thumb, for younger children, you will need to keep your approach more simple and concrete. For instance, when using the Detour Method with an older child, your "replacement plan" might include four distinct steps for handling frustration. With a younger child, in contrast, you would only use a two-step plan. Similarly, when teaching your child to think more accurately about a situation, you will need to move more slowly with younger children, giving them one or two "true thoughts" to learn, while an older child can handle more. To help you with this even further, I have provided a simple developmental guide (Appendix B: Your Child's Development) that you can use to help you gauge your responses to your child's developmental level.

Chapter 1

Accepting Consequences

The case of the broken record. Whenever Mr. or Mrs. Wagner told Andrew, ten, that he had earned a negative consequence, Andrew would launch into a routine of arguing and complaining that could have earned him an Emmy. Even though the Wagners would talk with Andrew and explain why he had earned the consequence, tempers eventually would rise, leading to a shouting match. Sometimes Andrew's mom and dad would forget what the original consequence was in the first place and be too worn out to enforce it anyway. Mrs. Wagner, especially, couldn't shake the feeling that Andrew was getting the best of her.

Why Does This Happen?

This is unfair! Sometimes a child will think that a consequence is unfair. Occasionally, he may be right. He may be getting into trouble for something his brother or sister did. Or an angry parent may give consequences that are overly punitive compared to the child's misbehavior.

While claiming that "This is unfair!" can also be used as a reaction against a justly deserved and reasonable negative consequence, older children tend to develop a pretty good barometer of what is fair and what is not. If your child honestly thinks that a consequence is unfair and does not know that he can talk to you about it at a later time, arguing may be the result.

Rewarding negative behavior may play a role in keeping your child from accepting his consequences. Remember that being given a negative consequence is an unpleasant experience for a child. If the inappropriate behaviors (for instance, whining, arguing, or shouting) are effective in delaying or (heaven help you) getting rid of the negative consequence, then those behaviors will be almost guaranteed to happen the next time you give a negative consequence.

Well-intentioned discussions can come at the wrong time. Many parents will talk with their children after the misbehavior in order to help them learn a lesson from the experience. It is a great idea to discuss the problem situation with your child in order to help him understand the relationship between his behavior and the negative consequences and to identify how he could have handled the situation differently. However, timing is everything. Having this type of discussion immediately after the negative behavior gives the child extra attention (which is a reward!) at exactly the wrong time and may inadvertently reward the negative behavior. On top of that, both you and your child are probably frustrated or angry immediately after his misbehavior, and your discussion will be more productive once everyone has had a chance to cool off.

What Can I Do?

Refuse to argue. If you don't want it to happen, don't do it. As long as you listen to your child's arguing, he will think that he still has a chance to make some headway and will argue even harder. When negative consequences are given, the only behavior that should be rewarded is appropriately accepting the consequence. Anything else, such as arguing, shouting, and so on, should never be rewarded. Once you have given the negative consequence, you should leave the area. It is harder to argue with you if you aren't there.

If you have given your child a consequence to be carried out at a later time, such as going to bed early, and he starts arguing, whining, or throwing a tantrum, just turn around and walk away. If your child becomes a "nomadic arguer," one that follows you from place to place, simply offer him a choice between stopping his arguing or going immediately to Time-Out.

Talk about it later. When you give a negative consequence, matter-of-factly tell your child why he is receiving the consequence and then administer it immediately. As a general rule, discuss your child's behavior and any lessons that can be learned from it *after* the negative consequence has been completed. This way, your child can experience a negative consequence *immediately* after his misbehavior, which will help him to learn that his misbehavior wasn't such a hot idea.

Talking about it later means that everyone will have had a chance to calm down and think about the situation, which will lead to a more positive discussion. If the negative consequence is one scheduled at a later time, you can discuss the situation with your child before the consequence is experienced, but only if he talks in an appropriate and respectful way. If he launches into argue mode, tell him that the discussion is over and you will talk later.

Depending on the situation, it may not be appropriate or possible to immediately discuss things, but your child needs to know that you will take the time to listen to his point of view. This does not mean that you are going to change the consequence or sit through an arguing match, but it does mean that you are committed to really listening to what he thinks and feels. Knowing that there will always be an open ear can go a long way toward building a strong relationship and reducing his need to argue when consequences are given.

Teach your child how to accept consequences. No two ways about it—accepting negative consequences is difficult. So, invest some time in teaching your child how to do it. During a positive time, tell your child that you want to help him get better at accepting consequences so that he can avoid getting into trouble. Let him know that you understand this can be difficult, but that you know he can learn how.

Using a child-friendly translation, read Proverbs 13:18 together ("He who ignores discipline comes to poverty and shame, but whoever heeds correction is honored"). Discuss why this is so. Think together about the following questions: What are the benefits of discipline and correction? What can discipline teach you? What kind of lessons does God want us to learn? How can discipline make a person wise?

Then, using the Detour Method, come up with a plan together for how he should respond when negative consequences are given. The plan can include things to think, say, or do. Make sure that the plan is specific and age-appropriate.

For example, even though your child may be upset when told to go to his room, he can learn to think, "Arguing will just get me into trouble," "I need to listen to Mom," or "I should listen now and talk about it later." A younger child should be given one simple sentence to think, such as, "I should listen to Mom." Then he can say, "Okay," and then go to his room. Once in his room, he can work on calming himself down by taking deep breaths and thinking about the best way to handle the situation.

In another example, if your child thinks that being sent to Time-Out is unfair, he can ask, "Mom, can we talk about this later?" and then go to his Time-Out, knowing that he can talk to his mother about it when the Time-Out is over. Pick common problem situations and talk about positive ways that your child can respond to receiving a negative consequence.

Reward the desired behavior, using the Pour-It-On Technique. After you have taught your child how you would like him to respond when consequences are given, you can remind him to use his new plan when you see a problem situation coming. When you see him use his plan, or even take a small step toward accepting his consequences without arguing, let him know that you appreciate his efforts and point out the specific positive behaviors that you noticed. If you make him glad that he made an effort to improve, a second effort may not be too far away.

Make sure arguing never pays off. In addition to teaching your child how to accept consequences and giving him positive feedback when he does it, negative consequences need to be used to help him learn that arguing doesn't pay off. You can ignore the behavior and just walk away. Or you can calmly give your child a Fork-in-the-Road, allowing him to choose between stopping the arguing (in other words, talking respectfully) and experiencing a Time-Out or loss of a privilege (such as going to bed thirty minutes early).

Response/Cost can also be used with this behavior. For example, each day your child would start out with a set amount of points, such as three. He would lose one point for each display of inappropriate behavior when given a consequence. Each point could be traded in for a daily privilege, such as thirty minutes of television or computer time. If he kept two points, he could watch television or play on the computer for one hour. If his points were gone—no television or computer for the day.

Be consistent. If your child has had trouble accepting consequences for the past year, do not expect the habit suddenly to vanish after a few days of making some changes. He should begin to change his behavior when *he* realizes that the rules have changed and that they are going to stay that way. In order for this to happen, you must come up with a good plan and stick to it.

 ## How Do I Put It All Together?

The case of the broken record. Mr. and Mrs. Wagner decided their arguing days were over. They spent some time thinking about the approach they wanted to take and then talked to Andrew. "We feel really frustrated when you argue about your consequences," they said, "and we want to help you come up with a plan to handle things better." "But, I don't argue ..." Andrew began instinctively, but Mrs. Wagner refused to enter into this argument.

She matter-of-factly explained to Andrew that from this point on, she and his father would expect him to promptly follow through with the consequences without arguing. If not, she would give him a choice: "If you start to argue with me about your consequences, I will give you a Fork-in-the-Road. You can choose to immediately stop arguing or you can choose the additional consequence of thirty minutes early bed" (a fate worse than death!).

Andrew's parents also explained that there would be times when he may have a legitimate question about the situation or consequence. "If you have a question," Andrew's dad explained, "you can ask it *after* you've done your Time-Out. If the consequence is for later on, such as no TV or early bed, then we can talk about it after waiting ten minutes and only if you talk in a respectful way."

Mr. and Mrs. Wagner figured this would give Andrew time to cool down and to think about the best way to ask his question. They reminded Andrew that after their discussion, they would still expect him to accept their final decision about the consequence. Occasionally, Mrs. Wagner quizzed Andrew on the new steps and they briefly role-played a few practice situations, allowing Andrew to get used to using his new plan.

Mr. Wagner took time to talk with Andrew about discipline. Together they read Proverbs 13:18 from Andrew's Bible and discussed the benefits of following God and learning from your mistakes.

"Why do you think the Bible says that about discipline?" asked Mr. Wagner. Andrew said he didn't know. Mr. Wagner asked him whether or not he might think that discipline is supposed to help us learn something."

Andrew said yes, and Mr. Wagner continued: "What kind of things do you think discipline can help us learn?"

Andrew thought for a moment, "Well, it can help us see what kind of things don't work out too good." Mr. Wagner smiled. "That's a good way to put it."

Mr. and Mrs. Wagner were also faithful with the Pour-It-On Technique. For example, they would say things like, "Hey, Andrew, that was a real nice job of staying calm when Mom told you to go to Time-Out." They made it a point to provide lots of positive feedback when they noticed Andrew controlling his arguing.

Initially, Andrew continued to argue following his consequences. But he began to realize that his parents had truly changed their tune and arguing didn't pay off as it used to. Mrs. Wagner simply walked away when he began to talk back, and he found himself going to bed early on many occasions, which he did not like at all. Andrew's parents remained consistent with their approach even though Andrew's arguing habit did not suddenly stop. They felt confident they were helping Andrew to learn the right lessons. As time went on, Andrew's behavior did begin to improve. He learned that things worked out much better for him when he accepted his consequences and decided that arguing wasn't such a hot idea after all.

Chapter 2

Bedtime

The case of the midnight intruder. "What I wouldn't give for Shawna to just stay in bed," said Mrs. Hawkins, looking as if she hadn't had a good night's sleep in weeks. "It's a battle every night. She must get out of bed at least ten times between nine and twelve o' clock. And by the last time, I'm about ready to strangle her!" Shawna was the first Hawkins child and she had just turned three. Mr. and Mrs. Hawkins had tried changing Shawna's bedtime and threatening her with a spanking if she got out of bed. Sometimes they just let her stay up until she fell asleep and then quietly carried her off to bed.

Why Does This Happen?

Going to bed is no fun! What child likes to go to bed? In a child's mind, going to bed means missing out on whatever else is going on in the rest of the house. They don't want to miss out on the action! And to make it worse, they don't even get a vote in the matter. It is perfectly natural for a child to show resistance to bedtime. You probably did the same thing when you were a kid. Remember to think about it from your child's point of view.

Parental attention is very rewarding to a child. In a situation like this, many children find that they get extra attention by getting out of bed. Sometimes Shawna would get to stay up, sometimes she would get a backrub, and so on. This served to reinforce the getting out of bed behavior. In short, Shawna has learned that getting out of bed equals more attention from Mom and Dad.

Inconsistency is another common culprit. Sometimes Shawna would be marched right back to bed. Sometimes she would get a glass of water. Shawna learned that there is a fifty-fifty chance of getting something good. So, why not get up?

Putting themselves to sleep is a skill children learn. If they are not going to sleep regularly without too much of a problem, chances are that they have simply not yet learned how to. It is a significant task for young children to learn how to stay in bed all alone (knowing that others are awake and having fun), soothe themselves, and put themselves to sleep. And much like toilet training, this is a task that they often have no intrinsic interest in learning. They would be very happy to fall asleep in your arms every night or watch TV until they can no longer stay awake. But, with a little encouragement and guidance, most children learn how to go to sleep on their own without too much trouble.

What Can I Do?

Have reasonable expectations. Most children have some amount of difficulty learning how to stay in bed and put themselves to sleep, but most eventually learn how to do it. Remind yourself that this is normal childhood behavior and that if you respond in a thoughtful manner, chances are that your child's bedtime behavior will fall into place.

A calming bedtime routine will make bedtime enjoyable and predictable. Clearly, this does not mean having a version of Wrestlemania in your child's bedroom. We want enjoyable but *calming* activities that will happen in the *same order* every night.

Doing things in a consistent order makes the evening predictable for your child and signals that bedtime is coming. There are many different ways you can arrange a good bedtime routine. I recommend activities such as having a drink or small snack, telling stories, talking about the day, reading a book, singing songs, saying prayers, and other quiet but fun activities. If you're having trouble getting the less pleasant tasks done, like teeth brushing, make sure it's tackled *before* the fun stuff.

The bedtime routine that we currently have with our children includes getting pajamas on, brushing teeth, taking vitamins, going to the bathroom, having a small glass of water, saying our prayers, and reading a short story or talking for a short while—in that order. Sometimes, we will have a thumb wrestling contest or play a bedtime game. For example, we might tell a silly story (reminiscent of church camp days) where I make up a story and my boys get to provide either silly adjectives or nouns to help create the story ("There once was a big, *(adjective)*, *(noun)* who liked to wear *(adjective)* *(noun)* on his head . . .").

As you might imagine, bedtime can take up to fifteen or twenty minutes each night. But it is worth every minute. Not just because it helps reduce nighttime problems, but also because it is a rewarding time that I wouldn't trade for anything in the world.

Make sure that "out of bed" behavior is not rewarded. Parental attention, getting to stay up later, a glass of water, a snack, and so on, will only reward the getting out of bed behavior. When your child gets out of bed, she should receive as little attention as possible.

Instruct her to get back into bed and guide her there if you need to, providing as little attention as you can. If you walk her to her room, then get her into bed, say "goodnight," and leave. Don't be mean, just firm. Remember, the only behavior that should be rewarded is staying in bed.

Give attention for appropriate bedtime behavior. If it is attention that your child wants, give it to her. But not for getting out of bed! How about for staying in bed! Using a timer, tell her that you will come in to see her again if she stays in bed until the timer dings. Set it for only two or three minutes the first time, to make it easy.

When the timer dings, go in and spend about a minute giving her a kiss and a hug and telling her what a great job she did staying in bed. Let her know that you will come back again if she stays in bed, this time in five minutes. Slowly increase the amount of time on the timer. This way, she is motivated to stay in bed for longer periods of time and will have an opportunity to learn to soothe herself and fall asleep on her own. Staying in bed is being rewarded and getting out of bed is not.

Use Response/Cost to address this behavior. Buy a bunch of stickers (or pennies, chips, or whatever you would like) and place a few of them on the dresser, out of reach. Let your child know that she will lose one sticker each time she gets out of bed. The stickers that remain in the morning will be hers to keep.

Create a simple menu that will allow her to trade her stickers in for a fun activity or privilege, such as picking a special cereal in the morning if she keeps four of her five stickers. Sometimes, just earning fun stickers is enough of a reward for some children to improve their behavior.

When she gets up, guide her back to bed, let her know that she has lost one sticker, remove it, encourage her to stay in bed and thereby keep the rest of her stickers, and leave. In the morning, provide her with lots of positive attention for the stickers she has kept and encourage her to do as well or better next time. This approach will be most successful if you keep it fun. As she improves, require more stickers for the special privilege until you do not need to use the stickers anymore.

Give a Time-Out. If your child repeatedly shouts or gets out of bed, you can administer a Time-Out. If you have chosen a good Time-Out spot, then lying in a warm, cozy bed will start to look pretty good to your child after a few Time-Outs. When the Time-Out is completed, quickly escort your child back to bed and encourage her to stay in bed and go to sleep.

Be consistent. Whatever plan you choose, stick with it. Don't give in and allow the out-of-bed behavior to be rewarded. Inconsistency will confuse her and make the problem that much more difficult to resolve. Being consistent may mean some temporary inconvenience for you, but believe me, it's worth it in the long run.

Once a pattern of appropriate bedtime behavior has been well established, you can make exceptions now and then if you want to. But in the initial learning or training phase, come up with a reasonable plan and stick with it!

How Do I Put It All Together?

The case of the midnight intruder. Mr. and Mrs. Hawkins decided to put together a plan to address Shawna's out-of-bed behavior. Just having a plan and reminding themselves that this is an extremely common preschool-age problem helped them reduce the pressure they had placed on themselves to "fix" Shawna's behavior.

They decided on a bedtime routine that consisted of getting pajamas on, brushing teeth, having a glass of water, reading a book or two in bed, and saying prayers. Once the routine was finished, they gave Shawna a big kiss and hug and then set a timer (just outside the door) for two minutes. They told Shawna, "If you stay in bed until the timer dings, then one of us can come back and see you for a few more minutes and rub your back. If you get out of bed before the timer dings, then you have to get right back in bed and we have to start the timer all over again. Remember, we can only come to see you if the timer dings!"

The timer was initially set for two minutes, then five, then ten, and so on. If Shawna got out of bed at any time, she was quickly marched back into bed, with only enough parental attention (and no glasses of water) given to get her back into bed. The timer was then reset and Shawna was encouraged to stay in bed.

Initially, Shawna cried when her parents left the room and proceeded to get out of bed several times a night. However, Mr. and Mrs. Hawkins calmly and firmly escorted her back to her bed each time, encouraging her to stay in bed until the timer dinged. When Shawna did make it until the timer dinged, her parents were very excited and let her know what a great job she did staying in bed ("Hey, you did it! That's a great job staying in bed by yourself! Now, I can come and see you for a little bit more!").

Despite the tears, Shawna began to learn that getting out of bed did not result in anything fun, while staying in bed got an extra visit from her mom or dad. Within about a month of consistently following this routine, Shawna's excursions from the bedroom decreased considerably, and like most other children Shawna eventually learned to stay in bed through the night, much to her parents' relief.

Bedwetting

The case of the soggy sheets. Jonathan, almost five, had never managed to stay dry during the night for more than a week or two in a row. Occasionally, he would wet the bed two or three times a week. Mr. and Mrs. Davis were beginning to wonder if there was something wrong with him.

A few months ago, Jonathan began making good progress and his parents thought that this issue was finally behind them. But then the family moved, and the change seemed to flush away whatever gains had been made. Mrs. Davis was getting tired of constantly changing his sheets and was starting to think that this problem would never go away.

 ## Why Does This Happen?

Developmental maturity plays a big role. Kids can develop differently from one another and still be within the "normal" range. Some children are quick to develop one ability and slow to develop another. In this way, establishing the ability to maintain a dry bed is no different than many other developmental tasks.

Approximately 20 percent of five-year-olds struggle with bedwetting. Almost all of them grow out of it by their mid-teens. For some children, the communication process between their brain and their bladder has not fully matured. Others have simply not yet learned how to control their bladder well enough to stay dry for a full night. Others may have a relatively small bladder, which can make staying dry overnight understandably difficult.

Basically, children have to be physiologically able to sense the signals that indicate a need to urinate, learn to respond to those signals, and be able to hold a full bladder long enough to get to the bathroom. Patience, reassurance, and a little training are usually enough to do the trick.

Emotional upset is behind the bedwetting of some children, but not most. Stressful circumstances, such as moving, starting school, the birth of a new sibling, and so on, can result in increased bedwetting. The goal, of course, is to help your child adjust to the new circumstances and learn to keep a dry bed at the same time.

A physical cause is a possibility but not a probability for most children. A legitimate physical problem, such as a urinary tract infection, can contribute to your child's bedwetting problem. This is why a physical examination is always the first step in addressing this problem if it persists past the age of five.

What Can I Do?

A physical examination should be the first step to addressing bedwetting that persists past your child's fifth birthday. Your child's pediatrician needs to rule out any physical problems that may be making it difficult for your child to stay dry overnight. If physical obstacles to nighttime bladder control exist, then your doctor will advise you on how to proceed. If not, then you can proceed with the recommendations below. If your child is under five and you are really concerned about bedwetting, you can still check with your pediatrician about it.

Keep your cool. Chances are that your young child's bed-wetting is perfectly normal. If your child is in the elementary years, there is a good chance that he will naturally grow out of it or that you will be able to do something that will help. Remind yourself that if you take the appropriate steps, your child's ability to hold a full bladder through the night should develop with time.

Use a mattress pad. One good idea during a bedwetting period is to use a plastic mattress pad. Not only will this extend the life of your child's mattress, but it will make the clean-up easier and can help reduce your child's embarrassment.

Never embarrass your child. Bedwetting is not your child's fault. Most children want very much to stay dry during the night. Help your child to understand that staying dry overnight is an ability that develops with time. Do not scold, punish, or embarrass your child for wetting the bed. Instead, calmly supervise the clean-up, reassure your child, and express your confidence that he or she will master this skill in time.

Sphincter control and urine retention exercises are helpful for some children. It is the sphincter muscle that controls the flow of urine; greater control over this muscle can increase your child's ability to hold a full bladder until the bathroom can be reached. When your child urinates during the day, this muscle can be strengthened by having the child stop and start the flow of urine several times during urination. This type of practice should be gently guided by parents at first. It may even become fun as your child experiences greater control over urine flow.

Urine retention refers to your child's ability to hold a full or partially full bladder. I'm sure you know what a valuable skill this can be, especially when you are driving cross-country and have just passed the last rest stop for thirty miles! In order to improve this ability, have your child drink as much as comfortable and then pay attention to the signals indicating the need to urinate (this exercise is best done at home!). At the first urge, have your child tell you and then "hold" the urine for as long as possible, up to ten or fifteen minutes. Start with a minute or so if that is all your child is able to do. With practice, most children are able to hold their urine for ten to twenty minutes with ease. The combination of sphincter control and urine retention exercises will help your child improve the ability to control the release of urine and can have a positive effect on nighttime control.

A urine alarm is effective in helping a child learn to keep a dry bed. There are different versions of this approach. Some use a pad that is connected to a bell or buzzer; others have metal snaps that attach to the child's underwear and are connected to a wrist alarm. The main idea is the same: an alarm goes off when urine is detected. The child is awakened and, if all goes as planned, heads for the bathroom to finish urinating. Pajamas and bedding must then be immediately changed. The challenge is for your child to learn to "beat the buzzer" by waking up to urinate prior to the buzzer going off.

This is one of the most effective approaches currently available and can effectively be used in conjunction with many of the other suggestions described in this section. Once your child begins to stay dry regularly, slowly reduce the number of nights that you use the urine alarm. I recommend a urine alarm for children who are experiencing consistent problems with bedwetting and are at or close to five years of age (or older). You can check with your pediatrician about where to purchase a urine alarm in your area.

Positive practice can help increase nighttime dryness, particularly when used in conjunction with a urine alarm. Before you turn the lights out, have your child lay in bed for about thirty seconds and imagine feeling the need to urinate. Then have your child contract the sphincter muscle, get up, and go to the bathroom. The child must sit on the toilet for twenty to thirty seconds, whether or not any urination occurs. Repeat this exercise ten or fifteen times each night before bed during the initial phase of using the alarm. As bladder control improves, you can have your child practice fewer nights each week.

Have your child help clean up after wetting the bed. This means that immediately after discovering a wet bed, you have your child go to the bathroom, clean himself, change pajamas, and help change the bedding. If the child sleeps through the wetting, he will do the clean-up routine immediately upon waking up.

If your child is young, be prepared to help with the bedding change; older children can learn to change the bedding by themselves. This is not meant to be a punishment and should definitely *not* be presented as such. In fact, parents should make this a very straightforward process. The message is simply that when your child wets his bed, he helps clean it up.

Chips or stickers can also be given for keeping a dry bed. The chips can be used to purchase special privileges or activities from a menu. For instance, five dry nights may earn a special new set of sheets, or a trip to the zoo. Have your child keep a record of dry nights by placing a sticker or writing a "D" (for every dry night) on a calendar. However, the primary emphasis should not be placed on the chips earned, but rather on your child's effort and his success at learning a new skill, namely, staying dry during the night. The stickers or chips are just to help make it fun and to reward good effort.

Be encouraging. Give lots of positive feedback as you observe your child making an effort to keep a dry bed. Remember, he is learning a new skill and we want him to feel encouraged about his efforts to do so. During sphincter control and urine retention exercises, clean up, positive practice, or urine alarm use, let your child know that you admire his efforts and that you are confident that he will succeed.

How Do I Put It All Together?

The case of the soggy sheets. Mrs. Davis took Jonathan to his pediatrician to discuss her concerns about bedwetting. The doctor warmly reassured her that there was nothing physically wrong with Jonathan and that this was a very common problem for children his age. He also underscored that Jonathan had already begun to make good progress in staying dry that had been temporarily upset by the recent move—another common occurrence.

Given the doctor's reassurance, Jonathan's parents decided to take a low-key approach. Mrs. Davis reminded herself that this is a very common preschool problem and bought a plastic mattress pad. Thinking about their recent move, they decided to delve a bit deeper into how their son was handling the new changes in his life.

"So what do you think about our moving here and going to a new school?" Mrs. Davis asked Jonathan.

"It's okay," he answered quietly, shifting his gaze to the ground. As they continued to talk, Mr. and Mrs. Davis discovered that Jonathan was missing his old friends and was still adjusting to his new environment. His mother provided reassurance that he would make new friends at his new school. They prayed together that God would watch over Jonathan's old friends and help him meet new friends. They even decided to write a letter together to a few of his old friends and send them a picture that he had drawn and photos of Jonathan's new house and school.

"Honey, why don't you pick a boy from your preschool class that you think is nice, and I'll talk to his mother and see if we can meet together to play at a park." Mrs. Davis suggested.

After thinking for a couple seconds, Jonathan's eyes opened wide, "Maybe I could ask Bobby." His mother couldn't help but notice the anticipation on his face.

Mr. and Mrs. Davis assured Jonathan that bedwetting happens to many children his age and that most children learn to stay dry overnight with time. "Y'know Jonathan," his father said, "lots of kids your age wet their beds sometimes at night, but they all grow out of it sooner or later. If you want to, there are some things that you can do that can help your body learn to stay dry at night a little faster. Would you like to try some of them?"

Jonathan was very interested, so they developed a nighttime dryness plan. Mr. Davis taught him how to do sphincter control and urine retention exercises to help build his ability to control and hold his urine flow. With a little practice, Jonathan mastered these exercises easily and thought the sphincter control exercises were fun. They also agreed that Jonathan would help clean up after nighttime accidents and came up with a routine where Jonathan was responsible for sitting on the toilet to finish urinating, cleaning himself, changing his pajamas, putting his wet clothes in the hamper, and helping to change his bedding. Jonathan did positive practice right before bed every night for the first two weeks and every other night for the next two weeks. Following that, he did positive practice only if he had wet his bed the previous night.

They decided to have Jonathan keep a sticker chart for dry nights, with every five stickers earning a special privilege. When he saved a total of twenty-five stickers, Jonathan would get a new Star Wars sheet and pillowcase—something he was really excited about! Jonathan's parents regularly praised his effort to stay dry and emphasized the fact that he was beginning to learn an important new skill.

Mr. and Mrs. Davis were careful not to criticize or embarrass Jonathan in any way for wetting and treated accidents in a calm and matter-of-fact manner. They decided that they would talk to the pediatrician about getting a urine alarm if significant problems continued past Jonathan's fifth birthday.

In their nightly prayers, they thanked God together for helping Jonathan get better at staying dry: "Lord, please help Jonathan to keep getting better at staying dry at night. Thank you that he is such a hard worker and we know that you will help his body to learn to stay dry at night, even if it takes a little while. Thanks for loving us and for listening to us and please help us to keep working and not give up."

As Jonathan gradually started to make some new friends and followed his nighttime dryness plan, it wasn't too long before he began to pick up where his progress had stopped before the move. He occasionally complained about his positive practice and having to help change his sheets, but stuck with his plan fairly well. Within six weeks, Jonathan had managed to go five consecutive nights with a dry bed and was wetting only one or two times a week. By three months, he was often going seven to ten days between accidents and had earned his Star Wars sheets. Everyone, including Jonathan, was delighted with his progress. While occasional nighttime accidents occurred into the next year, Jonathan continued to make progress and achieved regular nighttime dryness well before his sixth birthday.

Breaking Toys

The case of the broken spaceman. Mr. and Mrs. Taylor looked very perturbed as they described how their eight-year-old son, David, failed to care for his toys. Although they had explained to him that toys do not grow on trees, they said he was still so rough with them that he cracked, broke, or maimed about one a week.

The latest broken toy was a new spaceman that his grandparents had bought for him. David was pretending that the spaceman could fly and threw him across the room. Unfortunately, a wall stopped his flight and cracked his helmet in the process. David was entirely unaffected by the incident and simply turned to play with another toy, of which he had many. Two weeks later, after some award-winning begging and pleading, David got a new rocket ship that he had seen on television.

 ## Why Does This Happen?

Too many toys. In David's case, he did not mourn the loss of his spaceman because he had a whole warehouse of other toys to turn to. Having too many toys and possessions can result in a child not learning to appreciate their value. While retailers may try to tell you otherwise, fewer toys on birthdays and Christmas can go a long way in helping a child to realize that toys really do not grow on trees.

Overlooking the positive. It is easy to get so busy with the everyday details of life that you forget to give your child positive feedback for good behavior. When is the last time you pulled your child aside and told her what a great listener she is or that you saw her put something away without being told to? If you are overlooking your child's positive behavior, then don't be surprised if you don't see it as often as you would like. Remember, plants grow much better with a little water and sunshine.

Ineffective discipline is another common culprit. When a child chooses to treat possessions in a careless or destructive manner, what is the result? Your child's immediate experience should consistently lead to the conclusion that being reckless or destructive with toys is not a good idea.

Inconsistent or ineffective negative consequences, such as yelling or lecturing, will not get the job done. Consistent and effective negative consequences are a must if a child is going to learn that positive behaviors pay off and negative behaviors don't.

Emotional upset is another reason why a child may "act out" with his toys. Watch for a sudden change in the way your child interacts with others or plays with toys. A sudden change in behavior is often a clue that something may be upsetting your child. Problems with family members, friends, grades, or peer pressure (among other things) can be difficult to contend with, and negative behavior may be a way of expressing frustrated and angry feelings or a method of getting your attention.

 ## What Can I Do?

Talk with your child about what is going on. Let him know that you are concerned about the way he is playing with his toys and that together you need to find a better solution. Explore the possibility that something might be upsetting or bothering him, doing your best to listen in an open and non-threatening way. This will make it easier for him to be honest about what he is thinking and feeling.

If there doesn't seem to be an emotional upset at the root of the problem, then find out what your child thinks appropriate play behavior actually is. What does he think about breaking his toys? What does he think will happen after he breaks a toy? What consequences does he think should happen when he is reckless or destructive with his belongings?

You can also have your child recount the many ways that God has blessed him. Then ask, "If God wants us to be grateful for the blessings he has given us, how can we show him that we are thankful?" Your child's responses to these questions will likely be both helpful and insightful.

Take care of your own things. If you are reckless, careless, or destructive with your possessions, it is extremely likely that your child will conclude that this is the way to care for his things as well. Books, magazines, CDs, clothing, furniture—everything counts. If you would like your child to take care of his toys and belongings, make sure that he sees you doing the same with yours.

Provide an outlet for "rough and tumble" activities. If your child enjoys more rigorous physical activities, then provide him an opportunity for this type of play. Let him know what the rules are (such as no pushing, waiting for a turn, no breaking things) and let him go. Take him to a park, play baseball, wrestle, enlist him in sports, go to a play area located at a fast food restaurant, or just go to an unpaved road and throw rocks. The good thing is that you will be burning off energy and having fun.

Set clear guidelines. Take the time to clearly explain the different rules that apply to "outside" and "inside" play. Make them simple and understandable and then stick to them. If certain toys can be thrown, such as a soft ball in the playroom, then make this clear. Physically demonstrate for your child what he can and cannot do with his toys so that there will be absolutely no misunderstanding.

Take the time to explain the reasons why he needs to look after his things. For example, he should take good care of his belongings because they will last longer; if he breaks them, he will not have them to play with any more; God wants us to take good care of the things he has given us. Review the guidelines and the reasons for them as often as needed.

Point out positive behavior. Using the Pour-It-On Technique, watch carefully for your child to play appropriately with his toys. If you have determined that he plays too rough with a toy about once for every hour of playtime, then watch for him to play appropriately for about thirty minutes. Then, immediately go over to him, placing your hand on his shoulder, and say, "Johnny, you are doing a great job of playing nicely with your toys! That's just how God wants us to look after our things!" Regularly pointing out his positive play behavior in this way will make looking after his toys a rewarding, and repeated, experience.

Respond immediately to destructive play behavior. Your child has to learn that purposely reckless or destructive play never pays off. This is not done just by telling him, but by showing him. A Time-Out after breaking a toy will help him learn that destructive choices result in an immediate loss of playtime.

In certain situations, the loss of a privilege (such as playtime, having friends over) is an appropriate negative consequence. The broken toy will not be replaced any time in the foreseeable future and, if your child is older, he can pay for the toy out of his allowance. If your child consistently plays too rough with a certain toy, that toy can simply be taken out of circulation for a while. Let your child know what the consequence is and what he did to earn it. Then without shouting or lecturing, let the consequence do the work.

Overcorrection is another good way to teach appropriate respect for toys and possessions. If Johnny rips a page in a book, not only must he tape this page back up, but he must go through all of his books, look for ripped pages, and similarly repair them. This approach is not only logically connected to the misbehavior, but it gets a lot of pages taped as well!

 ## How Do I Put It All Together?

The case of the broken spaceman. Mr. and Mrs. Taylor decided to devise clear rules for David's toys, with David's participation.

They specifically targeted the toys that David tended to misuse. The rules were simple: No throwing, banging, or breaking the toys. They told David which toys he could be more rough with and made sure he clearly knew the difference.

David's father sat down with David and modeled appropriate and inappropriate use of his toys, to make sure that David understood. Using the Pour-It-On Technique was a big part of their plan as well, providing David with immediate positive attention whenever they saw him playing appropriately with his toys, especially with the toys that he used to throw or break. ("Hey buddy, you're playing great with your toys right now. Good job!")

Mr. Taylor explained to David that if he broke or hurt a toy by playing too rough with it, "the toy will either be thrown away if it is broken or it will be off-limits for a long time." Depending on the situation, David might have to pay for the toy out of the "birthday money" he had saved.

Finally, in order to help David develop an appreciation for material belongings and to instill a spirit of compassion and sharing, Mr. and Mrs. Taylor limited the amount of toys David received on Christmas and birthdays. They also started a regular family tradition to donate toys, clothes, and other possessions that were in good condition to a local shelter for needy families.

Despite all their good planning, David broke another toy within about two weeks. The toy had to be discarded and it was not replaced. David had to spend about thirty minutes cleaning up the toy room and had to help pay for the toy. On other occasions, David had several other toys removed due to excessively rough play. His parents were diligent in using the Pour-It-On Technique for positive behavior and stayed consistent in providing Logical Consequences. As David's toy stockpile gradually diminished, he slowly came to realize that playing more carefully with his toys was much more fun than the alternative.

Chapter 5

Cleaning Up Toys

The case of messy Melissa. "Ouch!" exclaimed Mr. Johnson, lifting up his leg and looking at the imprint of a Lego™ still painfully fresh on the bottom of his bare foot. Neither Mr. nor Mrs. Johnson had been successful at getting Melissa, their five-year-old daughter, to clean up her toys after playing with them.

When Mrs. Johnson asked Melissa to clean up her toys, Melissa usually ignored her and continued playing. Continued requests occasionally resulted in a few toys being picked up, but that was usually as good as it got. Frustration and shouting often followed and when all was said and done, Mrs. Johnson wound up putting the toys away, and Melissa was sent to her room, where she found something else to play with.

 ## Why Does This Happen?

What does she see? If your child regularly sees you leave messes around the house, such as scattered piles of dishes, clothes, magazines, unfinished work, CDs, and so on, it is only natural to expect her to learn to do the same. After all, if Mom and Dad do it, it must be all right. Right?

Ineffective negative consequences are another heavyweight contributor to this behavior. If your child is not listening when you make a request, then think very carefully about what happens immediately following her choice to disobey. In Melissa's case, she ended up playing in her room while her mother picked up her toys. She behaved in an inappropriate way and did not experience the right consequences as the result of her choice. No wonder she didn't pick up her toys.

Inconsistency can sabotage your efforts at solving this problem behavior. Inconsistency takes place when you respond to your child's negative behavior in a variety of different ways, including shouting, giving a negative consequence, ignoring it, and picking up the toys for her. You and your spouse can also respond to the behavior in ways that are inconsistent with each other. Either way, if your child learns that she can get away with the negative behavior a fair amount of the time, then the misbehavior has a pretty good chance of continuing.

 ## What Can I Do?

One mess at a time. This is a nice way to prevent this problem from becoming too big to handle. Observe your child as she plays and when you notice her losing interest in one toy and moving to another, kindly but firmly let her know that she can begin to play with the second toy *only* after she has cleaned up the first. Make this a general rule and stick to it.

Make sure you clean up your own messes. While it is not necessary to strive for perfection, give serious thought to the example that you set. If you would like your child to develop habits of neatness and caring for her belongings, give her a head start by showing her what that looks like and letting her see first-hand the benefits (things last longer, look nicer, don't get lost or broken) that come from a little extra effort and a little less procrastination.

Break it down into small steps. Sometimes a bunch of scattered toys seems like a colossal clean-up job to a child. You can imagine how overwhelming a fully demolished room must seem! The command, "Clean up your room" may be a little too "big" for some children. It is much more effective to help your child break this large task into smaller and more doable steps by having her complete one small step at a time. Think of yourself as the fore-man and your child as the worker. Consider this approach:

"Okay, first pick up your Legos and place them in the blue box over there. Great job! Now, pick up these horses and put them on this desk. Hey, we're almost done! These dolls here go in the cor-ner, all in a row. That's great. You did it!"

As your child gets older, you can have her do more on her own, for example, telling her "OK, please put away everything on this couch." The idea is to break this large task down into bite-size chunks.

Make clean up fun. Sound like a contradiction? Well, maybe. But do the best you can to make it enjoyable. With younger chil-dren, singing a "clean-up song" or another favorite song that they like to sing is a great idea. You can even play "Beat the Clock." This is where you set a kitchen timer for, say five minutes, and have your kids race to get the toys picked up before the timer dings. If they do, a simple reward, such as a snack, glass of juice, or other small special privilege, is given.

Use the Detour Method. Make sure that your child under-stands exactly what you expect of her when you ask her to pick up her toys. Make it simple and clear. For example, when you instruct her to pick up her toys, you want her to (1) say "Okay, Mom" or "Okay, Dad"; and (2) begin putting her toys away at a reasonably quick speed.

Make sure that she understands this. Then, lay out some toys and demonstrate this "clean-up plan" for your child. Show her what to do, what not to do (for example, move very slowly, get distracted, throw a fit), and what to do again. Have her repeat this procedure, providing lots of positive attention as she learns her clean-up plan. Talk together about what will happen if she picks them up and what will happen if she does not. Conduct future practice sessions every other day until she has mastered her plan. This procedure will help increase the likelihood that she will remember to do her plan the next time a "real-life" situation occurs.

Provide positive attention. After you have taught your child what to do, you need to make sure that this behavior is consistently rewarded when it happens. Using the Pour-It-On Technique, look for any amount of compliance to your command to clean up the toys and make sure that this is followed by a specific verbal reward. If your child picks up two toys and then gets sidetracked, then redirect her, but make sure that you verbally reward her for her initial compliance. For instance, gently guide her back to the still-to-be-picked-up toys and say, "That was great! But let's keep it up, there are more toys over here." Now she is back on track and she knows that you have noticed and appreciated her compliant behavior. Find something to reward every time she moves in a positive direction!

No clean up, no fun! There are several Logical Consequences that can be used if your child refuses to pick up her toys. One common-sense approach is to simply not allow your child to play with anything else or do anything else until the current toys are picked up. If you actually follow through with this approach, it should be effective. Alternatively, if your child refuses to pick up her toys, she can choose a Time-Out. After the Time-Out, she should immediately be instructed to come back out and pick up her toys.

Another approach is to tell your child that if the toys are not picked up within a certain amount of time (use a timer), then you will pick them up, put them in a bag, and store them in the garage for a day or two (or longer). As always, negative consequences are most effective if given in a matter-of-fact way, without lecturing or scolding. Let your actions do the talking! Immediately notify your child of the consequences she has earned. Make them fair but strong enough for your child to remember them.

Be consistent. You are trying to teach your child that a certain set of rules applies to picking up toys. She will learn this more quickly if the same set of rules is applied every time she is instructed to pick up her toys. If you are consistent in your approach to cleaning up toys, she will soon learn the new rules and be more likely to make a good decision.

How Do I Put It All Together?

The case of messy Melissa. First of all, Mr. and Mrs. Johnson talked together about Melissa's refusal to pick up her toys. They decided to come up with a plan that they would both implement consistently to teach Melissa to clean up her toys.

For starters, they agreed to be more consistent with picking their own things up around the house. "Well, I do leave my ice cream dishes and drinking glasses around the family room after watching TV," Mr. Johnson admitted. "And I guess I do scatter my magazines all over the house," Mrs. Johnson sheepishly confessed.

Secondly, they decided to allow Melissa to only make one mess at a time, as a general rule. "When you are finished playing with a toy, you will need to put it away before you can play with another one," they explained to her. Then, they took out some of Melissa's toys and showed her how they wanted her to pick them up, with Dad pretending to be Melissa and Mom asking him to clean up his toys. Melissa thought that was pretty funny. Melissa had a chance to practice and both parents poured on the positive feedback as she began to pick her toys up and they pointed out the benefits of good listening. For example, "There's much more room to play now!"; and "It's so much more fun when you listen!" They had short and fun practices every other day for about a week until Melissa had it down pat.

The Johnsons also started making clean-up fun by regularly singing a "clean-up song" with Melissa when they cleaned up messes together or when Melissa was asked to pick up her toys. They used the Pour-It-On Technique when Melissa did pick up her toys, to let her know what a wonderful job she was doing.

Finally, on occasions when Melissa refused to pick up her toys following two requests, Melissa immediately went to Time-Out: "Okay, you just chose a Time-Out. Let's go." Following the Time-Out, Melissa was required to go back and pick her toys up. If she still refused, this time after only one firm request, she was sent back to Time-Out and the toys were picked up and put away (out of sight and reach) for one week.

Mr. and Mrs. Johnson put their plan into action, hoping for the best. While Melissa initially responded well to the practice and social rewards, she was not so quick to change her behavior in "real-life" situations. However, her parents stuck with their plan and worked hard at using the Pour-It-On Technique whenever possible. Melissa experienced many Time-Outs and had several toys taken away over the next few weeks.

The Johnsons almost made the mistake of concluding that, "She doesn't care if we put her in Time-Out or take away her toys!" However, they wisely sidestepped that negative thinking trap and reminded themselves that Melissa was learning a new behavior and that learning will include some mistakes and will take some time.

As they continued to be consistent with their plan, Melissa's behavior did begin to fall into place. Melissa continued to experience positive parental attention when she picked her toys up without arguing and realized that she could easily avoid the Time-Outs and loss of toys by simply cleaning up when she was asked. In short, she learned that picking up her toys wasn't so hard after all.

Chapter 6

Dealing with Divorce

The case of mixed-up Mike. Mike was seven years old when his parents divorced. His dad had a girlfriend and was soon to be remarried. Mike and his three-year-old brother, Jordan, lived with their mother, who had custody, and visited their dad every other weekend and one weekday evening.

The last six months prior to his parents' separation were very tense and Mike and Jordan witnessed a lot of shouting and arguing. Now, ten months after the separation and one month after the divorce had become final, Mike was having a pretty hard time adjusting. He missed being able to see his dad more often and was angry his dad had to leave, although he didn't express these feelings openly.

Mike's mother, Ms. Simpson, was working full-time and had to use day care for the boys after school. Mike had become more oppositional during the past three months and found that often if he pushed hard enough, his mother eventually gave in. And, given some of his father's comments, Mike was starting to think that the divorce was his mother's fault.

Why Does This Happen?

This is a difficult time for the custodial parent. In most cases, this is the mother. She may have to work full time, her income usually decreases, and she and the children may have to move to a less expensive home. Arranging day care and babysitters can also be difficult. There often is less family time and Mom must play the role of full-time parent, provider, and housekeeper, all at the same time. (This is not to discriminate against dads. Many of the above can also be true for the custodial father.)

On top of it all, a newly separated mother has just gone through her own crisis—the loss of her marriage, her hopes, her dreams. The realities of life use up much of the parent's physical and emotional resources during the first couple of post-divorce years. That means there is less for the children.

The absence of a father is an unfortunate result of many divorces. While some fathers make a strong effort to stay positively involved in their child's life, others do not. For daughters, this means the loss of an opportunity to see how a husband should treat his wife. Boys may lose the chance to see first-hand what it means to be a strong and loving man, husband, and father devoted to God and to his family. This is particularly unfortunate, as the presence of a strong and loving father can provide not only an irreplaceable role model, but a sense of security and a source of practical guidance, for both boys and girls, through the difficult and confusing teen years.

A change in environment can also be a difficult factor for many children. The custodial family may have to move, and the child may have to begin a new school and make new friends. On top of that, there may be regular visitations with the non-custodial parent or a joint parenting arrangement. This means that the child will be spending time in two homes and may eventually have to learn to deal with stepparents and stepsiblings. Participation in sports and other activities can become a scheduling challenge between the two families, and special events and birthday parties may also conflict with the visitation schedule. All of these can be very stressful situations for the child. In younger children, they can lead to emotional upset and regressive behaviors.

There are many unanswered questions. Divorce raises a lot of issues for children. It is not uncommon for children to think that their behavior may have been responsible for the divorce. They may dream about their parents reconciling (although most parents do not) and experience feelings of disloyalty toward one of their parents. Children may question God's role in the situation and struggle with the issue of why God didn't keep their parents together.

When one parent speaks negatively about the other parent in front of the child or inappropriately shares personal divorce-related struggles with the child, it can cause a high level of confusion and conflicted feelings for the child. Due to their own confusion and desire to help things get better, some children will keep these feelings and concerns inside. The result can be depression and irritability, difficulty concentrating on school work, and behavioral acting-out.

 ## What Can I Do?

Do all you can to make it work. While divorce is never God's intent for marriage, the choice is not always entirely in your hands. You may have extremely difficult issues to deal with. In certain situations, such as physical abuse, a separation and possibly a divorce become the only healthy options left.

However, it is important to approach the issue of divorce slowly, prayerfully, and with much wise council. Many marriages that were on a greased one-way street to the divorce courts have been salvaged and mended. It may be possible that with the help of the right marriage therapist, support from your pastor and friends, and an extended amount of forgiveness, commitment, and work, your marriage *can* be restored to health. Don't make the mistake of throwing in the towel too soon.

Minimize conflict and change. Continued parental conflict is one of the factors that makes it more difficult for a child to successfully adjust to a divorce. Factors that improve children's adjustment include a supportive relationship with both parents, authoritative and consistent parenting styles, positive parent adjustment to the divorce, effective coping strategies, consistent daily routines, and reduction of overall stress.

Don't give in to the temptation to blame, criticize, or speak poorly of your former spouse in front of your child. Decide instead to model a high degree of integrity and positive communication for your child—it will pay off in the long run. Conduct serious or heated discussions with your former spouse only when your children are not present. As much as it depends on you, keep pick-up and drop-off meetings business-like and as pleasant as possible. While you don't have to be best friends, you do have to be co-parents.

Get some support—for yourself! Many counseling agencies and churches offer support groups for divorced persons. This type of group will help you more effectively handle your own loss, provide support and understanding from people in similar circumstances, and supply you with valuable information on the divorce recovery process essential in your own healing and recovery. If you find that you need more support than a group can provide, talk to an individual therapist. Remember, the better you handle this difficult time, the more you will be able to help your children adjust successfully.

Answer questions honestly. Explain the separation or divorce to your children in a simple and honest fashion. However, be careful not to go into details that are inappropriate for your children or that will further confuse them. Calmly explain the practical details in order to calm their anxiety, including details about living arrangements and visits. Be honest about the fact that things will be different now and perhaps a little harder for a while. Make it clear that the divorce had *nothing* to do with them and that both you and your spouse always will love them just as much.

This can be an opportunity to discuss how God is faithful, even in the most difficult and painful times of life. While being careful not to minimize their feelings of hurt and confusion, help your children look to God as a source of comfort and security through this difficult storm. Passages such as Psalm 23 and 2 Corinthians 1:3–5 remind us of God's faithfulness through even the darkest hours of life.

It also may be helpful to buy a book on divorce written just for children, such as *Why Don't We Live Together Anymore? Understanding Divorce*, by Robin Prince Monroe (published by Concordia). This short book provides basic information about the divorce process, and is designed to help young children process their thoughts and feelings about divorce from a Christian perspective. *Dinosaurs Divorce*, by Laurene Krasny Brown and Marc Brown (published by Atlantic Monthly Press), is an excellent book for children and, although it doesn't provide a uniquely Christian viewpoint, it is very useful in educating children about the divorce process, helping them identify their confusing feelings, and suggesting practical ways to cope with the many changes that divorce brings.

As you read together, periodically put the book down and explore your child's experience, using the book as a launching pad for meaningful discussion. Regularly pray together, encouraging your child to tell God about his struggles and feelings, and committing your lives and family to God's care. Reaffirm your trust in God's love and that he is able to make good things happen in your lives, even in the midst of the most difficult and painful circumstances (Romans 8:28, 38–39).

Maintain appropriate behavioral limits. While it is important to allow children time to grieve the loss of their family as they knew it and to express upset, confused, and angry feelings, a divorce is not a license for your child to become disrespectful toward others or to develop bad habits that will be difficult to change later on.

It is important that both parents maintain consistent and appropriate behavioral expectations regarding basic household rules, school behavior, and relating with others (such as parents, siblings, friends). Given the challenges that often follow a divorce for the custodial parent, getting some professional assistance if your child's behavior becomes difficult can really pay off.

A support group for kids can also be an excellent investment. By talking with your pastor, school, or local counseling agencies or hospitals, you should be able to locate a group for children that deals with divorce issues. These groups are often geared toward elementary-age children (or older), and are short-term, lasting twelve to fifteen weeks. Groups for children of divorce focus on providing education about the divorce process and help children realize that their worries and feelings are normal. They also teach children the type of coping skills that will aid them in their adjustment to post-divorce life.

How Do I Put It All Together?

The case of mixed-up Mike. At the advice of some friends and her pastor, Ms. Simpson joined a divorce recovery group at a local church and found a short-term group for children of divorce for Mike. The support and camaraderie she felt from her group helped her when times were tough with Mike's father and she learned many practical ideas for holding things together at home.

Ms. Simpson sent some of the material that she got from the group on co-parenting to Mike's father. She also included a letter, respectfully asking that they speak only neutral or positive things about each other when the children are around and that they reinforce the children's need to respect both parents. Mike's father never responded to the letter, but Ms. Simpson felt better knowing that she was doing her part.

Ms. Simpson bought a book on divorce for children and read and discussed it with both of her children, allowing them plenty of opportunity to share their feelings and concerns. "How are you feeling about our family?" Ms. Simpson asked.

"I still wish you and Dad could get along," Mike replied sadly.

"Sounds like you're still feeling sad about the divorce," Ms. Simpson summarized.

Mike sighed and looked at his mother, "I wish it never happened."

"What kind of feelings do you have about it, Mike?"

"Mostly mad . . . and sad," he replied.

"Y'know, those are pretty normal feelings," reassured Ms. Simpson, "I have them too."

They also regularly prayed together, asking God to help them and thanking him for loving them and being faithful to them during this difficult time for their family. Sometimes, Mike didn't pray, but he would listen.

Using ideas she had gotten from her group, Ms. Simpson talked with Mike about his behavior and let him know that while this was a tough time for everybody, they still needed to treat each other with respect. She reminded Mike of the good things that follow respectful behavior as well as the negative consequences (such as Time-Out and Logical Consequences) that would follow his negative behavior. She made sure to use the Pour-It-On Technique for both boys to let them know when they were being helpful and respectful ("I sure appreciate you boys playing nicely and talking respectfully today. That really helps our family a lot.").

With lots of support and encouragement from her group, Ms. Simpson was able to find the strength to remain consistent in her responses to Mike's challenging behavior. She had also resolved herself to call a child therapist if her attempts to help Mike were not working.

Relations with Mike's father, however, remained conflicted and eventually resulted in Ms. Simpson having to consult with her attorney and go back to court to clarify details surrounding visitation. While Mike made some headway with his home behavior, he became more angry and sullen at school, withdrawing from friends.

Ms. Simpson finally decided to take him to a therapist, where he could talk about his feelings and learn better ways of coping with things. Mike mostly met with his therapist individually, but occasionally they all met together to work on family issues, although Mike's dad refused to come.

As time passed, they went through some rough periods, but Ms. Simpson looked to her group for support and took comfort in the fact that she was doing all that she could to help her children. Over the next couple of years, Mike's ability to handle things did slowly improve and, through it all, Ms. Simpson never let go of her trust that although it would be hard, God would be faithful.

Chapter 7

Death

The case of the great grandfather. Joey's grandfather was not just any grandfather. "Papa" was a *great* grandfather and nine-year-old Joey loved him very much. This is why it was particularly hard for Joey when he died.

During the six months after receiving the news of Papa's cancer, Joey spent as much time with him as he could. One day Joey came home from school and his mother told him that his grandfather had died that afternoon. While Joey had known that Papa was going to die soon, the finality of the real news hit him hard.

During the next few weeks, Joey's parents handled the funeral arrangements, and the whole family began the process of coping with their sadness. Mr. and Mrs. O'connor knew that this was hard on Joey and wanted to help him get through this difficult time the best way possible.

 ## Why Does This Happen?

Death is hard. There is nothing easy about saying goodbye to someone you love. Few things can shake up a child's world like the death of a parent or a loved family member. The security and dependability of life gets the air suddenly knocked out of it as, sometimes without warning, a person who was supposed to always be there is now forever gone. Life will never be the same.

There are so many questions. The death of a loved one strikes at the central nerve of our existence. As adults, we become painfully aware not only of the immense loss of a loved one, but also of our own mortality—the fact that we also will die one day. Understandably, the passing of a loved one also causes many significant questions to rise to the forefront of children's minds: "Why did this happen?" "What happens when you die?" "Did God take _____ away?" "Could this happen to me or you?" And, "How will things be different now?"

These can be challenging questions to answer because they tap into the deepest questions of life many of us find ourselves coming face to face with during times of tragedy. It is all the more difficult when they come from children, who are hoping that you can provide some answers that will help them understand why God allows painful things to happen.

A child's developmental level as well as past experience affects his ability to understand death. A glimpse of this process was nicely captured in Dandi Daley Mackall's book, *Kids Say the Greatest Things About God* (published by Tyndale House). Children aged two to ten gave the following answers to questions about death and heaven:

Q– *What happens when you die?*

A– "When you die, you go to the hospital and never come out."

Q– *How do you get to heaven?*

A– "Oh, you get to heaven in a big, black limousine that goes really, really slow. I saw it in a funeral."

A– "They bury you in the ground, and you go straight down through the ground to heaven. So I don't know why everybody thinks heaven is up."

Children whose thinking abilities have matured or who have had previous experience with death are better able to understand that death is irreversible and that all people die. As children enter into adolescence, they become better able to comprehend the abstract theological aspects and implications of death.

What Can I Do?

Take care of yourself. Your ability to cope with death will affect your children by influencing the stability and emotional climate of your home as well as the amount of emotional energy you have left over to help them with their own grieving and adjustment. Finding support from family members, friends, a support group, or a therapist is very important during this time. If you need to, don't hesitate to ask your close friends or church for temporary assistance with some of your everyday duties such as child care, cooking, and housework. This can go a long way toward helping you manage this time of grief and transition.

Talk about it. The best way to address all of the questions and feelings that death stirs up is to have a twenty-four-hour-a-day open-door policy on the issue. As you talk about death and how it has impacted each of you, give top priority to honoring and carefully listening to your child's thoughts and feelings. There is no guarantee when these thoughts and feelings will surface, so be ready for them whenever they come.

Difficult questions are best answered in a simple and honest way. Don't go into more detail than your child can understand. For instance, you can say something like:

"You know that God made our souls (which is who we are inside) to live forever, but everyone's body will stop working one day. And when that happens, the person's body doesn't start working again. It's really sad when a person that you love dies and it is okay to say how you feel and ask questions about it."

With regard to heaven, keep your discussion simple, while staying consistent with biblical teaching. Your child's ability to understand the abstract concept of life after death as well as the difficult theological issues surrounding eternal destiny will gradually develop with age, so gauge the conversation to fit your child. For instance:

"God promised us that people who have asked Jesus to forgive their sins and have done their best to listen to him will go to heaven when their body stops working. And God even said that he will give them a brand new body that will last forever!" (see Romans 6:5, 1 Corinthians 15:42–44).

If your child asks what happens to people who have not asked Jesus into their hearts, honestly tell him that people who have not committed their lives to Jesus will not go to heaven. This makes God very sad because God wants everyone to be with him in heaven.

In response to questions about the eternal destiny of any specific person who did not appear to be a believer, be gentle but honest with your child about your concerns that the person had not given his or her life to Jesus. Make it very clear that God alone knows our hearts and that some people have accepted Christ even a short time before their death. For each of us, the issue of our eternal future will ultimately be settled between us and God.

"I don't think that Uncle Ted ever asked Jesus into his heart, which means he may not be in heaven. But sometimes before a person dies, they realize the truth about God and ask him to forgive them. That's what happened to the thief who was on the cross beside Jesus. I don't know if Uncle Ted did that or not, but God knows if he did. And we can trust that God will always do the right thing."

Providing your child with clear information about death as well as plenty of opportunity for discussion will give him a supportive environment where he can begin to process this difficult issue within the context of his growing Christian faith.

Allow your child to grieve in his own way. Children do not grieve in exactly the same way that adults do and usually do not sustain feelings of grief for long periods of time. As such, you might see younger children revert back to play and mistakenly assume they don't care. It is also common for young children to use play to process feelings about difficult issues and you may see themes related to death or the deceased person surface in their play.

Older children may find it helpful to write a letter, compose a poem, draw a picture, or make a gift for the deceased person. Looking at picture albums and remembering the person as current situations spark their memories is also a wonderful way of cherishing the impact of those who have been so important to us.

In your prayers with your children, thank God for his promise to always be with us and for his comfort during times of sadness. If the deceased person was a believer, make sure to connect with your child's feelings of sorrow but don't stop there. The reality is that the person is not dead, but is now with God in heaven, embarking on an incredible journey of unthinkable joy and excitement. On top of that, the Bible teaches that there will be a jubilant reunion someday, when we can all be together again.

As you walk with your child through this difficult time, remind him of these truths and help him to grieve in a way that both embraces the pain and sadness of death and combines it with the hope that God has graciously given us.

Model and encourage appropriate expressions of feelings. It is perfectly natural and healthy for you to express feelings of sadness and loss in front of your children. However, you need to do so in an appropriate manner that will not unduly upset or worry them. Explain to your children why you are crying or feeling sad or angry so that they do not mistakenly think that you are unhappy with them. Let your children know that it is normal to feel sad and that there will be times when they will feel sad too. When this happens, it is okay for them to show and say how they feel. Be sensitive and supportive of your children's feelings, reaffirming your deep love for them and your shared sense of loss.

Minimize change. The death of a loved one means regular activities will be disrupted, perhaps by funeral arrangements, travel, and other necessary details. Such disruption of routine can increase stress for children, who find comfort in predictability. You can help your children by minimizing such disruptions and getting them back to a regular schedule as soon as possible. This helps to bring a sense of familiarity and safety back to their lives and communicates that life can go on, even after the death of a loved one.

Maintain reasonable rules and expectations. The changes in family composition and in the range of emotions following a death can result in the inappropriate expression of feelings at times. While you want to be understanding of this and allow everyone a little room for being human, it is not appropriate to allow your children to slip into negative habits of treating others disrespectfully during this time.

Remind your children that while this is a difficult time for everyone, you still expect them to follow the family rules and treat others with respect. Make sure that instances of inappropriate behavior are followed by negative consequences and that specific positive feedback is given when your children behave and relate to others appropriately.

How Do I Put It All Together?

The case of the great grandfather. Mr. and Mrs. O'Connor decided to be proactive with their family as they went through this difficult time. Their church and close friends were providing meals for two weeks and both parents felt supported and held up in prayer by their friends and Bible-study group. Mrs. O'Connor knew that she could call several of her girlfriends and get extra help with watching the children or other daily responsibilities if she needed it.

The O'Connors allowed plenty of opportunity for Joey to talk about the issue of death as well as how he was handling things. Not only did they have an open-door policy, but they purposely checked in with Joey: "Hey Joey, how are you doing with everything? Do you feel like talking about anything right now?"

During their discussions, Mr. and Mrs. O'Connor were honest about their own feelings of sadness and loss and did their best to answer Joey's questions about death in a simple and honest way.

As the months went by, everyone lived out their own schedule of grief. Some days were good, others were very painful as the reality of Papa's absence set in. Joey's parents spent time with Joey's grandmother, helping her with practical issues as well as providing lots of emotional support as she dealt with the loss of her husband.

Joey had both up and down days. Mr. and Mrs. O'Connor reminded him that the sad feelings would come and go and they all agreed that anyone could be sad about Papa's death whenever they wanted to be. Mr. O'Connor came up with a helpful idea: "If anyone needs time to talk together, pray, or just be alone, all you have to do is ask for it. Agreed?" They all agreed, and Joey thought it was a good idea.

During some of their family times, the O'Connors looked at family picture albums, spending extra time on the pictures of Papa. They shared their favorite memories of Papa and talked about what exciting things he might be doing in heaven. "I wonder if God will give Papa any beef jerky?" Joey wondered out loud, as this was one of the favorite snacks that he and Papa had shared together.

Mr. and Mrs. O'Connor did everything in their power to keep Joey's schedule as normal as possible. Joey chose to attend the funeral and they later talked about what that was like for him. Following the funeral, Joey's family got back into their normal schedule of work, school, church, and soccer.

Joey greatly missed his Papa but knew that he could talk about his feelings with his parents whenever he needed to.

"Dear God," he would pray each night, "I know that Papa is in heaven with you. Tell him 'Hi' for me and I hope he's having fun. I'm glad I'll get to see him when I go to heaven too."

While Papa's death was difficult for Joey and his family, their approach helped it become a time of family bonding as Joey's family remained close to God and to each other through one of the most difficult storms life has to offer.

Chapter 8

Expressing Angry Feelings

The case of the human volcano. Jason was an eight-year-old boy who had trouble expressing angry feelings. When mad, he would sometimes say nothing and stomp off to his room. Other times, he would say mean things to his siblings or his parents. He often felt he was being treated unfairly.

It was hard to predict what would make Jason angry. Mr. and Mrs. Smith said that he had been "difficult" and "moody" since he was a young child. Jason's parents usually responded to angry behavior by sending Jason to his room. He had received a spanking on more than one occasion as well. Still, the behavior continued and the Smiths were worried about what was going to happen when Jason became a teenager.

❓ Why Does This Happen?

A difficult temperament can magnify the built-in challenges of childhood. A child who is temperamentally irritable, aggressive, sensitive, or slow to adapt to new situations can be at risk for developing inappropriate ways of expressing his angry feelings.

What does he see? How do you handle conflict and express your own angry feelings? Children will mirror the habits that are modeled by their parents. If you shout, engage in "cold wars," or strike out with barbed comments when you are mad or hurt, you should be more surprised if your child *doesn't* do the same than if he does.

Does aggression pay off? If it does, your child will be more likely to continue. You must think carefully about what usually takes place after your child explodes or hits someone. If a behavior has continued for some time, then it probably benefits the child in some way. Your job is to make sure that the only behavior that pays off is appropriate behavior.

What does your child think? Children who display aggressive behavior often view their world in a distorted way. They misinterpret neutral events, like someone bumping into them, as an act of hostility, and react with aggressive words or actions. In addition to making sure that aggressive behavior is not rewarded, parents must work hard to help their children develop an accurate way of viewing these situations.

 ## What Can I Do?

Get closer. If talking about school and chores results in your child getting defensive and edgy, then talk about something pleasant and spend time doing activities that your child finds enjoyable. Have some experiences together that are just fun, with no strings attached. In spite of his tantrums, let your child know that you love him by regularly telling him you do, as well as by talking together about things that are important *to him*, such as his interests, goals, and activities. Spending regular, quality time with your child will communicate your love, improve your ability to talk together about difficult things, and help your relationship stay strong even when the going gets tough.

Do it right yourself. Make sure that you are setting a healthy example for how to respond to frustrating situations. Ralph Waldo Emerson penned a phrase that rings true all too often: "What you do speaks so loudly that I cannot hear what you say." It is sad when our example is so strikingly different than our instruction that the end result is confusion and disillusionment for our children. Everything that you tell them about anger control applies to you too and they know it. When you are angry, remember that your children are watching. And learning.

Make an appointment if your child is older and you have something unpopular to talk about. Surprising your child with a discussion about negative behavior right after he walks in the door after school, or out of the blue in the evening, is not a wise approach. Instead, respectfully let your child know that you would like to talk with him about a few things and together decide upon a good time. If you really want to get through to him, take him out for a cola or hamburger while you discuss a particularly difficult subject. It can also be a nice idea to let your child know that your appointment book is always open if he has something that he would like to discuss.

Teach your child to control his anger. Make a list together of the things that make him angry and explore his ideas about the best way to handle these situations. Keep this discussion very simple for younger children. Examine what happens when he blows up or gets disrespectful, and contrast that with the benefits of showing more self-control.

Using an age-appropriate translation, read and talk about how God wants us to learn to handle our anger, using the following verses (all from the NIrV) as your starting point:

> Scripture says, "When you are angry, do not sin." Do not let the sun go down while you are still angry. Don't give the devil a chance. (Ephesians 4:26–27)

> My dear brothers and sisters, pay attention to what I say. Everyone should be quick to listen. But they should be slow to speak. They should be slow to get angry. Human anger doesn't produce the kind of life God wants. (James 1:19–20)

> But Lord, you are a God who is tender and kind. You are gracious. You are slow to get angry. You are faithful and full of love. (Psalm 86:15)

Foolish people let their anger run wild. But wise people keep themselves under control. (Proverbs 29:11)

As you discuss these verses, ask why God thinks that controlling our anger is so important. What are the benefits of being kind and slow to anger? What are the negative results of uncontrolled anger? Relate that handling frustration is difficult for everyone at times, but that God can help us do it.

Then, using either the Detour Method or Problem-Solving Steps (depending on your child's age), together come up with a plan for handling frustrating situations and expressing angry feelings. Your plan can include:

- asking God to help you stay calm
- saying your feelings with your words
- ignoring the behavior
- taking two deep breaths
- respectfully asking the person to stop
- respectfully asking the person to stop a second time
- counting to five
- walking away
- talking to a parent about the situation, after he has tried two of the above

In addition, the following statement can be a helpful way to express feelings:

"When _____ (what happens that makes your child angry), I feel _____ (how your child feels), and would like _____ (what your child would like instead)."

For example, if Jason is angry about his brother always wanting to go first when playing a game, he could say, "Bobby, when you always have to go first when we play anything, I feel kind of mad, and I wish that we could just take turns, so it would be fair for everybody." If Bobby still insisted on going first, Jason could respectfully repeat the sentence a second time. If Bobby responded inappropriately again, then Jason could decide if he wanted to play with Bobby, excuse himself from the game, or go and get some help from his parents. Either way, he has responded respectfully to his brother in a frustrating situation.

Make sure that the plan is simple enough for your child to both memorize and perform. Practice the plan together, using as examples situations that typically make your child angry, whether about home, school, friends, or anything else. If needed, model the steps for your child so that he can see how it looks when they are done right.

Once your child has learned the plan, review problem situations regularly, helping him think about how he could have used his plan instead of blowing up. Give him lots of positive feedback and encouragement—you are helping your child to learn a difficult and important skill.

A change in perspective may be needed. If your child is getting angry because he is misinterpreting the actions of other people, then take some time to help him examine how he views things. Help your child learn to think about the situation from the other person's point of view. Ask him if he can think of other ways of viewing the situation or other reasons the person may have responded as they did. Give him some ideas if he has trouble with this. Suggest short sentences that your child can tell himself to keep things in better perspective: "Maybe he's just having a bad day." "She probably didn't mean it that way." "I'm kind of frustrated, but God wants me to handle this the right way."

Reward healthy anger expression. Watch very carefully for signs of your child handling frustrating situations well and expressing his angry feelings appropriately. Using the Pour-It-On Technique, immediately acknowledge good behavior and let him know that you notice his efforts. If anger control does not come easily for your child, then make extra sure you notice any effort to better control his temper.

Negative consequences are a must. Specifically define the types of anger expression that will result in negative consequences. Time-Out is a good negative consequence for temper problems, as it gives your child a chance to cool down and regain control of himself. Logical Consequences, such as a loss of privileges (early bed, no television), can also be used with good effect. With some children, it can be wise to remove privileges in shorter time segments so that you don't run out of consequences to use. For example, your child can earn twenty or thirty minutes of early bed for every instance of inappropriate anger expression.

When you see mild or moderately negative anger expression (in other words, he's just starting to lose it), you can give your child an immediate Fork-in-the-Road. This will give him a better chance of redirecting himself and reminds him of the negative consequences that are right around the corner, but still avoidable.

You can also use a simple contract with a Response/Cost approach. Design your contract so that your child starts each day with five points. One point will be lost (in addition to an immediate Time-Out) each time your child expresses his anger inappropriately. The points remaining at the end of the day can be saved and traded in for special privileges. Certain daily privileges will be lost if your child loses more than a predefined number of points. For instance, losing two of five points can mean no television for the day, losing three points can mean no friends over plus no television, and so on.

Get additional help if needed. Aggressive or explosive behavior is not a habit you want your child to have. If your initial attempts at addressing this behavior are not successful, consult with a child therapist who can evaluate your child and help you further.

 ## How Do I Put It All Together?

The case of the human volcano. Mr. and Mrs. Smith talked together about how they should approach Jason with this issue. Mr. Smith decided to spend more regular quality time with Jason. He decided to take Jason out to breakfast every third Saturday morning and to make more time for them to play chess together, one of Jason's favorite games. Jason was elated at the thought of spending more time with his dad.

On one of their first breakfast dates, Mr. Smith had Jason bring along his Bible. They looked at Ephesians 4:25–32 and Proverbs 29:11 and talked about how God wants us to handle our anger. "I have a tough time with my anger sometimes too," Mr. Smith shared, to Jason's surprise. "I can get frustrated at work or sometimes at home and I need to cool down too."

"I never thought about that," Jason responded.

"Oh yeah," his dad continued, "I have to stop and ask God to help me think about things right and treat people respectfully, no matter how frustrated I feel. And sometimes, as you know, I blow it too. But I keep working on it, just like you are."

It made Jason feel good to know that his dad understood. Jason's parents made a "talking date" with Jason at his favorite fast-food restaurant. They expressed their concerns about Jason's behavior when he gets frustrated and took time to listen about the things that made him angry. Jason agreed that he needed to improve the way he handled his frustration and together they came up with a plan to help him handle his angry feelings in a more acceptable way. The plan consisted of several steps:

1. Take two deep breaths
2. Think about what you want to say
3. Say it in a respectful way
4. Walk away or get help from parents

As a "safety-valve" measure, Jason could ask for a "cool down" minute (sixty seconds) any time he needed to when he became angry to help him collect his thoughts and calm down so he could appropriately express himself. To help him calm down, Jason decided to memorize a short prayer: "God, help me stay calm and be respectful." His parents reminded him that they would give him a Fork-in-the-Road if they saw him start to lose control, to help remind him to use his plan.

Mr. and Mrs. Smith also used a Response/Cost chip system. Jason started out with three chips a day and could earn a highly desired fishing afternoon with Dad when he saved twenty chips. "I like this idea," Jason nodded, giving his approval. However, in addition to an immediate Time-Out, he would also lose thirty minutes of television time for the second chip lost and go to bed thirty minutes early for the third chip lost in one day. He wasn't so enthused about the second part, but he realized that there was no use arguing about it.

Mr. and Mrs. Smith had decided that if Jason's behavior did not improve, they would call a child therapist for some additional help. While Jason showed some initial improvement, he was seldom in the mood to "review" situations where he had lost a chip and still felt that others were treating him unfairly. His progress reached a plateau, and he started to resist going to Time-Out or early bed. There were even instances when Jason's anger was getting worse. As Mrs. Smith picked up the phone to schedule an appointment with a child therapist, she knew that both they and Jason needed more help and that she was taking the right step.

Chapter 9

Fears

The case of nervous Nikki. "I think it's getting worse," Mrs. Mann said about their six-year-old daughter, Nikki. "She seems to be nervous around dogs and got really scared during that last thunderstorm," Mr. Mann explained. Nikki's parents usually tried to console and comfort her when she became noticeably nervous but no matter what they said, Nikki remained unreassured. Mr. and Mrs. Mann were starting to worry too.

 ## Why Does This Happen?

Fears are common in preschool- and elementary-aged children. While most children learn (with time and a little parental encouragement) to handle these fears effectively, there are plenty of things that can spark worry in a child during these years. The list includes the dark, monsters, separation from parents, animals, catastrophes, failure in school or sports, and being different.

Anxiety runs in families. Research on anxiety is finding that problems with worry are often a family affair. This suggests a genetic predisposition to the problem for some people that might warrant professional help.

Kids can learn to worry. Even if anxiety is not in a child's genes, a tendency toward worrying and anxiety can still develop. If Mom or Dad are "worriers," children can learn to take an overly cautious or fearful approach to life by simply observing their parents respond to life's challenges in an anxious manner. On top of that, if a child discovers that anxious behavior usually results in lots of extra attention or can get her out of difficult situations, the behavior can be strengthened because of the immediate consequences that it brings.

 ## What Can I Do?

Talk with your child about worrying. Let her know that it is normal to worry sometimes. Acknowledge your child's fears—don't call them silly or discount them; they are very real to her. The goal is to get your child talking about her fears and to gain an understanding of what she is afraid might happen. For instance, when a dog walks by and she looks nervous, ask her about it. "How did you feel when that dog was close to you? Can you tell me what you were afraid was going to happen?"

Teach realistic thinking. This will be most effective if you keep it simple and tailor your guidance to your child's age and reasoning abilities. You want your children to develop an underlying trust in God's promises along with a sense of mastery over the situation that is frightening them.

To remind your child of God's faithfulness and his promise to always be with us, read together passages such as Psalm 23, Psalm 32:6–7, and Psalm 57:10. The stories of Esther, Gideon, and David and Goliath also provide memorable examples of how God rewarded those who bravely trusted him.

If your child's fears are common ones, then help her to realize that her fears are normal. Remind her that lots of kids get nervous during a storm. Help her to think about the most likely outcome of the feared event. Her worrying could be caused by an exaggerated fear of what might happen (for example, "A tornado is going to come and blow our house over"). If you live in tornado country, you can acknowledge that tornadoes sometimes do come. Whether or not you do, emphasize that tornadoes are the exception rather than the rule and that the vast majority of storms are not followed by catastrophes. Have your child do some research by going to the library and finding some age-appropriate books about storms. Read them together, making sure to learn about how and when they occur and procedures that have been developed to keep people safe. Help your child identify the most probable outcome and then turn that into a short sentence or two, such as, "The worst thing that will happen is that the power may go off for a few hours. Most of the time, that doesn't even happen."

The goal is to help your child keep her thinking accurate and reality-based. This should be done in a gentle way, helping your child to conquer her worry by increasing her sense of trust in God as well as her knowledge and control over the feared situation.

Develop a plan. For younger children, the plan will have to include the concrete steps of prevention (such as using a night-light), reassurance (for example, "Daddy won't let the monsters hurt you"), and *gradual* and safe exposure to the feared situation (looking at books about dogs, petting calm puppies, and so on).

For an older child, you need to teach her how to keep her *body* and her *mind* calm. Taking several deep breaths is a great way for your child to calm her body down—it is hard to breathe slowly and be anxious at the same time! Calming her mind can be accomplished by having her memorize two or three simple statements, such as, "Stay calm," "God will help me to handle this," and "If _____ (I see a dog; there is a storm; and so on), I know how to stay safe." Make sure to customize the statements to fit the particular situation. You may also identify a few relaxing activities that your child can do to help her stay calm and get her mind off her worries. They might include reading a book, talking to someone, or playing a quiet game.

Once you have a set of steps for helping your child to calm her body and mind, write them on paper and post them. Have your child practice the steps, pretending that she is in the anxiety-producing situation. Remember also to show your child how you would use the steps, and have her identify the likely outcome after using them. Of course, when a real-life opportunity comes, such as a storm, make sure to have your child use her steps and provide plenty of encouragement as your child uses her new coping skills.

Take small steps to help your child master the feared situation. For instance, if your child is hesitant around dogs, you might start by reading a book on dogs or looking at dogs through the window at a pet store. You can learn about all the different types of dogs together by going to the library. You can talk about the rules for petting dogs and guidelines for how to stay safe around dogs that you don't know. This will help increase your child's sense of mastery and control over the situation. With younger children, you can practice together, with you pretending to be a friendly dog or a grouchy dog.

It can also be very helpful for your child to observe other children petting and playing with animals, perhaps at a children's zoo if you're near one, where the animals are tame and opportunities for watching other children are plentiful. Eventually, she may be willing to pet the back of a calm dog or a gentle puppy in your presence and progress from there.

Don't push your child past the level of exposure she is comfortable with. Let her move at her own pace. This type of gradual approach will help your child to warm up to the feared activity at her own speed, develop a sense of mastery and control over the situation, and experience for herself that she can do it.

Use positive reinforcement. Use the Pour-It-On Technique to provide specific verbal rewards and positive encouragement when you see your child use her new steps in fearful situations. Remind yourself that she is showing a lot of courage and be proud of her for being so brave. You can also use a simple contract to strengthen your child's new skills by allowing her to earn a point each time that she uses her coping steps to effectively handle a fearful situation. The points can then be traded in for a fun privilege.

 ## How Do I Put It All Together?

The case of nervous Nikki. Mr. and Mrs. Mann decided to help Nikki learn to handle her fears. While there was not a history of anxiety problems in their family, they agreed that they would seek a professional consultation if she did not improve following their efforts.

During their next few family times, they read the biblical stories of David and Goliath and of Esther, and talked about how God wants us to have courage and to trust in him. They all took turns listing things that they used to be nervous about or that used to be hard for them, but now are easy. "I used to be afraid that I would fall off my bike," Nikki recalled, "but now I'm not."

"Well, I used to be afraid to climb very high on a ladder," said Mr. Mann, which surprised everyone, given the ease with which they had seen him hop on a ladder to fix anything that needed fixing.

They turned the discussion to Nikki's hesitancy around dogs. "Nikki, when that lady walked by the house yesterday with her dog, you seemed pretty scared. What do you think might happen if you got close to a dog?"

They discovered that while at the grocery store with her grandmother about six months ago, a large dog had growled and snapped at her when she reached out to pet it. She hadn't said anything about it and had been afraid to get near a dog ever since.

Nikki and her mother found a big, colorful book on dogs, which they read together. They were surprised at how many dogs the book said were friendly. They also made rules for staying safe around dogs and for how to figure out if a dog is friendly or mean.

"Let's see, if a dog is friendly," began Mr. Mann, "he would probably be wagging his tail, he wouldn't growl, and he would act friendly when other people pet him." Nikki volunteered the idea that she could also ask the owner if he is a friendly dog.

"Yes," said her mother, "and if you're not sure, you can just watch him for a while. No one will force you to pet him." Then they practiced these rules together with one of Nikki's stuffed dogs.

Mr. Mann helped Nikki to come up with some "true thoughts" to memorize that would help her to stay calm, such as, "Most dogs are really nice," and "I don't have to pet a dog until I'm sure that he is nice." He also took Nikki to visit a friend who had a gentle golden retriever. With the owner's permission and her father's encouragement, Nikki slowly and carefully took her first step, by petting the friendly dog, first gingerly on the lower back and eventually touching him behind the ears. She was elated at how fun it was to pet a nice dog.

They took a similar approach with thunderstorms. With the help of a nicely illustrated library book, Mr. Mann explained what a storm was to Nikki. They talked about the usual effects of a storm, such as rain, thunder and lightning, and an occasional loss of power. With a flashlight, he showed her where their sump pump was located and explained to her that this pump kept the rain water from coming in the house during a storm. He showed her where they kept the flashlights and candles in case the power went out. With a gleam in his eye, Mr. Mann told Nikki, "If the power ever does go out for a couple of hours, it will be an adventure, like we were camping. You can help me get the flashlights, bring in some firewood, and light the fireplace, so we'll stay warm. Maybe we'll even roast marshmallows," he added with a grin.

Nikki's parents also wrote down a few calming thoughts for Nikki to refer to during a storm. They helped her memorize "We have storms every year, and we've always been safe"; "Mom and Dad will keep me safe"; and "We can have fun during a storm."

When the next storm came, Nikki's parents began by calmly reminding her that God is always watching over them. They had her repeat her calming thoughts and gave her lots of positive encouragement, "Nikki, we're proud of you for working hard on your plan and being so brave." They also had her look for evidence that her "true thoughts" were true. "Nikki," they asked, "is our house safe right now or is it getting knocked over by the wind and rain?"

Mrs. Mann fixed them all a favorite snack and they kept busy by reading stories and playing dominoes during the storm. Mr. Mann took Nikki downstairs with him to listen to the sump pump working and had her check the flashlights and set them out on the kitchen counter. Nikki felt nervous, but all the evidence that they were safe made her feel just a little better. Before they knew it, the storm had passed and Nikki's parents congratulated her on staying calm and being such a big helper. Nikki felt proud of her accomplishment and her parents felt comfortable that she was on the road toward learning to handle her fears.

Chapter 10

Giving Up

The case of fallen Freddy. "I'm not playing anymore!" had become Freddy's favorite phrase. Freddy's parents were concerned that their nine-year-old son was beginning to give up when things got difficult. If a homework problem was too hard, if he dropped a pass in football, if he was losing at a board game, Freddy would just quit trying.

Mr. and Mrs. Drane had encouraged him to try again, but nothing seemed work. "I really didn't want to do that anyway," is what they would hear. Mrs. Drane said that Freddy had been teased by some kids on occasion, and wondered if that had anything to do with his behavior. Recently, Freddy's parents had noticed that he was starting to spend more time alone and less time with his friends. That is when they knew he needed some help.

 ## Why Does This Happen?

An overemphasis on performance instead of effort can get a child started on the wrong track. If a child thinks that winning, being the best, or getting A's is what it's all about, then he will probably strive for this at the expense of more important things. He may feel ashamed if he is not able to deliver. Nobody can deliver perfection all of the time. Most of us do well to deliver it now and then, if at all. If your child believes he cannot live up to such a high standard and anything less is unacceptable, feelings of failure and inadequacy are sure to follow.

Negative thoughts are almost guaranteed to be in this picture. If a child is giving up quickly or refusing to try something, this is because he *expects* a negative outcome or doesn't think that he can do it. You may not know exactly what negative outcome your child is fearing, whether it's failure at the task, getting teased, or parental disapproval, but you can be sure that some negative thinking is lurking around somewhere.

Leaving doesn't promote learning. When a child quits an activity because of a fear of failure, one thing is surely *not* going to happen: Your child will not learn to succeed at that activity! This is one of the ironic and vicious circles that causes fears and worry to persist. If you avoid the activity, your avoidance keeps you temporarily "safe," but becomes the very thing that stands in the way of your learning to master the activity. You can't learn what you never do.

What Can I Do?

Examine your expectations. While expecting the best from your child, you need to make sure that you are not expecting more than your child can realistically deliver. Not every child is going to be musically talented, a top student, popular with peers, an athlete, and so on. But every child has a unique set of God-given traits that lay waiting to be discovered and nurtured.

For example, it can be an adjustment for a "sports-minded" dad to realize that his son is not gifted in sports. But it is an adjustment that he needs to make without penalizing his child for having different interests or abilities than his own. Dad may have to learn something about computers, science, or music if he wants to share some wonderful experiences with the child that God has given him. You need to know your child's strengths and weaknesses, likes and dislikes, and then help to bring forth the best that he has to offer.

Emphasize effort and perseverance instead of performance. After all, it is not the grade or outcome that counts as much as the effort. Success is not usually the result of undisciplined raw ability but of moderate ability paired with perseverance.

The apostle Paul wrote candidly about his own failed attempts at obeying God (see Romans 7). However, in Philippians 3:12–14, Paul identified his goal, not of attaining perfection, but of pressing on "toward the goal to win the prize for which God has called me heavenward in Christ Jesus." The goal is to keep running, to keep moving, to keep trying, in spite of all our failures, to live into all that God has destined us to be.

On the one hand, if you teach your child that winning, earning top grades, and so on, are all that counts, he will be adopting a shallow and flawed perspective and will be set up for feeling inadequate whenever he is less than perfect. On the other hand, if he gets the message that making his best effort with the abilities that God has given him is what is really important, then you will help him to develop traits that will serve him well for a lifetime.

In your family times, talk together about the importance of sticking to it when things are tough and not giving up. Take turns listing things that once were difficult for each of you, but now are easy. Examples may include tying shoelaces, riding a bike, learning to swim, reading, skating, gymnastics, and so on. Talk about what you did to succeed in those activities, actions like not giving up, asking for adult help, and so on. Identify what you thought that helped you succeed, like, "I can do it if I don't give up."

Then, identify things that are difficult for you *now*. Talk about what you tell yourself now to help you to stick with it. Explain to your child that not giving up takes courage. Reread the stories of Gideon, Esther, and David and Goliath. Talk about how they had courage and didn't give up when things were hard or looked impossible. Instead, they trusted God and did their very best. Not a bad combination.

Give your child a model of how to respond to difficult situations in a positive way. Your child will learn to cope with difficult situations more easily if he can see real-life examples of you doing the same. When you lose a game or find yourself up against a difficult obstacle, remind yourself that this is your golden opportunity to show your child how to respond to a challenge positively and effectively.

You can do this by "thinking out loud" so that your child can learn from your response to the situation. You can say, "I'm not sure how to handle this, but I'll figure it out"; "That was tough, but I'll try it again tomorrow"; "I lost today, but I had fun anyway." In a natural and unassuming way, your child will be exposed to a powerful, living example of how to keep on trying, how to find the positives in a seemingly negative situation, and how to put things in perspective.

Ask yourself why. Children who have difficulty responding to failure often tend to assume that the failure is due to something wrong with them. Consequently, they neglect to consider other valid possibilities for why things went wrong. For example, if Johnny failed a math test, he might think, "I failed the test because I'm stupid." However, his low test score could be because the test was very hard, math is a difficult subject for him, he has a hard teacher, he didn't spend enough time studying, he missed several days of class last week, and so on.

Together with your child, gently examine his "failed" experiences, asking him why he thinks they happened. Then ask him, "Why else do kids sometimes have trouble with _____ (whatever the failed effort was)?" See what possible reasons he can think of, and together identify the reasons that seem to best fit his situation. Several of the reasons are likely to be factors that he has either some or full control over. He cannot change the fact that his teacher gives difficult tests, but he can control how much time he spends preparing and reviewing for them. Help him realize that he is not powerless and that he can change things. If he changes the things that are within his control, he can create a more successful experience next time.

Straight thinking is as important for your child as a straight arrow is in an archery contest. Just as a crooked arrow could mean defeat for the archer, thoughts that miss the mark can spell disaster for your child when the going gets tough.

When your child approaches a challenging situation, what goes through his mind? Ask him what he is thinking or what he is afraid will happen. You may hear common negative thoughts like these: "I can't do it." "I'm going to look stupid in front of my friends." "I'll never learn this." "I might as well not even try." If this is what your child is thinking when things get tough, failure is not far behind.

To combat this, help your child develop a set of thoughts that will promote a positive attitude and perseverance. Encourage him to memorize three or four thoughts. Here are some suggestions: "God will help me to do my best." "I won't give up." "Everyone makes mistakes." "This is hard, but I can do it." "I don't need to be the best." "If I need help, _____ can help me and I'll keep on trying." "This is hard for a lot of people when they're just starting." "Even if this is hard for me, I can still try my best." "If I keep on trying, I'll get better at it."

The beauty of these thoughts is not that they are positive— though they are—it is that *they are 100 percent true!* Everybody does make mistakes and rewarding things are only learned through practice and by not giving up. There is no other way. This is the lesson that your child needs to learn.

I recently had the opportunity to see the fruit of these thoughts when my oldest son learned to ride his bicycle without training wheels. He certainly had had his share of spills over several days and had at times felt like giving up. I remember so clearly the words he said after that one final push when he beamed back at me while riding down the sidewalk on his own. He didn't say, "See Dad, I'm riding on my own." Instead, he looked back and shouted with a proud and confident grin, "See Dad, I didn't give up!"

Safe practice. You don't learn to play basketball by jumping into the middle of an NBA playoff game. If your child has not developed his skills at something, that is just how intimidating it might feel for him to be involved in that activity with peers who are already skilled in that area.

Your child needs to practice in a safe setting, where he can develop his skills at his own pace. If a lack of skill is the problem, then get together and practice throwing a football, talking to a group, asking a question in class, reviewing the multiplication table, introducing himself to new people, or whatever he is struggling with. Make sure to give him lots of positive encouragement for his effort and for being brave enough to risk learning something new. Sometimes, tutoring or involvement in other extracurricular activities can help your child learn the skills he needs to succeed.

Once your child has begun to develop his skill, then encourage him to *gradually* use his new skills in other situations, going only as fast as he feels comfortable. This allows him to safely accumulate experiences of success and build up his sense of self-confidence at his own pace.

 ## How Do I Put It All Together?

The case of fallen Freddy. As Mr. and Mrs. Drane sat down with Freddy and talked about his recent behavior, they soon discovered that he was afraid of looking "dumb" in front of his friends and was beginning to think that he just was not good at very many things.

They helped Freddy to consider other ways to look at his "failed" situations and pointed to examples of how learning almost anything takes lots of practice and mistakes. "Freddy," Mr. Drane began, "let's think about that last football game, when you dropped the ball. You're thinking that means that you're not good at football, right?"

Freddy agreed. Mr. Drane asked him if anyone else dropped a ball during that game.

"Yeah, Tommy did," Freddy said.

"Do you think that Tommy is lousy at football just because he dropped a pass? If you remember, he caught some passes too. And he made a touchdown."

Mr. Drane underscored the point, saying "So then, even though he dropped some passes, he kept on trying and didn't give up. Is that right?"

With his parents' help, Freddy soon recalled that he had seen other kids drop the football, even some of the best players, and no one had laughed at them. He also acknowledged that most people (even good students) find homework to be hard at times. And Mr. Drane humbly pointed out that everyone (even dads!) loses at board games.

Freddy and his parents came up with some helpful thoughts that Freddy could use to keep his thinking positive ("Everyone makes mistakes," "God will help me to do my best," "If I keep trying, I'll get it next time") and printed them out on the computer so they could review them with Freddy.

Mr. Drane offered to help Freddy improve at throwing and catching a football. With a little practice and encouragement, Freddy learned to throw and catch quite well. "Good try, pal. You'll get it next time," Mr. Drane would say whenever Freddy dropped the ball.

Mr. and Mrs. Drane took turns sitting with Freddy during homework time. Together, all three came up with things that Freddy could think and do (instead of give up) to help him handle it when his homework became frustrating: "This is hard, but I can figure it out," and, "If I get really stuck, I can ask for help." They taught him to skip the most difficult question and come back to it later or ask his mother or father for help. Again, they printed these thoughts and actions out on the computer and taped them to the wall in Freddy's homework area.

While Freddy still needed reminders to keep his thinking straight when things got tough, he began to "hang in there" more often. When he did, his parents made sure to give him plenty of positive feedback for making his best effort and sticking with it.

Mr. and Mrs. Drane continued to review what they called Freddy's "never give up" thoughts. During their family times they practiced how to respond to difficult situations. (Think: "If I keep trying, I'll get it next time," and then try it again.) Over time, Freddy's perseverance grew and resulted in making some touchdowns, working through some difficult math problems on his own, and having fun even when he lost a game. Freddy was learning how to keep things in perspective and to be satisfied when he did his best.

Chapter 11

Grocery Store

The case of the runaway child. At times, Kelly, who was three-and-a-half years old, was a handful. This was never more evident than when she went with her mother to the grocery store. It was all that Mrs. Thompson could do to get through the shopping trip without making a scene. While Kelly would have periods of appropriate behavior, she would often run far ahead of the grocery cart. Worst of all, she would throw a tantrum right in the middle of the store if she found something that she wanted but couldn't have.

Mrs. Thompson would tell Kelly to "Get back here!" in a muffled shout, hurriedly put the unneeded items back on the shelf, and wait for Kelly to stop throwing her tantrum, all the while feeling extremely embarrassed as she turned new shades of red. When the trip was over, Kelly's mother was ready for a vacation.

 ## Why Does This Happen?

What do you expect? A short attention span is normal for younger children. A long grocery store trip may be more than your child can realistically handle, especially if you already made a few other stops before reaching the grocery store. If you are expecting your young child to behave perfectly during a long trip, you are setting yourself up for frustration and a long afternoon.

So many things to touch. From a child's point of view, a grocery store has a lot of neat and interesting things in it. There are so many colorful boxes, cans, packages, and fun things to eat. It is natural for them to want to explore this smorgasbord of new and exciting things. Now, this does not mean that you just let her run all over the place, but it does mean that you can understand why she wants to.

Nothing else to do. Sometimes a child's misbehavior during a grocery store trip can be due to the fact that she is bored stiff. She is trapped in a metal prison (the cart), slowly traveling through an amusement park of fun things to explore, and prevented from touching anything. If you have not provided *something* for her to do then she will be left with nothing else to do but to sit there in torment. Or perhaps to torment you.

A lack of clear and consistent rules can also contribute to problematic grocery store behavior. It may be that you have not yet developed a simple set of "grocery store" rules and taught these to your child. Or it may be that the rules for the grocery store have not been consistently reinforced. A lack of either clear rules or consistency could be a key to your problem.

What Can I Do?

Provide your child with things to do. Prevention is one of the keys to a successful grocery store trip. If you can keep your child busy with appropriate behavior, she will have less time left over for inappropriate behavior.

There are several ways that you can keep your child busy while you gather the items on your grocery list. First, you can bring along a small toy or book that is reserved just for the grocery store. This keeps them special and novel and will help maintain your child's interest in them during your trip. Or, you can just use a few toys or books from home that you know your child enjoys.

Second, a little bag of favorite snacks and some juice can go a long way in keeping your child occupied. You can even make them a reward for appropriate behavior by saying, "If you sit there quietly, I have a snack for you in a little while."

Third, you can make your child your "little helper" and have her assist you in getting things from the aisle. This may take a little longer but can be a lot of fun. In fact, some stores even have child-size grocery carts that can be used for this purpose. Either way, have your child stay close to the cart until you spot the item you need. Point it out to her and have her get the item and place it gently in the cart. Let her know that she is really helping you and doing a great job.

Develop clear and consistent rules for grocery store behavior. Decide what you want your child to do, make sure it is reasonable, and let her know. For instance, you may decide that she can walk on either side of the cart or up to about five feet in front of the cart and is not to touch any items without your permission. Explain these rules to her and make sure that she clearly understands them.

Just before you embark down your first grocery aisle, remind her of the rules and the positive and negative consequences that will follow her choices. For example, you can say, "Remember Sally, if you follow our grocery store rules, you can help me get things from the shelves and have a snack a little later. If you don't, you will have to hold on to the cart, you won't be able to get things for me, and you will have to do a Time-Out when we get home. Do you understand? Okay. Let's have a fun time!"

Practice doing it right. Whoever learned anything without a little practice? Both at home—and at the grocery store—review and practice the "grocery store" rules. If you want your child to walk no more than about five feet in front of the cart, then get a cart and show her how far that is. Have her start at the cart and walk forward, stopping at about five feet. Be a teacher! Do a dry run down a few aisles just for practice. Walk together down the aisles and have your child practice getting items from the shelf and putting them gently in the cart. Remember to give her lots of positive feedback on her performance as she learns the grocery store rules!

Look for signs of progress. If you think you can't find anything to reward, you are probably not looking hard enough. Watch carefully for your child to abide by the grocery store rules, which you have reviewed and practiced with her beforehand. When you see her walking close to the cart or sitting quietly in the cart as you have asked her to do, let her know how thrilled you are about her behavior. Use the Pour-It-On Technique to give her plenty of specific verbal rewards. Make sure that she knows *exactly* what she did to get this rewarding parental attention.

Other ideas for rewards include snacks or juice, getting out of the cart, riding on the front of the cart, pushing her own small cart, a fun sticker, a small twenty-five-cent toy when you leave the grocery store, a snack on the way home, or a special privilege when you get home.

Weaken negative behavior. If you do not want your child running out of your sight or throwing a tantrum in the middle of the store, then you must make sure that these behaviors do not "pay off" for your child. When your child begins to misbehave, immediately give her a Fork-in-the-Road, kindly but firmly telling her exactly how to correct her behavior and what the consequence will be if she does not.

A good Logical Consequence for the grocery store is to have your child lose various amounts of freedom in response to inappropriate behavior. For instance, she may have to ride in the top part of the cart, or hold on to the cart with one hand if she does not follow the grocery store rules. Inappropriate store behaviors can also keep your child from experiencing rewards. Remind your child that she is missing out on some fun things because of the choices she has made. Then, encourage her to begin making better choices and, if appropriate, give her another chance.

You can also have your child do a Time-Out right there in the store. Quickly find the most boring and unpopulated spot available and have your child sit there for a minute or two. This, of course, is a customized version of the regular home Time-Out. Once the Time-Out is over, remind your child of what you want her to do and move on.

If a store Time-Out is too difficult to pull off, you can give your child a "Time-Out ticket" for misbehavior in the grocery store. This means that you actually purchase some tickets (from a party store) and keep them with you (at all times!). When your child begins to display inappropriate behavior, give her a choice between behaving appropriately and receiving a Time-Out ticket. A Time-Out ticket is good for one Time-Out immediately upon returning home. The fact that you actually hand your child the ticket helps to make the negative consequence more immediate and tangible.

Finally, you can offer your child additional consequences if her misbehavior begins to reach epidemic proportions. For example, after using loss of freedom and rewards, Time-Out, or Time-Out tickets, you may need to let your child know that continued violation of the grocery store rules will result in an additional consequence at home. The loss of a preferred activity or other privilege is often very effective. Knowing your child and the things that she finds enjoyable will help you to pick the right consequence.

Cut your trip short. Some days are just not meant for the grocery store. If your child is having "one of those days" where she has already earned a grocery store Time-Out ticket, *and* early bed, *and* is beginning to gear up for her next tantrum before you've even reached the frozen foods, it may be time to cut your losses and leave.

When you get home, immediately administer the Time-Out and then sit down and take a deep breath. Perhaps your spouse can pick up a few items from the store later or you can have a friend watch your child while you come back to the store tomorrow.

Having one of these days may be a sign that your child needs more positive practice at using the grocery store rules, that your grocery store bag of toys and snacks needs revamping, or that your child may just be having a bad day. Either way, showing a little flexibility can go a long way towards saving a lot of sanity.

 ## How Do I Put It All Together?

The case of the runaway child. Mrs. Thompson decided that until Kelly learned better "grocery store behavior," she would prevent the problem by saving her big grocery store trips for times when her husband could watch Kelly. This kept both her and Kelly from having to endure a long and torturous battle. However, for the times when she needed to go to the store and bring Kelly with her, she decided to be prepared.

For starters, Mrs. Thompson promoted Kelly to the position of "little helper" and sat down and explained to Kelly the "little helper" job description and benefits. "To be a little helper, you have to stay close to the cart, so that you can always touch it with your hand. You can help me by getting things from the shelves, but *only* when I ask you to. Then, you can lay them *gently* in the cart so that they don't break or get banged up." (No three-point shot attempts!) "If you do a good job, we can visit the live lobsters (Kelly loved them) and have a special snack."

Mrs. Thompson continued, "If you don't listen at the store, then you can't be a little helper and will have to sit in the cart. This means that we might not be able to see the lobsters or have a snack." If while sitting in the cart Kelly decided to throw a tantrum, a Time-Out ticket or loss of privilege would be given. However, if Kelly sat in the cart quietly, she may get another chance as the little helper and earn back *either* the lobster tank or the snack, but not both.

Mrs. Thompson made a few special trips to the store just to practice this with Kelly. They walked up and down the aisles, with Kelly staying close to the cart and practicing getting only the things that her mother asked for. Kelly actually loved this special practice and did her best to be a great little helper. Mrs. Thompson beamed, "Kelly, you are doing such a great job at staying close to the cart and putting the things in so carefully. You are a super little helper!"

She also had Kelly pretend to do it *wrong* a few times by walking too far ahead and pretending to throw something in the cart. They reviewed what would happen if Kelly broke the grocery store rules and how it would make her feel. "I'd be sad," Kelly said. "Yes, it would be very sad," echoed Mrs. Thompson.

Mrs. Thompson was amazed at how well Kelly responded to their positive new plan. About half a dozen times Kelly lost her rewards and earned a Time-Out ticket, but she did appear to relish her new job and quickly learned the predictable structure of the grocery store rules. On the occasions where Kelly did not want to be a "little helper," Mrs. Thompson gave Kelly the choice of walking close to the cart or sitting in the cart.

Mrs. Thompson regularly used the Pour-It-On Technique and Kelly thrived on the positive attention from her mother. Mrs. Thompson occasionally threw in a surprise reward for exceptional grocery store behavior, such as a quick trip to the ice-cream store next door or allowing Kelly to pick out a special snack to bring home. Before long, Mrs. Thompson began to actually enjoy her trips to the store with Kelly, her new little helper.

Chapter 12

Homework

The case of the popular procrastinator. Sabrina was a bright, well-liked twelve-year-old girl who did not enjoy the burden of homework. In fact, she avoided it like the plague. The problem came when, two weeks before the end of the grading period, Sabrina would go into overdrive trying to catch up on late assignments. Unfortunately, she was never quite able to do it. Mr. and Mrs. Erickson would help her as much as they could, quizzing her on study material and helping her with projects. But as a result of her procrastination, Sabrina's grades were typically lower than they otherwise could have been.

Believers in letting children learn from their mistakes, Mr. and Mrs. Erickson were unsure about how much they should get involved in her decision-making and whether or not they should make home privileges dependent upon school grades. As a result, the situation continued year after year.

 ## Why Does This Happen?

Homework is not fun. I just wanted to remind you of this fact that we parents can so easily forget. While some children (what planet do they come from?) actually enjoy reading about U.S. history and studying pre-algebra, many would rather be doing something else. We all have to do our share of duties that are not fun and homework falls into that category for many kids. Remember to think about things from your child's point of view as well.

Homework can be very difficult for some children. Not only is homework not always fun, for some children it can be downright hard. For children whose gifts do not lean toward reading, or writing, or math, homework can be a struggle. The same can be true for children with Attention Deficit/Hyperactivity Disorder, who often are very disorganized and find it very difficult to sustain their attention on these types of tasks. For these children, homework represents a formidable challenge. Their resistance to doing it is not hard to understand.

Avoiding homework pays off. If your child perceives doing homework as a "negative situation," then whatever she can do to get out of that situation will be reinforced. If avoiding homework, procrastinating, whining, arguing, and so on, result in delaying homework or getting her out of her homework duties, then you shouldn't be surprised if she begins to exhibit these behaviors often. You should expect it.

Undetected physical problems can result in problems with class work and homework. Sometimes children are not clearly hearing instructions or find reading to be difficult because they cannot clearly make out the letters. Other times, children with delays in fine motor skills (in other words, strength and coordination of hand and finger muscles) or poor visual-motor coordination may find writing to be quite laborious. These are not problems with motivation, but are problems with certain abilities that make school work very difficult.

What Can I Do?

Check with your pediatrician. This is especially important if you think that there is a physical problem contributing to your child's resistance to homework. Problems with vision and hearing are among the most common. You should also check with your pediatrician if you think your child may have greater than average problems with sustaining attention or with overactivity. Make sure you clearly describe any signs or behaviors that you have observed. If your physician thinks that you may be right, further examination and testing may be required to fully assess the nature and severity of the problem.

Talk to your child's teacher. If your child appears to be making a legitimate effort to complete her work and yet spends an unreasonable amount of time doing homework each night, or if certain subjects seem to be a real obstacle to your child, schedule a conference with your child's teacher. If your child has several teachers, you should talk to the school guidance or academic counselor to help coordinate a meeting.

If the problems do not subside within a reasonable time frame, explore your options with the school counselor, and bring the principal or school psychologist into the conversation as well. It could be that modifications to the assignments may be helpful or that further academic assessment is needed to rule out the possibility of a learning disorder and to find out what is slowing things down for your child.

Have a regular routine and place to study. Sit down with your child and together decide upon an afternoon and evening schedule for school days. Sketch out a calendar-type weekly schedule and fill it in, with a sufficient block of time each day for homework, preferably at the same time each day. It can be immediately after school, following a short after school break, or right after dinner.

Decide where the best place is in your house for your child to do her homework. Try to pick a place that is quiet, well-lit, and will provide the least amount of distractions. I must mention here that I have met a few older children who actually were able to get their homework done with music in the background (possibly through headphones). In these cases, the music did not seem to be a distraction and made the homework a more enjoyable task for the child. The homework was getting done accurately and in a reasonable amount of time. I can live with that.

Teach your child to organize. Occasionally, problems with homework will be the result of lost homework sheets or forgotten homework assignments. If your child's notebooks look like they have just been hit by a nuclear bomb, then you may want to help her become better organized. You can start by providing a pouch for writing tools. Using a different colored tab or notebook divider for each subject is another idea. You can also make a folder for homework to be done that day and a folder for completed homework to be turned in the next day.

One way to help your child learn to plan for longer assignments is to teach her to break them down into smaller parts. You can do this by purchasing a fun calendar and marking down the due date for an assignment. Then, together with your child, determine logical dates when certain portions of the assignment should be completed by and write these on the calendar. Check with your child on these dates to make sure that these "mini-goals" are met. You can even use small fun rewards for meeting these goals. Your child's teacher should be able to give you even more ideas for helping your child learn to organize. Be creative and make organization fun!

Use a homework log. One method for keeping track of homework assignments that is becoming increasingly popular is to use a homework log, or assignment notebook. This is where the child writes down the homework for the day and, if needed, the teacher can initial it. This provides the child and parents with an accurate record of daily homework assignments. If you have not been using a homework log and homework completion or organization has been a problem, talk with your child's teacher about using one. I have included a sample homework log for your convenience at the end of the book. However, your child's teacher may have a particular homework log or assignment notebook that he or she prefers.

Develop a plan for homework frustration. Homework is often difficult for one of two reasons: (1) the subject is difficult for your child, or (2) your child simply has a lot of homework to do. Help your child develop a practical plan for handling these difficult situations. Homework strategies can include these:

> *Prioritize.* Decide what assignments need to be done first and which can wait until later or for another day.

Break it down. Break a large task down into several smaller parts and then start with one small part.

Divide and conquer. Do the ones you can now and save the rest for later.

Use your resources. Keep close at hand your dictionary, glossary, chapter summaries, class notes, and computer aides, and get help from parents and teachers when you need to.

Take a short break. If feeling frustrated or mentally drained, take five.

Give yourself a hand. Make your very best effort and don't worry about the rest. If something doesn't get finished after you've made your best effort, you can usually finish it another time. Congratulate yourself for making a good effort in a difficult situation.

Explain and teach these strategies to your child, modeling exactly what they would look and sound like. Write them on a sheet of paper and post them in your child's homework area. Refer your child to these strategies when she gets frustrated and use these moments to help her put the strategies to work. Make sure to let her know how proud you are of her effort in handling this frustrating situation.

Make homework come first. If your child is able to engage in afternoon and evening activities and still get her homework done by a reasonable time, consider yourself fortunate. However, if your child just seems to never have enough time to get her homework done, it is probably because she is spending too much time playing or watching television and is not leaving enough time for homework.

If you want homework to get done, then require that it be completed *before* any of these other fun activities are allowed. If you want her to have some afternoon free time, then make evening activities dependent upon getting her homework finished. If your child realizes that you mean business and that she will not be playing until her homework is done, then she will be much more motivated to get right to it.

Regularly check your child's work. This type of accountability is made easier if your child uses an assignment notebook to record her daily assignments. Until you feel that it is no longer necessary, conduct daily homework checks where you review your child's homework to make sure that it is reasonably and accurately done, *before* she gets to play. This will help ensure that it gets done and can prevent messy or rushed work. Make sure that your child knows what types of errors or mistakes will cause her to have to make revisions.

To help her learn to check her own work, make a checklist of the things that you would like your child to do *before* she calls you to check her completed homework. The checklist can include completing her work, double checking the work for accuracy, and checking for neatness. After you have checked her work, she will need to put all of her materials (pencils, pens, papers) away in the correct places and straighten up her homework area. The important thing is that the checklist is completed and checked off before she is released to play.

Reward homework completion. Remind your child that getting her homework done is naturally rewarded by good grades, feelings of accomplishment, and the freedom to play. Use the Pour-It-On Technique to let your child know that you like the effort and work she is putting forth. You like it when your boss tells you that you are doing a good job, don't you? Do the same for your child when she completes her homework.

If homework completion has been a significant problem, you might even consider putting together a simple contract. Set it up so that a daily point can be earned for accurate and timely completion of the assignments listed on the homework log. When your child saves five points, she can earn a special privilege.

Don't reward procrastination. The classic fable of the ant and the grasshopper drives home the importance of daily perseverance. In Proverbs 6:6–8, Solomon also points to the ant as an example of faithful endurance and the rewards it brings. In training your child to have "ant-like" perseverance, the last thing that you want is for your child's "grasshopper-like" procrastination to be rewarded. To teach your child the lesson of the ant, set things up so that procrastination on homework means delays of fun daily activities. If needed, you can also make it so that your child does not participate in any weekend activities (with the exception of organized sports, clubs, and so on) until her homework for that week is finished.

Make sure that arguing, whining, and so on, do not get your child out of her homework duties. Instead, encourage your child to use her homework plan and send her back to her homework area. If she needs to have a break, then let her have a break *after* a certain amount of homework is completed—not as the result of arguing, complaining, or procrastinating.

Provide a reasonable amount of assistance if you think that your child is legitimately "stuck," but don't let yourself get talked into doing your child's homework for her. Remember, you have already been through school, now it is her turn.

 ## How Do I Put It All Together?

The case of the popular procrastinator. Mr. and Mrs. Erickson knew that there was no problem with Sabrina's vision or hearing as her last checkup had shown her to be in good physical health. They also knew that she was very capable of getting good grades. They decided that it was high time for Sabrina to learn to manage her time better and to quit playing the "catch-up" game.

"Honey," Mr. Erickson started, "it is really important that you learn good study habits, because school isn't going to be getting any easier. We've got to talk about how you can start getting your homework and studying done properly and on time." "And," chimed in Mrs. Erickson, "what will happen if you do and if you don't."

Sabrina hesitantly agreed that she should make a more consistent effort on her homework. "The desk in my room is the best place to do my homework," Sabrina concluded. Her parents said that she would be given the opportunity to get her homework completed by bedtime each night, at which time they would check it. This was new for Sabrina.

"If you start having trouble getting your work done, and done properly, by bedtime," Mrs. Erickson explained, "then you'll have to start right after dinner, regardless of what television shows are on."

"And I suppose that you'll have to check it before I can do anything fun?" Sabrina asked with a little attitude, not liking the new approach too much so far.

"You've got it," Mr. Erickson confirmed.

The next day, they reviewed helpful homework strategies with Sabrina, which her dad had printed out on a sheet of paper and taped to Sabrina's desk. They also scheduled a meeting with Sabrina's guidance counselor. "You guys are taking this kind of seriously, don't you think?" Sabrina asked in typical preadolescent fashion.

With her guidance counselor, they discussed Sabrina's progress and asked for tips on how Sabrina could better organize herself. The guidance counselor suggested that Sabrina use an assignment notebook to keep track of daily homework assignments and offered some helpful ideas to Sabrina on how to organize her school notebooks and study for tests.

Within the first week, it quickly became clear that Sabrina was not getting her homework done by bedtime. Despite some sarcastic protests, Sabrina was then required to begin her homework each night after dinner. Mr. and Mrs. Erickson stuck with their plan and did not allow Sabrina to watch television, use the computer, or take phone calls until her homework was satisfactorily done each night.

This put a serious cramp into Sabrina's social life, which her parents encouraged her to fix by getting her homework done properly, so she had time to talk with her friends before phone time was over. They watched for Sabrina to make a positive effort and gave her plenty of encouraging feedback when she did. They also let Sabrina know that any grade falling below a "C" on a quarter or semester report card would result in the loss of her stereo until the grade was improved on her next progress report or report card.

As time went on, Sabrina experienced the painful consequences of her choices and she lost the use of her stereo for several weeks as the result of earning a "D" in science on her first quarter report card. Sabrina' s parents asked her science teacher to initial Sabrina's assignment log for the rest of the semester in order to ensure accuracy and arranged for Sabrina to meet with her teacher after school when she needed extra help.

By the end of the semester, the message had sunk in. Sabrina had pulled her grades up substantially, had her stereo back, and was feeling proud of her academic accomplishments. While doing homework was still not on her "top-ten" list of favorite things to do, she was learning that getting her homework done definitely had its benefits.

Chapter 13

Insecurity About Physical Appearance

The case of perfect Pamela. "I look fat!" declared Pamela, with a frown on her twelve-year-old face.

"What are you talking about?" Mrs. Meyer asked incredulously, taken aback by her daughter's unexpected comment.

"Rachel and Tammy are so thin," Pamela explained, "and they can wear all the latest clothes. All the boys think they're cute. I look so fat compared to them."

"Honey, you're not fat at all," Mrs. Meyer said, still amazed that this discussion was even taking place. "You look just fine. You're just the right size for your age. All girl's bodies go through changes during these years," she explained, as she gave Pamela a reassuring squeeze. "You'll be just fine."

"I'm still too fat," Pamela said, unconvinced by her mother's supportive efforts. While she didn't panic, Mrs. Meyer knew that she would need to keep her eye on this issue over the next several years.

Why Does This Happen?

Preadolescence. For both girls and boys, preadolescence is a time of great change. Not only do they no longer view themselves as children, their social landscape changes as well. Peer acceptance becomes increasingly important as these soon-to-be teenagers try to figure out who they are and how they fit in to their social group.

In addition, the young adolescent body goes through a predictable set of hormonal and physical changes. As a result, there are awkward growth spurts, weight changes, and the final stages of physical sexual maturation. During the teen years some experience these changes sooner and some later.

Not surprisingly, mood swings, social insecurity, and body-image concerns are common experiences during these tumultuous years. The goal is not to make these challenges go away, but to help your child make it through this passing storm and emerge with a balanced view of who she really is.

The messages we hear. It's not a pretty sight. The television programs, movies, magazines, and music that children see and hear routinely contain distorted and unhealthy messages about the importance of physical appearance. Perfectly shaped and conditioned bodies, stunningly beautiful or ruggedly handsome faces, the latest hair styles, and provocative clothing trends are held out as the gold standard of what it takes to be accepted and valued by others.

In addition to promoting a false basis for self-worth that is totally at odds with why God says we are valuable, another problem surfaces. None of us can ever attain these unrealistic standards, which often results in a never-ending struggle to achieve the elusive state of physical perfection. The great deception of these cultural messages is that they encourage your children to look to external physical factors to provide the meaning and value that God wants them to find in him.

The words we believe often come from those closest to us. Some of us fail to recognize the lasting impression our words make on our children. Referring to children with derogatory terms such as tubby, chunky, toothpick, twiggy, even if said in jest, will heighten their uncomfortableness with their physical appearance, rattle their social confidence, and leave them feeling deeply wounded by the very people who should be the safest and most encouraging.

What Can I Do?

Listen and learn. Sit down with your child over a Coke and find out what it is like to be a preteen nowadays. It may be very different than what you remember.

Ask your child what she enjoys about being twelve years old. What does she find difficult? What are some of the pressures she feels? What kind of good decisions does she see her peers making? What kind of bad decisions does she see some of them make? What does she think about God's commands regarding the issues of honesty, hard work, loving and accepting others, and obeying God in all she does. What are the current "cutting-edge" issues in her young Christian life?

Get reacquainted with your child on a personal level and let her teach you about the challenges of being a young person today. Showing this level of genuine interest in your child's life will build your relationship and help set the stage for the important discussions about physical appearance to follow.

Explore the messages your child hears. By this age, your child has been exposed to the subtle messages our society gives about the importance of physical appearance. What does she think about the importance of a person's physical appearance? Does a person have to look "perfect," to be pretty or handsome, or to have a wonderful smile? Does she think it is any different for girls than for boys? Does she see children at school get accepted or rejected purely on the basis of their physical appearance? If so, what does she think about that?

You want your child to not only identify the messages she hears about physical appearance, but also to explore the truth about those messages. Is physical appearance the most important thing about a person? What does God say about why people are important? Passages such as Psalm 103:8–18; Psalm 139:1–18; John 3:16; and Ephesians 3:17–18 teach us about God's great love for us and the value he places on us. First Samuel 16:7 reminds us that while people often look at a person's outward appearance, God looks at what is on the inside.

Help your child to examine honestly the distorted messages she sees and hears and contrast them with what God tells us is important about people. This is a discussion that may take place over time, and it will give your child invaluable experience at thinking through real-life issues from a Christian perspective.

Find a balance. Much of life comes down to our ability to find a healthy balance—work balanced with play, God's command for obedience balanced with our continual need for his grace. The issue of physical appearance is no different. We want to avoid the extremes of inaccurately over- or under-emphasizing the importance of physical appearance.

God chose to create us with physical bodies and declared that they were good (Genesis 1:31). He wants us to enjoy and care for our bodies and to make good decisions with them (1 Corinthians 6:19–20). The truth is that our physical appearance is important and does have an impact on our relationships with other people. People do make certain judgements about us based on our physical presentation. If you don't believe me, just walk around for a couple days with your hair uncombed and your pajamas on and see what kind of looks you get!

As Christ's ambassadors (2 Corinthians 5:20), we need to take care of our bodies as part of God's wonderful creation so that all aspects of our lives will bring glory to him. This includes making decisions about eating, exercise, and clothing that will promote a healthy body and positively reflect our relationship with God.

However, while our physical presentation is important, it is not the most important thing about us. Our value is found not in our external features, but in the very nature of who we are, being created in God's image. While our physical presentation does play a role, it is our personalities, unique characteristics, and chosen attitudes that make us attractive and desirable to others over the long run. Only the most shallow and fickle of relationships are determined solely by physical characteristics. Deep, lasting relationships only happen between people who develop the enduring qualities that God wants to instill in us, such as honesty, integrity, compassion, kindness, and joy (Galatians 5:22; Ephesians 4:25–32; Colossians 3:5–17).

When viewed from a Christian perspective, the pursuit of perfect physical appearance is not only misguided, it is very sad. To borrow a phrase from the writer of Ecclesiastes, it is "chasing after the wind." And even if physical perfection could be attained, what would it bring with it? Acceptance based on the most external part of who you are, which can only lead to inevitable feelings of being devalued and used. Again, the Bible is proved true when it tells us to base our value in who we are to God, not in how we look.

The balance we want our children to achieve includes making decisions that will promote a healthy body and positive physical presentation, and understanding that their worth and deepest attractiveness come from their value to God and the type of person they choose to be. In practical terms, this means that we want them to take reasonable steps to eat well, exercise, and dress fashionably and appropriately, while at the same time keeping their physical "imperfections" in proper perspective.

This balancing act takes place in the arena of your child's thoughts and beliefs. Here are some balanced thoughts you can discuss with your child:

- Everyone has a different body type (e.g., bigger, smaller).
- Everyone can look attractive (handsome or pretty) in his or her own way.
- I have (a) very handsome/pretty/attractive _____.
- I can do my best to look nice and stay healthy.
- When I keep my body healthy, my body gives glory to God.
- The most attractive part of a person is what is on the inside.
- God loves me because he made me and planned me on purpose.
- Some people think that looks are what count, but I think that it's the kind of person you are.
- I pick my friends because of the kind of person they are, not because of what they look like.
- People will like me because of the kind of person I am, not because of what I look like.

Discuss these statements with your child and see what she thinks about them. Share with her why you think that these statements are true and encourage her to choose two or three of them to memorize. Talk together about how God wants us to take good care of our bodies and how we can do that in a balanced way. If your child is having difficulty with eating and exercise habits, help her come up with a balanced eating and exercise plan. Consult with your pediatrician or a nutritionist for ideas if you need to. The goal is to help your child begin to develop a balanced view of her physical appearance that will contribute to healthy lifestyle choices and a positive self-view.

Look for models. I don't mean runway models here. What God says about loving everyone is true, and because it is true, the evidence is often plentiful. Keep your eyes open for examples of people who are funny, friendly, likeable, intelligent, and dynamic. If you look closely, you will find that few of them are without various physical flaws when compared to Hollywood standards. Some will be short and some tall, some will be skinny, some will have larger body types, some will have braces, some will have freckles, and so on. While they will all have attractive characteristics, there is another thing they will all have in common: None of them is perfect! Open your child's eyes to the evidence around her that God's beauty really does shine from within.

Affirm your child. The words your child hears from you everyday have the potential to shape her life forever. So make sure that your comments affirm the truth about who she is. Comment positively on her effort, her perseverance, her sharing, her friendliness, her compassion, her great sense of humor, her kindness, her joy, her helpfulness, her hard work, her not giving up, her being a good sport, her talents, her listening, her respectful talking, her standing up for others, and how fun it is to be around her. Let her know that you are glad that she is your child and how proud you are of her. And don't forget to remind your child regularly that he or she is very handsome/beautiful, has a wonderful smile, and looks great.

Build self-esteem. Positive self-esteem is built by teaching a child to think accurately and positively and by helping her to successfully handle the challenges that come with each stage of life.

Using the ideas for building self-esteem provided in the section on "Poor Grades," help your child to develop positive thinking habits and build a track record of positive interpersonal experiences.

Encourage healthy eating. Food is meant to be enjoyable, and tasteful meals and snacks are one of the pleasures God has given to us. As always, balance is the key. Treat food as a natural part of good nutrition, designed to help us stay healthy. Use mealtimes as a chance for enjoyable family relating, a time for family closeness and bonding. Discuss each other's lives and have fun, meaningful, and intelligent conversation during mealtimes. Prevent unnecessary weight problems by stocking your shelves with healthy foods and snacks and keeping reasonable limits on more sugary treats.

Keep your eyes open. Most boys and girls experience periods of insecurity about their physical appearance during their preteen and teenage years and do not develop an eating disorder. But there are many who do. While the large majority of eating disorders are experienced by females, males can also fall prey to these same distorted messages. If you find that your child is not responding to your efforts to help balance her thinking about her physical appearance and if you notice unusual eating habits, fluctuating weight, excessive efforts to lose weight, frequent trips to the bathroom following meals, or a continued preoccupation with weight and body image, consult with your pediatrician and a qualified mental health professional.

 ## How Do I Put It All Together?

The case of perfect Pamela. Mr. and Mrs. Meyer decided to put some extra effort into understanding the reasons for Pamela's recent dissatisfaction with her appearance. Mrs. Meyer took Pamela out for a movie and dessert to give them a chance to talk. "What did you think about the girls in that movie?" Mrs. Meyer asked. "Did you think they were pretty?"

"Yeah," Pamela replied, "they were beautiful."

"Do you think a girl has to look that beautiful to have friends and to be married someday?" Mrs. Meyer asked, getting right to the point.

Pamela paused, then answered, "No, I guess not."

"What do you think about how important it is to look like one of those girls in that movie?" Mrs. Meyer continued.

"Well," Pamela blurted out, "Jessica at school is so perfect looking. All the boys think she is so cute. I can't stand it."

Pamela and her mother continued to talk about her worries that she wasn't as pretty as Jessica. "Honey, you are very pretty," Mrs. Meyer eventually reassured her troubled daughter. "You have beautiful eyes, a great smile, and most important, you're a wonderful friend. I've got something else to tell you," Mrs. Meyer continued. "While it's great to try to look your best, it's not how you look that wins you friends or eventually attracts boys, when it's the right time for that; rather, it is the kind of person you are inside that makes people want to be with you."

Over the next few months, Mr. and Mrs. Meyer talked with Pamela from time to time about this issue. During a family devotion, they took a look at God's love for us and contrasted that with liking someone just because of how they look. "Is that how God wants us to treat people?" asked Mr. Meyer.

"No, it's not," replied Pamela, "that would be pretty bad. He wants us to love them for who they are on the inside."

Mr. Meyer talked with Pamela about being balanced in her desire to look nice and be the right person on the inside. "Which of these sentences do you like the best?" Mr. Meyer asked Pamela, after going over some positive statements about physical appearance and self-worth.

"I like the one that says everyone can look handsome or pretty in his or her own way," said Pamela, "and the one that says people will like me because of the kind of person I am and not just because of how I look."

"Do you think those are true?" asked her dad.

"Yeah, I do," replied Pamela. "Look at Ricky Johnson," she continued. "I think he's cute but Sara doesn't. And she thinks that Joey Martin is cute, but I think he's just okay."

Mr. Meyer smiled as he asked Pamela what God thought about Ricky and Joey. "He thinks they're both great," she replied, "because he made them."

Pamela enjoyed playing soccer, which gave her plenty of exercise. Mrs. Meyer put more effort into planning healthy meals for their family, and they started to keep more healthy snacks around the house. Whenever an opportunity presented itself, Mr. and Mrs. Meyer made sure to tell Pamela how proud they were of her positive behaviors and frequently pointed out her positive characteristics ("Pamela, you did a very nice job working hard on your homework just now. Way to stick with it until it was done!"). They also regularly affirmed her positive physical appearance by saying things like, "Honey, you look nice today," and "Sweetie, that sweater looks great on you."

Pamela's concern about her physical appearance seemed to come and go unpredictably over the following months. Mr. and Mrs. Meyer gave her space to have these feelings and didn't try to solve things for her. They stayed consistent in their support, positive affirmation, and overall plan to help Pamela keep her body healthy and develop a balanced view about her physical appearance and her self-worth.

As with many preadolescents, Pamela's growth spurts took her on a physical and emotional roller coaster at times, which wasn't easy for anybody. As time went on, however, Mr. and Mrs. Meyer saw that some of their discussions were starting to sink in. Pamela began to seem less concerned about her physical "imperfections" and more confident about her appearance. During one of their discussions, Pamela told Mrs. Meyer, "Mom, I like who I am. And I have some really good friends too." While they knew the battle was not yet over, the Meyers were thrilled to see their daughter begin to show signs of self-confidence about how she looked, and more important, about who she was.

Chapter 14

Interrupting

The case of the human magnet. "I swear, it's like he has radar," exclaimed Ms. Hudson. "Whenever I'm on the phone, he just appears out of nowhere, like a magnet." She was speaking of her five-year-old son, Jimmy, who had a remarkable talent for needing something whenever his mother picked up the phone.

"It is *sooo* aggravating, I can hardly stand it!" said Ms. Hudson. She usually responded to Jimmy's interruptions by trying to wave him off with a variety of hand signals that made her look like a confused referee. "Be quiet!" she would say in a muffled scream while trying to walk away (with Jimmy trailing along behind). Sometimes, she would grab a bag of pretzels and give it to him, hoping that this would be a temporary distraction. It worked, if Jimmy was in the mood for pretzels.

Why Does This Happen?

He hasn't learned the rules. This type of interrupting is in part due to the self-centeredness that is a normal part of being a young child. However, it is also due to the fact that some young children have not yet learned what to do instead of interrupt when they have a question. Most children are not born radiating with manners; you have to teach them.

Is interrupting rewarded? Your child wants your attention. Make no mistake about it. If he loses your attention to someone else, he may try to get it back. If your child finds that interrupting is the best way to get your attention back, he will probably continue doing it. If he is continuing to interrupt, that probably means that you have not yet taught him that there is a better way to get your attention.

 ## What Can I Do?

Keep your cool. Remind yourself that occasional interrupting is normal behavior for young children and that chances are that, given time, your child too will learn not to interrupt. *Expect* to be occasionally interrupted as your child is learning this new behavior. This way you'll feel less frustrated when it actually happens. Put things in perspective; your problems could be a lot worse. Tell yourself that it's okay to feel a little frustrated and then lighten up and laugh a little. You'll live longer.

Occupy your child when you have to make an important telephone call or have an important conversation. One way to do this is to have a few special toys or books that are reserved just for "phone time." These toys will have a novel appeal to your child because he doesn't get to play with them regularly. You can also direct your child to other toys or activities that you know he enjoys if you think this will work. Occasionally providing a little snack just before you begin an important phone call can also be a helpful distraction.

Develop a set of clear rules for getting your attention during phone calls and other conversations. Using the Detour Method, the first step is to develop a simple set of clear rules that you might call his "telephone plan" or "interrupting plan."

The first step should be for your child to decide if the issue is important enough for an interruption. Regarding the telephone, with the exception of an emergency or very important request (such as if someone is hurt, or needs to go to the bathroom), your child should try to wait until your phone call is completed. If your child has a question he feels he must ask, teach him to stand beside you and softly say, "Excuse me," or give you a little tug on your wrist—some respectful sign that he wants to ask you something. Of course, then he must wait until you break from your conversation to speak with him. This plan would look something like this:

1. Ask myself, "Do I really need to interrupt?"
2. Politely say, "Excuse me," or gently touch my parent's wrist
3. Quietly wait for them to answer me

Practice what to do. Once you have decided upon the steps for appropriately getting your attention while you are on the telephone or talking with someone, practice them together. In my family, we have used the Detour Method to teach our sons simple steps for various things (sharing toys, telling the truth), and *they* often ask *us* if we can practice them! It is easy to see the pride they take in their accomplishments of successfully learning the plan. The rehearsals are short and fun, with plenty of positive encouragement thrown in.

So, get a toy phone and practice, taking turns being the interrupter and the interruptee. Grab one of his stuffed animals and pretend that you and the animal are talking. Have him then practice the rules for getting your attention when you are in the middle of a conversation. You can then practice using a real phone, or while you and your spouse, or you and a friend have a mock conversation. Have a lot of fun doing this, use plenty of specific verbal rewards, and watch your child's face glow as he begins to master this new skill.

Instruct your child clearly before phone calls or other conversations. This is particularly important in the initial learning phases of this behavior. While you will not always be able to do this, do it whenever possible. Remember, you want your child to succeed in using his steps for getting your attention appropriately. This will be more likely to happen if you prepare him. Let him know that you are going to make an important phone call and you want to see him use his steps. Exude excitement and confidence as you communicate that you know he can do it—and be thrilled when he does. Have him recite his steps to you, give him a "high five," provide him with something else to do, and make your phone call. The same procedure applies to other types of conversations as well.

Provide positive attention. When you are actually on the phone or in the middle of a conversation, watch carefully for your child to be doing his new plan. Look for any sign of even the first step. If you have been regularly practicing the steps and have prepared your child beforehand, you should be able to see some signs of the steps.

The next step for *you* is very important. When you see your child playing quietly and not interrupting while you are on the phone, excuse yourself from your phone call or conversation for about ten seconds and let him know with no uncertainty that you have noticed his effort, appreciate it, and that he is doing a great job! If your child comes up and softly says, "Excuse me," smile at him and then break from your conversation in a reasonable amount of time to see if there is an important request or emergency. If his request is important and it is something that you can help him with right then, then do so. If it is not, then instruct him to wait until you are off the phone. When you are done with your call or conversation, let him know that he did a wonderful job with his plan and that he is learning exactly how to do it!

On the other hand, if while in the middle of a phone call or other conversation your child loudly or abruptly interrupts you, don't go ballistic. *Calmly* excuse yourself and remind your child to do his plan. He has started to veer off of the road, so gently and firmly redirect him back on to the road. Then, *immediately* after you see your child beginning to use his steps, give him some sort of a sign, like a thumbs-up or a squeeze on the shoulder, indicating that he is back on track.

Use Time-Out for continued interrupting. Make sure, of course, that you have done everything you can to help your child learn the appropriate replacement behavior, such as practicing his steps and consistently rewarding them. However, if interrupting continues, then adding a negative consequence will be essential and a Time-Out is a logical choice.

If your child interrupts inappropriately, refer him back to his steps, letting him know that a second interruption will result in a Time-Out. If he chooses to interrupt again, stay calm; this will be a good learning experience for him. If possible, administer a Time-Out right then and there. Depending on your situation, you may have to improvise on the Time-Out spot, but that is okay. The point will have been made. He chose to continue to interrupt and the result was a modified Time-Out and no parental attention. You can also calmly let him know that he has just earned a Time-Out, needs to go sit down, and will go to Time-Out immediately when your call is over.

Once the Time-Out has been completed, review the "telephone plan" with your child and have him practice the situation with you again, this time using the appropriate steps. In contrast to your earlier displeasure, provide lots of attention and plenty of social rewards as he does it right this time. Remember, the Time-Out is over. If possible, end the situation on a good note, with your child feeling positive about himself and his ability to do his steps the next time. You should also feel good, because you have just taken a negative situation and turned it into a positive learning experience for your child.

 ## How Do I Put It All Together?

The case of the human magnet. Ms. Hudson talked with some other mothers and immediately felt much better after hearing that Jimmy's habit of interrupting was very normal. In fact, she heard some stories that made her feel fortunate! Even so, she decided to take action. "Jimmy, let's come up with a plan to help you learn how to get my attention the right way when I'm on the phone." They decided upon a simple "phone plan":

1. Interrupting immediately if there was an emergency
2. Not interrupting if it wasn't an emergency
3. Softly saying, "Excuse me," if a question was necessary, and waiting quietly for the parent to respond

They practiced this plan together once a day for a week with a toy phone, until Ms. Hudson felt comfortable that Jimmy knew the rules well. Next, Ms. Hudson had one of her friends call her each day to allow Jimmy an opportunity to practice. When the phone rang, she excitedly encouraged Jimmy, "Now, remember to do the phone plan!" During the call, she repeatedly gave Jimmy positive nonverbal feedback and broke away once from each conversation long enough to whisper, "Jimmy, you're doing great!"

Following a successful phone call, Ms. Hudson poured on the positive attention, "Jimmy, that was perfect! You didn't interrupt one little bit. Brenda (who had been on the phone) thought you did a great job too!" The phone rules also included a Time-Out if Jimmy interrupted more than once during any phone conversation (they practiced this too!).

The practicing paid off. As the real phone calls came, Ms. Hudson reminded Jimmy of the phone plan and tried to get him involved in an activity before picking up the phone whenever possible. For instance she would say something like "Jimmy, why don't you color this picture until I'm done on the phone." She also made it a point to give Jimmy a little extra attention *after* a successful phone call to let him know that he had done a great job following his plan.

As the result of all of her planning and practice, Ms. Hudson found that Jimmy was interrupting much less than before. During the first couple of weeks, she had to review the rules and do a few more practice sessions, and Jimmy earned his fair share of Time-Outs for repeated interruptions. However, once Jimmy learned that the phone rules were here to stay, it wasn't long before his interrupting became the exception rather than the rule.

Chapter 15

Lying

The case of tall-tale Jessica. Jessica was a ten-year-old girl who had recently developed a habit of lying. She had seen some of her friends lie to their parents about their homework and figured that it might work for her too.

Mr. and Mrs. Kim did not realize that Jessica was being untruthful until they were shocked by a progress report indicating a drop in grades due to numerous missing assignments Jessica had told them were completed. They asked Jessica about the missing assignments, and Jessica said that she didn't know that she had to do them. Mr. Kim almost exploded (but didn't), as the thought of his daughter lying to him was almost more than he could take.

Why Does This Happen?

What your child observes at home plays an extremely important role in the development of moral decision-making skills. Does your child see you regularly engage in small "white" lies with your spouse, friends, or coworkers? Are you untruthful with your children, shading the truth to your benefit? Do you ask your child to cover for you on the phone (as in, "Tell him I'm not here")? Or does your child regularly observe respectful, caring, and thoughtful honesty, even when it is difficult? If you are not modeling honest behavior, don't expect the apple to fall too far from the tree.

Peer influences can contribute to a child's untruthfulness. From direct pressure to lie about a certain situation to observing other children being untruthful, the pressure to be accepted by one's peer group can be very strong. Additionally, if a friend's twisting of the truth or telling a small lie appears to pay off, your child can be tempted to try it out for herself.

Avoiding trouble or embarrassment is a common reason for being untruthful, regardless of the age bracket. When a child realizes, usually in a terror-stricken panic, that she has done something wrong and is going to get into trouble, lying can appear to be quite an attractive option! A few experiments with being less than 100 percent candid is a normal part of learning for most children. While it is admirable to learn from the mistakes of others, most of us need to make a few of our own.

Short-sighted thinking is the cause of many childhood lies. Your child does not yet fully understand all of the moral implications of lying. This comes only with time, maturation, and experience. All she knows is that she wants that new toy or that she doesn't want you to see her latest report card. She has made the mistake of thinking that being untruthful will actually help things to go better for her. Instead, she needs to learn that honesty is always the best policy and that lying never, never, never pays off.

What Can I Do?

Don't overreact. You want to be a parent who your child will confide in when she does something wrong, not a parent she'll learn to avoid. Your response when she is untruthful—or commits any type of misbehavior—will teach her what kind of parent you are.

Just around the corner are many important issues that are difficult to talk about, such as drugs, sex, friends, peer pressures, and so on. Lay the groundwork now that will help your child feel comfortable talking to you when she has made a mistake or when she is faced with a difficult situation. While it is perfectly okay for you to express to your child your feelings of hurt or anger about being lied to, make sure that you express those feelings in a way that doesn't make your child wish she had talked to someone else.

Model honesty. Doublecheck yourself to make sure that through your own example you are teaching your child how important honesty is. Communicate that you hold in high esteem God's command to be truthful. For example, if you break something in a store, honestly admit it and pay for it; if you find something of value, do your best to locate the owner instead of keeping it for yourself.

Once, while picking up some household supplies at a hardware store with my son, I found a $100 dollar bill. It likely belonged to the person who had just paid at the cashier ahead of me. For a moment I thought about all the things I could do with that money. But my son got to watch me return that $100 dollar bill to its rightful owner, which provided a great opportunity to talk about the importance of honesty and doing what God wants us to do. Remember, the best lessons in life are seen, not heard.

Talk about honesty. If you catch your child in a lie, take some time to talk together about what happened. Explore your child's reasons for lying, and place yourself in her shoes. Try to appreciate the bind that she was in and how she felt stuck between a rock and a hard place. We've all been there. Find out what she was worried might happen if she told the truth and how she thought that lying might help the situation. Since your child did lie, how did it work out for her? What were the results of her "experiment" with untruthfulness?

Individually with your child or together as a family, spend time talking about the importance and benefits of being honest. Verses such as Leviticus 19:11–13; Psalm 15; Proverbs 11:1, 16:11, 13; and Ephesians 4:25 make it clear that God places great value on honesty. Hebrews 6:18 even tells us that it is impossible for God to lie.

Why do you think that honesty is so important to God? As a parent, why do *you* choose to be honest when telling a lie might be easier? The benefits of being honest—especially when it is difficult—lead to developing a godly character, a clear conscience, causing people to trust you, strengthening friendships and relationships, not making things worse, and helping to solve problems the right way. Sometimes being honest about misbehavior will bring a price tag with it. But the benefits far outweigh the cost.

Find a better solution. Your child's choice to lie is, in part, a reflection of her inability to effectively solve the problem she was faced with. In other words, something in her decision-making process was terribly flawed if she came to the conclusion that lying was the best alternative. You need to help her find a better solution.

One way to do this is to use a positive problem-solving approach. First, have her clearly identify the problem she was faced with. Not wanting to do her homework? Trying to avoid getting into trouble? Second, help her to come up with several different things that she could have done instead of lie. Third, have her identify what would have probably happened if she would have done those things. Fourth, have her choose which solution or combination of solutions she would use if the situation were to happen again in the future and have her tell you why.

Discuss exactly what she would have to do to make her new approach work. If it lends itself, role-play the situation with your child and see how well she is able to pull it off. Finally, review how she thinks her final solution would actually work. This positive problem-solving approach gives you a chance to learn about your child's thinking process, teach her valuable problem-solving skills, and help her come up with a practical plan for making a better decision and obeying God in the future.

Catch your child telling the truth. I remember my wife and I doing this about a year ago with one of our boys. He said he hadn't done something (when he clearly had) as an obvious attempt to avoid getting into trouble. Our initial response included clearly instructing him about the importance of being honest and then watching closely for him to tell the truth so that we could immediately reward that behavior.

It wasn't long before our chance came, and you should have seen him beam with pride as we expressed our pleasure that he had chosen to tell the truth. Since then, he has voluntarily brought his truthfulness to our attention when he was honest about having done something wrong ("...but Dad, aren't you glad I told the truth?"). You bet I was—and we would always respond that we were extremely thankful that we could trust him—even though he might still get a negative consequence for what he had done wrong.

Watch for chances to use the Pour-It-On Technique when your child tells the truth *in situations where she has previously been untruthful.* Let her know how proud you are that she chose to be truthful, especially when telling the truth is difficult (such as admitting to doing something wrong).

I am also in favor of occasionally reducing the negative consequences for an offense when a child tells the truth about it, particularly if lying has been an issue in the past. Don't leave your child with the distinct feeling that lying would have been a much better choice. We want her to be glad that she told the truth. Letting your child know that the consequences have been lightened because she was truthful is a great way to reward her honesty while still providing appropriate negative consequences for the misbehavior.

Make lying your child's problem, not yours. Devise Logical Consequences that "fit the crime," such as an immediate Time-Out, the loss of privileges, or additional work or chores. For example, if a child has lied about school work, then having to complete the missing work and losing a privilege until it is completed may be an effective Logical Consequence. If a child has lied about finishing her chores so she could go to a friend's house, then having to come home immediately to complete her chores and losing the privilege of returning to the friend's house for a few days would be a Logical Consequence.

If lying becomes frequent, then let your child know ahead of time that even the slightest *suspicion* of a lie will result in an immediate negative consequence. You can also use a Response/Cost approach by letting your child know that she will be fined a certain amount from her allowance for every lie or that she will lose one or more privileges for several days each time she is untruthful.

How Do I Put It All Together?

The case of tall-tale Jessica. Mr. and Mrs. Kim sat down with Jessica to discuss her recent decisions to lie. "Okay, honey, let's talk about why you thought that lying would be a good idea."

"Mom," Jessica said, "some of my friends do it all the time...." Jessica went on to explain how she had seen some of her friends lie to their parents and thought it might be a good way to get out of having to do her homework. "I knew it was wrong, but I decided to do it anyway," she sheepishly admitted.

In an understanding way, Mr. and Mrs. Kim talked with her about why honesty is so important and had Jessica list the consequences that lying had brought for her. They looked at Leviticus 19, Proverbs 11, and Ephesians 4 and talked together about why God would value honesty so much that he put it on his top-ten list (in other words, in the Ten Commandments). "Jessica, why do you think being honest is so important to God?" Mrs. Kim asked.

"Because lying hurts people," Jessica said, "and God wants people to be able to trust you." Then, to prepare Jessica to handle things better in the future, they used their problem-solving steps to help her come up with other approaches that she could take when tempted to be dishonest or when school work became difficult.

Mr. and Mrs. Kim also decided to include Jessica in deciding upon appropriate negative consequences. Together, they decided that Jessica would have to complete all of her missing work *and* would lose evening telephone privileges until the work was caught up. Each night, she would be required to complete her regular homework and work on her make-up assignments as well. They also decided to use an assignment notebook, signed by Jessica's teacher, for the rest of the quarter to be sure that all of Jessica's homework was coming home.

Mr. and Mrs. Kim watched carefully to catch Jessica being truthful, particularly when she was truthful about having done something wrong, such as teasing her brother. When they saw this, they immediately let her know how proud they were of her for telling the truth. "Jess," said Mrs. Kim, "we're really proud of you for telling the truth about calling Matt a name just now. That's a great job of being honest. Now, I want you to apologize to your brother and any more name calling will earn you a Time-Out."

While Jessica was not too happy about losing her telephone privileges, this lesson in truthfulness was an influential one. With her parents' help, she was learning that dishonesty did not pay and had become much better prepared to make a wise choice the next time the temptation to lie came knocking at her door.

Chapter 16

Managing Electronics (TV, Video Games, Computers)

The case of the video junkie. Philip was a nine-year-old boy who loved his video games. And his Game Boy. And his computer games. And of course, the interactive Internet games. Let's not forget television, movies, and videos. In fact, Philip loved playing and watching electronic toys so much that if he could, he would choose to do nothing else with his free time. Mr. and Mrs. Douglas were concerned about Philip's preoccupation with his electronic toys. They also did not like Philip's habit of talking back ("Just a minute, Mom, I'm still playing") or ignoring his parents' attempts to set time limits on his computer and video game playing.

❓ Why Does This Happen?

Electronic games are captivating. An entire media industry is focused on one thing: getting your child's attention. And through the use of multimedia advertising, state-of-the-art graphics, booming sound effects, fast-paced music, and catchy games, they are doing just that. With all this technology, the fact that over 140 million Nintendo and Sony PlayStation systems have been sold worldwide is no surprise. Neither is it surprising that children find them hard to turn off.

Your children live in an electronic world. The only interesting "electronic" devices most of us grew up with were television and radio. Oh yes, don't forget turntables, cassette tapes, and the eight-track player. In contrast to our primitive technological upbringing, our children are being taught how to use complicated computers in elementary school. Times have changed, all right.

Our children are not to blame for their interest in computers and video games—an increasingly technologically sophisticated society is gearing them in that direction. However, while we must understand that our children are being brought up in a world much different from the one in which we were raised, we must still teach them how to keep things in balance.

A screen won't reject you. Some children latch on to various forms of video entertainment and interactive Internet games because it is safer than person-to-person interaction. Interacting with real people who have the power to accept or reject you carries more risk than interacting with a computer screen where you play games with people you don't really know. And who don't really know you. For some children, electronic games become a safe and entertaining sanctuary where they can avoid the risks that come with real people.

What Can I Do?

Get off the bandwagon. Don't fall into the trap of thinking that just because everybody has a certain video game system or Internet access that you have to as well. First of all, everybody does not have all of these things, and second, even if they did, it does not mean that you must have them. Be purposeful about what you allow into your home. While computers and video games can be healthy, fun, and educational, they can also contain inappropriate material and easily soak up far too much of your children's time. You decide what balance is best for your family.

Talk with your family about the dangers. Computer games, Internet access, television, and video games can bring inappropriate material and dangers into the family. While keeping the conversation age-appropriate, you can identify dangers such as bad language, pornography, violent graphics and themes, predatory adults who pretend to be children in chat rooms, and a reduction in quality family interaction.

As part of a family-time discussion, talk together about what types of computer access and video games are appropriate for your family. Discuss how you can use these tools in your family as sources of fun and education while safeguarding yourselves against the dangers that lurk in these electronic waters. Read together and discuss Colossians 3:17 and Proverbs 3:5–6 as a biblical basis for pleasing and honoring God in all that you do.

Encourage other activities. One way to get the kids off of the computer is to help them find other enjoyable and rewarding activities. Strongly encourage other fun "off-line" activities that build skill, character, and interpersonal relationships. Consider sports, photography, scouts, church groups, reading, summer camps, science club, chess club, archery, martial arts, art classes, music lessons, groups that care for animals, and so on. All of these activities can enrich your children and provide them with rewarding knowledge, experiences, and friendships that will shape their lives in a positive direction. And best of all, you don't have to plug them in.

Do fun things together. Families that have the least problems with the electronic invasion are often the families that are the most active and involved with their children. If your family basically just sits around most of the time, is it any wonder that your children find relief from boredom in an easy, convenient (and electronic) way? Instead, model an energetic approach to life and get out and do things together. Whether you go for walks, play board games, go bowling, look at tropical fish, play catch, shoot baskets, or whatever you enjoy doing together, be a family that has fun together.

Set appropriate time limits. Television, computers, and video games function much like candy for children. What child wouldn't overdose on Twinkies™ and doughnuts if they could? In the same way, and without the perspective and balance that usually come with age, many children would choose to spend hour after hour on various computer and video games.

Just as you limit candy and snacks, limit the amount of time that children spend with their electronic devices. Have a set amount of time each day, and monitor it with a timer. Some days, such as school days, may have very little, if any, time for electronic games and entertainment. Start your children off with good habits from the very beginning. Electronic games are not an unalienable right—they are an occasional privilege.

Require appropriate electronic behavior. Three things should be required to use electronic devices: Your child should: (1) get on right, (2) stay on right, and (3) get off right. Getting on right means asking to use the television, computer, or video game in a respectful way and reacting respectfully when the answer is no. Staying on right means exhibiting appropriate behavior while playing the game or watching the show (in other words, talking respectfully, sharing, being considerate of others). Getting off right means listening and talking respectfully when asked to turn the device off.

If a child has difficulty with any of these behaviors, then use the Detour Method to rehearse concrete steps for getting on, staying on, or getting off correctly. If problems continue, use the Logical Consequence of reducing the time available for the use of that device. If needed, you can remove that device all together for a while until your child has earned another chance to do it right by exhibiting appropriate behavior with the other electronic devices he still has access to. Remember, it will not mortally hurt your child to lose an electronic device for a while. Instead, it will help to reinforce the important lesson that people are more important than electronics.

Keep your eyes open for appropriate electronic behavior. Using the Pour-It-On Technique, watch carefully for your child to listen, share, take turns, talk respectfully, or exhibit any other positive behavior while engaged in an electronic activity. When he changes the television channel at a sibling's request, when he makes an encouraging comment to a friend who has just lost his last "life" in a video game, when he says, "Okay, Mom" and turns the computer game off at your first request, make sure that you let him know how happy you are about his choice to take turns, make an encouraging comment, or listen the first time. Walk over to him, squeeze him on the shoulder, flash a big grin, and let him know that he did a great job.

Be a watchdog. Making sure that your children are safe from inappropriate material on the computer, television, movies, and video games is a never-ending job, especially as they get older. If you have Internet access, make sure you use either a family-friendly Internet provider or an Internet filter to screen out inappropriate content. View your child's video games to make sure you are comfortable with the themes, graphics, and language they contain. Be selective about television shows and movies your children watch. Take the time to sit down with them and watch their favorite shows together from time to time. The manufacturers of these shows and products do not always have your children's best interests in mind when they create their products. That is why you must.

 ## How Do I Put It All Together?

The case of the video junkie. "Okay, guys, we've got to talk about how to handle our television and video games the right way," said Mr. Douglas, as he called a family meeting to talk about how to have fun with electronic devices without letting them get out of hand.

"I know how easy it is to watch too much TV," said Mr. Douglas. "I do it, and then I end up wishing I had spent more time with you guys." He and Mrs. Douglas talked with Philip about how anyone can spend too much time watching television or playing video games and how that would be harmful for that person. They turned their discussion to the content of various games and how some of them are fun and positive, while others are inappropriate and displeasing to God.

"Oh, you should see some of the games that Nick has," Philip said, as if he was revealing a world-class secret. "They have all sorts of stuff in them, like shooting and blood, even some bad words."

Philip was not enthused when the discussion turned to limiting the time he spent on his Game Boy and video game system. "But Mom, Dad—I don't spend too much time on them. You should see how much Bobby and Nick get to play theirs. They play way more than me. It's not fair!"

Despite his valiant effort, Philip did not dissuade his parents, who held firm to what they thought were reasonable time limits. They told Philip they would consider occasional exceptions depending on how well he handled these time guidelines. They also brought up the subject of appropriate play behavior. "Philip, if you want to be able to play these games—and remember, we want you to be able to play them—then you have to be able to do three things: get on right, stay on right, and get off right." They proceeded to give him clear examples, and also made it clear that inappropriate behavior while getting on, staying on, or getting off of an electronic device would result in losing the privilege of using that device for the rest of that day, or for longer if necessary.

Mr. and Mrs. Douglas also encouraged Philip to find other fun activities to get involved in. "Now, Philip, what are some other things that would be fun to do?" Mrs. Douglas asked. Philip said he didn't know. "Well, let's think of a few," Mrs. Douglas said, determined not to give up. "Didn't you say once that karate would be fun?"

As it turned out, Philip was interested in both karate lessons and scouts and he had several friends who did both. They decided to watch a group karate lesson at the local community center and have Philip attend a scout meeting with one of his friends. They also made a long list of fun family outings they could do together and decided to visit a game store to find a new board game to play as a family.

Philip had his fair share of unhappy moments when he lost his Game Boy for the day after arguing with his mother when she asked him to turn it off. After he lost the use of his video game system for two weeks as the result of whining and complaining about his reduced time limits, Philip gained a new appreciation for his video game privileges.

Philip's ear-to-ear grin and obvious excitement were plain to see on a family bike ride and he was an enthusiastic competitor in the family game tournament they started with their new board game. Mr. and Mrs. Douglas were consistent with their "electronics guidelines" and made it a point to emphasize the times when Philip demonstrated appropriate behavior with the electronic toys. ("Philip, that was a very polite way of asking to use the computer." "Philip, I really appreciate the way you turned your game off so quickly just now!")

While Philip ended up joining and enjoying scouts, his love for electronic games did not wane. He met new friends that shared his electronic fervor and had them over to play video games as well as other games. As Philip learned to respect his family's guidelines for electronic fun, he was able to develop other areas of interest, make new friends, have fun with his family, and enjoy his electronic games—all at the same time.

Chapter 17

Mealtimes

The case of the missing appetite. Four-year-old Maria Dominguez loved to eat. Anything not good for her, that is. Trying to get her to eat her dinner was another story. Maria would get down from the table, whine, pick at her food, and take forever to eat just a few bites. When the food got cold enough, Mrs. Dominguez felt bad about making her eat it and would make her a small peanut butter sandwich instead. Maria would take a few bites out of it and then report that she was full. Tired from the battle, Maria's parents would let her get down to play. Later on that night, she usually got a little snack if she behaved well.

 ## Why Does This Happen?

Some children have challenging appetites. At some point, meals become a battleground for most young children. However, some children are hypersensitive to the textures of certain foods and really do find them unpleasant. Others are hesitant to try new

things, want to exert their growing sense of autonomy by pre-
ferring certain foods, or simply enjoy the routine of familiar foods
to help them feel secure. Many children will like something one
week and insist that they have never liked it the next time you
make it. For most children, these common behaviors will pass
with time if you respond to them effectively. If you have not gone
through mealtime mania, then consider yourself more than a little fortunate.

A lack of consistent table rules can contribute to mealtime madness.
If you regularly eat in different settings, have the television or
radio on, allow your children to leave the table frequently, and
have no semblance of a consistent routine or consistent expectations during meals, your children are learning that during mealtime, anything goes.

Rewarding the wrong behavior will only add to mealtime mayhem.
Perhaps your child is taking forever to eat, getting down from the
table, or refusing certain foods. If, when she does such things, you
reward her by allowing her to avoid undesired foods, giving her
custom-made "meals to order," or providing evening snacks, then
you are teaching her that negative mealtime behavior is just the
ticket.

*Ignoring the right behavior will make it difficult for children to learn
positive mealtime manners.* If you are not pointing out instances when
your child eats politely, asks for the potatoes instead of reaching
across the table for them, or tries a new food, how do you expect her
to get excited about doing them? Learn to say things like, "Maria,
that was very polite when you asked to have a bun just now!"

What Can I Do?

Don't take it personally. Your children are not going to like
everything you make, no matter how good a cook you are. The
main point of meals is to keep your children healthy and well-
nourished, not to massage your cooking ego (that's your spouse's
job!).

If you think your child may be becoming undernourished
because of mealtime problems, check with your pediatrician.

Otherwise, accept the fact that your children will not always like what is good for them (or how you cook it); remind yourself that dealing with fluctuating appetites is part of being a parent; and resolve yourself to do your best to provide a well-balanced diet for your children. You can do that!

Prevent the problem by making some adjustments to your mealtime strategy.

1. *Give smaller portions.* A smaller amount on the plate looks more manageable to a child, and you can always add more if your child asks. If your child eats the smaller portion, rejoice and be glad!

2. *Get rid of competing distractions.* Turn off the television and radio and make meals a time for eating and family interaction. Period.

3. *Solids before liquids.* If your child tends to fill up on liquids before touching her meal, require several bites to be taken *before* you set the drink on the table. Then, make sure that your child continues to drink gradually with her meal. If she doesn't, limit fluids until a reasonable portion has been eaten.

4. *Minimize snacks between meals.* One reason that some children resist eating at meals is that they would rather save their appetites for the delicious snacks that will come later. Or perhaps they feel full because of having eaten too many between-meal snacks. If this is a problem for you, then get in the habit of providing only one snack between meals. If your child is still hungry, provide something to drink and let her know that lunch (or dinner) will be coming soon.

5. *Provide at least one food that your child likes.* When you have several items on a plate, make sure that you include something nutritious that you know your child likes. This will increase the odds that your child will eat something that is good for her and after all, don't you do the same for yourself?

Give dessert only if a reasonable amount was eaten. This is a nice way to use dessert as a natural reward. Just make it a general rule that dessert comes only if you have eaten your dinner. If you choose not to eat your dinner, then you choose to forfeit dessert. Leave the choice up to your child, with no negative aftertaste.

Provide an adequate amount of time to eat. Depending on how much interaction takes place during a meal, most meals can be finished within fifteen to thirty minutes. If your child is dawdling, let her know ahead of time that she will have five or ten minutes to finish up. Setting a timer at that point can be helpful for some children, or playing "Beat the Clock" for younger ones. When the timer rings, the meal is over, finished or not.

Encourage tasting new food, but don't force it. If you let some children live on peanut butter sandwiches, they probably would choose to do that. So, encouraging your child to try small tastes of different foods will give them the opportunity to realize that they like different things. However, once your child has tried a certain food, there's no need to force it if she really seems to dislike it. Let her observe other people enjoying that food and who knows, someday she might want to try it on her own. If she doesn't, that's okay. Encourage her to continue to try new foods as the years pass. Just like people, taste buds mature too.

Use forced choices. One nice way to sidestep battles over food choices is to offer what is called a "forced choice." Instead of asking, "What would you like for lunch?" which allows for many possible answers, including Jell-O™ and ice cream, ask, "Would you like a ham and cheese sandwich or a peanut butter sandwich?" By limiting the choices, you are making your child's lunchtime decision much easier.

Teach and reward positive behavior. If you want to see appropriate mealtime behaviors increase, make sure that your child knows what these are. In addition to modeling good eating habits, use the Detour Method to teach your child the behaviors that you would like to see during meals. Once you have decided what those behaviors are and have made sure that they are reasonable, sit down together at the table and demonstrate these behaviors to your child.

Appropriate mealtime behaviors may include: staying seated, eating with your mouth closed, finishing most of what is on your plate, and so on. Make the guidelines simple and clear. Pretend you are eating and have your child practice these behaviors. Then, remind your child about the "mealtime rules" before you sit down, and make sure that you use the Pour-It-On Technique to provide plenty of specific verbal rewards when you see these behaviors happen. Write the mealtime rules on a large sheet of paper and place it strategically so that it can be seen from the kitchen table. Also, remind your child of the natural rewards (such as dessert or a bedtime snack) that follow appropriate mealtime behavior!

Use Logical Consequences for negative behavior. Inappropriate mealtime behavior needs to be followed by negative consequences. When your child exhibits negative mealtime behavior, immediately give her a Fork-in-the-Road. ("Maria, you need to stop complaining about your dinner and eat up, or you will have to go to Time-Out and your dinner will get cold.")

Examples of Logical Consequences for mealtime include removing your child's plate for a period of time (for example, one or two minutes) or having your child serve a Time-Out. If her food gets cold during the process, don't warm it up! If your child continues to misbehave during the meal, then she can be excused from the meal with no snack later that night. If she gets hungry, you can give her a glass of juice and remind her to make a better decision tomorrow.

 ## How Do I Put It All Together?

The case of the missing appetite. After talking to a few other moms, Mrs. Dominguez quickly realized that picky eating habits were not uncommon for young children. It also dawned on her that Maria had not experienced the proper consequences for her mealtime behavior. They sat down together as a family and explained a simple set of mealtime rules to Maria. "Maria, the new rules for meals will be that you have to stay at the table until you're excused, eat politely, take at least a small taste of everything on your plate, and you can only have dessert and snacks if you eat enough of your meal."

Mrs. Dominguez also decided to give Maria smaller portions of food and to limit the amount of between-meal snacks. "Okay, now honey," Mrs. Dominguez would say with an encouraging smile before each meal, "let's say our rules together: stay at the table, eat politely, try a little of everything, and eat the right amount!" She always said the rules in the same order, and soon Maria was able to recite them on her own.

During meals, Mr. and Mrs. Dominguez did their best to give Maria specific positive feedback when she noticed appropriate mealtime behavior ("Maria, you're sitting at the table so nicely. I love it!"). When Maria began to argue or whine about eating, her parents gave her a quick Fork-in-the-Road and then either removed her plate for one minute or sent her to Time-Out if the misbehavior continued. When it was close to the end of mealtime, Maria's parents set a timer for ten minutes and let Maria know that when the timer rang, the meal was over.

Although Maria's parents worked hard to provide lots of positive reinforcement for appropriate mealtime behavior, Maria's mealtime habits were harder to change than they had expected. Initially, Maria threw temper tantrums when her plate was removed and she earned more than a few extended Time-Outs. While it pulled at Mrs. Dominguez's heart strings, there were several times when Maria went to bed feeling hungry because she had not eaten much dinner. However, Maria's parents held firm, gave her a glass of water, and reminded her that, "You can have lots to eat tomorrow if you follow the mealtime rules."

Over time, Maria slowly got tired of losing her snacks and sitting in Time-Out. Little by little, she began to improve her mealtime behavior and really enjoyed the positive attention (and snacks) that followed. With a few ups and downs, Maria's mealtime behavior continued to improve and her parents couldn't help but grin when they saw her trying to teach her younger sister the "mealtime rules."

Chapter 18

Morning Routine

The case of sleepy Sam. Eight-year-old Sam had a hard time getting up in the morning. As a result, the morning routine was always a challenge for Mr. and Mrs. Anderson. After the seesaw battle to get Sam out of bed, the rest of the morning was a mad dash to prevent everyone from being late for school and work.

Sam had always been slow to wake-up, but things had gotten worse during the past year. "Leave me alone! I'm tired!" Sam would grouchily respond when his mother tried to wake him. This escalated into arguing and shouting and Sam once got grounded for "the rest of the year." However, the groundings became impractical and were impossible to enforce consistently. Sam and his parents were locked into a no-win situation.

Why Does This Happen?

Getting up can be difficult for some children. Not everyone is a morning person, whether a child or an adult. However, this is not an excuse for inappropriate behavior. If your child is a slow riser, you may need to budget a little extra time for him to get moving in the morning. Remember, an ounce of prevention is worth a pound of cure.

Poor sleeping habits can also lead to morning problems. If your child is not going to bed consistently at a reasonable time, he may be understandably tired and uncooperative in the morning. Good nighttime habits can lead to fewer daytime problems.

Procrastination gets rewarded. Who wants to get up early? If your child has developed the habit of responding negatively to your attempts to wake him, he has found this behavior to pay off—by prolonging the time at which he has to get up.

The wrong routine can mess up a morning in a hurry. If your child is spending too much time playing or watching television and not enough time getting necessary tasks completed, then it is time to rearrange things so that the tasks come first and free time comes later.

What Can I Do?

Establish bedtime and morning routines. Don't make the mistake of overlooking the obvious. Make sure that your bedtime routine is reasonable (see the section on "Bedtime") and examine your morning routine. Do things the night before, such as setting out clothes, making a lunch, or showering, that can save valuable time in the morning. Together with your child, place the needed morning activities in a logical order, and write them down. Post them on a large sheet of paper in his bedroom as a reminder. The routine might look like this:

> Get up at 7 A.M.
> Go to the bathroom
> Get dressed
> Eat breakfast
> Brush teeth/hair
> Prepare backpack
> Free time (if available)

Then, determine when your child needs to get out of bed to be ready on time. While having a good routine will not guarantee that things will go smoothly, not having one guarantees that they won't.

Let your child warm up slowly to the idea of waking up. You can purchase an alarm clock that he can set twenty minutes early (you may have to help a younger child) and teach him how to use the ever-valuable snooze alarm, so that he feels more awake by the time he needs to get up. You can also get in the habit of turning on the lights in his room five or so minutes before it's time to get up. A creative variation on this is to get an alarm clock that slowly becomes light as it gets closer to the set time (yes, there is such a thing). All of these are ways to help your child warm up to reality—that it's time to get up!

Rewarding activities come last. For some children it can be helpful to identify the most rewarding parts of the morning routine, such as eating breakfast or having time to watch a morning television program or play with toys. Then, structure the routine so that these behaviors come *after* the less preferable behaviors, such as getting dressed, bathroom activities, and so on.

Make it your child's responsibility. Don't fall into the trap of being responsible to get your child out of bed. Do what you can, within reason, to help your child get up, such as providing a wake-up call or two and helping to devise a logical morning routine. After that, let your child make his decision and experience the positive or negative consequences that follow.

Respond to disrespectful behavior. Disrespectful behavior can be followed by either an immediate Time-Out or the loss of a certain amount of a daily privilege, such as an hour of television. Inform your child of the consequence in a clear and matter-of-fact manner, refusing to get caught up in arguing, shouting, or any other form of negative attention.

Use Natural and Logical Consequences. Choose the consequences that will be most effective for your child. Let your child be late and experience the Natural Consequences of this, such as getting detentions for unexcused tardies. Attach certain privileges to your child's morning timeliness. If your child is not ready by a certain time or if certain tasks are not completed, then your child can't watch TV that day or bedtime will come earlier that night. Let your child know what the consequences of morning slowness will be, and let him make his own decision.

Reward positive behavior. In addition to having negative consequences for slowness and disrespect, devise positive consequences for being on time. You can use a Simple Contract by telling your child that you want to come up with a fun way of helping him to learn this new morning plan. Emphasize that your child is learning a new skill that will help him have a fun morning.

For example, if your child completes his morning routine by the specified time for three days in a row, he may get to do a special activity with his dad. Five days in a row will result in a friend staying overnight. Ten days in a row could bring a special trip to a video arcade or a movie with the family.

As always, use the Pour-It-On Technique to give your child plenty of positive verbal feedback ("You're doing a great job at getting up in the morning") all through the morning and point out the natural rewards of his new choices as he learns to take responsibility for his morning behavior. Once your child is getting up and behaving appropriately on a regular basis, you can fade out the contract and congratulate your child for learning a new skill and for a job well done.

 ## How Do I Put It All Together?

The case of sleepy Sam. Sam's parents decided that it was time for Sam to take responsibility for his morning behavior—they were resigning from the job. They felt that his bedtime was reasonable and could not identify any extra tasks that he had to do in the mornings that could be eliminated. They sat down with Sam and expressed their concern about the constant morning battles.

"Sammy, we really want morning times to be enjoyable for all of us. Let's figure out how we can all make that happen." They reviewed the morning routine and decided how much time Sam needed to get ready, which would determine when he had to get up. They also came up with a checklist of morning activities that had to be completed *before* Sam could watch any television, draw, or play with Legos™. Mrs. Anderson took Sam to the store and had him pick out a fun alarm clock, which they showed him how to use.

Sam and his parents then had a discussion about the positive and negative consequences that would follow his morning behavior. "To summarize," Mr. Anderson reviewed, "if you are not ready on time in the morning, you will have to go to bed thirty minutes earlier that night. If you talk disrespectfully to Mom or me, you will go right to Time-Out. Sammy, if you get two Time-Outs before school, you will not be able to play computer or video games for the rest of the day.

On the brighter side, Sam's parents told him that the first time he completed his morning responsibilities for five days in a row, he could earn a pizza and movie rental night for the entire family. This sounded particularly good to Sam, as he happened to love pepperoni pizza. When he completed ten days in a row, he would earn an afternoon at the park with a friend and a trip to his favorite ice-cream store. That night before he went to sleep, they prayed together that Sam would have a good sleep and a good morning the next day. They made this a regular part of their nightly prayers.

While Sam was initially excited about the new morning plan, he quickly forgot about it the next morning. However, when he had to go to Time-Out twice for shouting, lost computer and video games for the day, and had to go to bed early that night, reality set in, though not without a fight.

While his morning behavior showed glimpses of improvement, he continued to have difficult mornings more often than not. Mr. and Mrs. Anderson stayed consistent with their plan and eventually had to add the loss of television on days when Sam was not ready on time. This turned the tide for Sam. Once he started having better mornings, Sam got excited about the prospect of a pizza and movie night, and his parents gave him lots of positive feedback about the new and improved choices he was making. They spoke such words as: "Sam, you got out of bed great this morning and you've been talking very respectfully. Keep it up and we'll be having pizza before you know it!"

Sam experienced how fun things were when he got up on time and treated others respectfully and enjoyed the positive morning interactions with his parents, not to mention getting to play on the computer again and stay up to his regular bedtime again. While mornings never became the highlight of Sam's day, he eventually learned to get up when he had to—and he really looked forward to Saturdays.

Chapter 19

Moving

The case of the unwanted promotion. "I got the job!" Lisa's father announced with a triumphant burst of energy as he came through the front door. However, this was not the news that eleven-year-old Lisa was hoping for. Her father had been working towards a promotion that would allow them to move to Chicago, closer to where her grandparents lived.

While Lisa thought it would be fun to live closer to "Papa and Grammy," she also did not want to leave her friends, many of whom she had known since preschool. On top of that, the thought of starting the fourth grade at a brand new school with all new kids (who already had all their friends) felt really scary.

Lisa couldn't hold it in any longer. "But I don't want to move!" she blurted out. "I want to stay here!" Taken aback by this sudden burst of emotion, Mr. and Mrs. Fraser weren't sure what to say. But they realized that their daughter was a long way from being ready to pack her bags.

Why Does This Happen?

Relationships count. It isn't often that a child doesn't want to move because she will miss a certain ice cream store. She will miss her friends. Relationships are a large part of what makes life meaningful for all of us—and your children are no exception. They will be leaving behind friends they have grown to be comfortable with and have shared wonderful memories with, of tag, soccer, gymnastics, school, and playing on the playground. These are the friends who helped them feel accepted instead of left out during the first few days of school. The friends who they have giggled with in their silliest of moods and predictably migrate towards every lunch hour. These relationships are important to your child and leaving them, while it may be a necessary part of life, is not easy.

The great unknown is scary for all of us. As adults, we're able to draw upon our logic, the experiences of others, and our own past experiences to help calm our anxiety in difficult situations. Our children, especially the young ones, are not as well equipped to tackle situations with such objectivity. They do not have as many experiences to look back upon. As such, the prospect of moving can feel to your child like her whole world is changing. One very important part of it is. And the new teachers she will have and friends she will meet are uncertain. Even though change can work out positively in the long run, it often feels safer to stick with what you already have.

"I didn't get a vote." When it comes to moving, the decision is often not a democratic one. There are times when you (or you and your spouse), after prayerfully weighing all the factors, will decide that moving is the best decision for your family. Other times, moving is simply a practical necessity.

While you discuss the possibility with your children and elicit their feelings about it ahead of time, it is you, the parents, who ultimately make the decision about whether to stay or go. If you decide to move, it means your child's world will undergo a significant change regardless of whether or not she would have preferred things to stay the same. This may have happened to you as a child. If it did, how did you feel about it? How would you feel if, right now, you had to pick up, leave your friends and close relationships, and move across the country, whether you liked it or not? That may be how your child is feeling.

What Can I Do?

Keep an eye on your child's "stress-o-meter." While moving can be a fun experience, it can also be a stressful one. Look for the things that children often do when they are upset about something. While some children will come right out and tell you their feelings, others will either "hold it in" or "act it out." When a child holds her upset feelings in, she may become withdrawn, clingy, fearful, anxious, or sad. She may show less interest in social activities and even regress to "younger" behavior, such as baby talk or bed-wetting. Children who act out exhibit increased irritability, frustration, anger, and disrespectful talking. Be aware that this may be a tough time for your child and watch for signs that she may need a little help.

Prepare, prepare, prepare. Talk together as a family about the upcoming move well in advance. Explain the reasons for the move in simple and honest terms that your children can understand. Model the honest expression of your own feelings (keeping them age-appropriate) and blend them with a positive, optimistic attitude. For example, it is possible to feel excited about the move, yet a little sad and scared—all at the same time!

Convey an unshakable trust that God will be with your family and will help your children handle every new situation. Read together the first chapter of Joshua. Talk about the similarities between the Israelites' situation and your own (for example: moving to a new place, starting a new adventure) and about how God has promised to help you be strong and courageous and to always be with you. Here are some other ideas for preparing your child:

• In your nightly prayers together, thank God for his promise to always be with you, no matter where you move. Pray for your child's current friends and for the new friends and teachers that she will meet.

- Go to your local library and check out a book about moving, designed especially to address the issues that children worry about the most. (We read a "Barney" book about moving with our boys prior to our move to Chicago.)
- Think together of ways your child can have a few special times with her favorite friends.
- Take pictures of your child with her best friends and pictures of her at her favorite places to make a memory scrapbook.
- For your child's best friends, she can purchase or make a "see-you-later" gift, that helps accent the specialness of that friendship.
- Make a plan together about how your child can stay in touch with friends after the move, such as by occasional telephone calls, e-mail, sending cards, or writing letters.
- Let your child be involved in the move. Give her age-appropriate jobs to help with the packing, particularly in her room. Allow her to pack a "My Special Stuff" box, filled with a few of her favorite things, such as a few toys, favorite books, a fun game, favorite pajamas, and a special stuffed animal. This box will be kept separate from the other boxes during the move so that it can remain easily accessible and can be quickly unpacked at your new home.
- Keep a one-month "countdown" calendar to help your child with organizing, heighten the sense of excitement, and give her a tangible sense of when the move will be.
- Familiarize your child with her new environment by visiting it if possible. If not, show her maps, pictures, and park-district catalogues of her new home, school, neighborhood, and special activities or clubs she can participate in.

Be understanding. As you talk together, place the emphasis on listening to your child and understanding *her* feelings. Remember, she is going to have to leave close friends, teachers, school, and familiar places and face the challenge of starting all over with new people—and none of this was her choosing!

She needs freedom to grieve about this loss, and she needs help in coping with this change in an adaptive way. Don't rush in to comfort her or point her to the exciting possibilities that lie ahead too quickly. Give her "permission" to shed some tears and express her feelings, such as fear, anger, or sadness. Acknowledge her feelings ("It's sad to think about leaving your good friends") and communicate that you understand. Your child can't move on to coping until she's had a chance to grieve.

Make it a family adventure. One of the things that bonds people closer together is going through difficult times together. Your children will take their cues about how to handle the move from you. If they see excessive anxiety from you, they will conclude there is a reason to be anxious. If they see a calm confidence that things will work out fine, they will find strength and comfort in your example.

Treat the move as a family adventure—because it is! No one knows exactly what will happen—what kind of people Daddy or Mommy will be working with, who your new neighbors will be, or what kind of experiences you all will have. But you do know that you have each other and that God will always be with you and will help all of you handle whatever comes your way. There will be new friends, new fun places, and new fun times. While you don't want to minimize the sad parts of a move, you don't want to make the opposite mistake of overlooking the exciting parts as well. This is one of life's adventures for all of you and a good example of the fact that life is always changing. The one thing that doesn't change is the fact that God will be with you—wherever you are.

Keep first things first. While the move will demand lots of your time and attention, make sure that you don't get so caught up in the moving details that you neglect what is far more important—your children. Adjust your goals and expectations and make sure you spend as much time as you need to attend to your most valuable and lifelong possessions.

Start growing new roots. Here are a few things that you can do as soon as you have moved to help your children begin to view this new place as their new home:

- Tour your new neighborhood and town. Locate the grocery store, the parks, the library, a good video rental store, the recreation center, your favorite ice cream store, and other family favorite places. Visit a few of these places and begin to make some new family memories.
- Walk through your child's new school and make an appointment to meet the new teacher as soon as possible.
- Within the first few days, have a "family night" together in your new house. Do a fun family activity and talk together about your feelings and hopes about your new job, school, friends, and neighborhood. Pray together that God will help you all make good friends, do well at school and work, and be a positive influence on the people that he will bring into your lives.
- Let your child have some input as to how her new room will be arranged and decorated. After all, some redecoration can be a nice "perk" to help counterbalance the stresses of moving.
- Find a church with a strong children's program and let the children's pastor know that you are new to the church and to the area. The pastor and children's workers can take a few extra steps to help make your child feel at home.
- If possible, talk to some of the parents at school and church to find out what types of activities, sports, or clubs their children are involved in. See if your child is interested in being involved in any of these activities.

 ## How Do I Put It All Together?

The case of the unwanted promotion. Mr. and Mrs. Fraser were excited about their move but were much more interested in helping their daughter handle this big change. They realized that they needed to do more preparation with Lisa, the most precious possession they were moving.

That night, Lisa's parents sat down with her to talk about the move. "Lisa, sweetie, we know that moving can be really hard," said Mr. Fraser, gently putting his hand on her shoulder. "It's sad to leave your friends and all the places that you know." Lisa's brown eyes started to tear up. "Could you tell us how you're feeling about everything, honey?"

"I don't want to leave Abby and Megan," Lisa said sadly, holding back her tears. "And I wanted to have Mrs. Klein as my teacher this year. She's got a guinea pig!" Mrs. Fraser hugged her daughter. As the discussion went on, they took the time to listen to all of Lisa's feelings about the move. Mr. and Mrs. Fraser agreed with Lisa that moving was hard and that leaving friends is one of the most difficult things to do.

"Let's see if we can think of any way that you can stay in contact with your friends," suggested Mrs. Fraser. "Moving doesn't mean never seeing or talking with your friends again. Y'know, Mommy's friend Sandra? She lives in Oklahoma, but we are still best friends. We just make sure to stay in contact. How do you think you can keep in touch with Abby and Megan?"

"I don't know," said Lisa. Her father stepped in with suggestions. "Well, you could write, occasionally talk on the phone, or send them an e-mail as often as you want," Mr. Fraser suggested.

"Yeah, I guess I could," pondered Lisa, thinking this through for the first time. They ended their discussion by praying together that God would help them with the move and that he would be with their old friends as well as with the new friends that they would make.

Over the next couple of months, Lisa's parents helped her by thinking of ways to have some special times with her best friends. They had several sleepovers and took lots of pictures; Lisa made special "Friends Forever" cards for each of her closest girlfriends. On their several weekend trips to Chicago to look for houses they made sure to drive by the schools that Lisa might go to and asked the realtor to take them by some parks and shopping areas as well. Lisa's eyes grew wide with excitement as she saw some of the fun sights and had a great afternoon at one of the downtown museums. Once they were back home, Mrs. Fraser had the Chamber of Commerce help her obtain catalogues from the park districts of the cities they were considering moving to in the Chicago area.

She went over them with Lisa and they talked about Lisa's play-ing soccer or taking an art class.

During their family times, the Frasers shared their different feelings about moving. Lisa was both surprised and comforted to hear that her mother had some of the same feelings she had. "Mom, you can stay in touch with your friends the same way that Megan and I are going to," Lisa said, trying to support her mom. "We decided that we will e-mail each other twice a week and take turns calling each other once a month. Just moving away doesn't mean that you can't still be friends."

Mrs. Fraser thanked her daughter with a smile. "That's a good idea."

As a family, they decided to look at the move as an adventure that God had for them and talked together about his faithfulness and great plans for them in their family devotions (Jeremiah 29:11). Mr. and Mrs. Fraser knew that there would be more tough adjustment times ahead (and that there was still lots of packing to do). But they felt reconnected with Lisa and had laid a good foun-dation of communication that would help all of them as they moved into the adventures that God had in store.

Chapter 20

Nightmares

The case of sleepless Susan. Six-year-old Susan had been waking up two or three times a week with nightmares for the past couple of months. When she could remember her dreams, they consisted of various monsters or were sometimes related to certain movies she had recently seen. Susan had also been very sad after the recent death of Curly, her pet turtle. Her mother, Ms. Jordan, had tried to comfort Susan by letting her climb into bed with her when she woke up with a bad dream. This did not seem to help Susan's nightmares and more often resulted in less sleep for Ms. Jordan.

 ## Why Does This Happen?

Nightmares are common. Nightmares are bad dreams that can wake a child up and are usually remembered. They are common for children and can be triggered by scary movies, television shows, or events a child is exposed to. Nightmares are more common during the preschool years, and most nightmares are eventually outgrown.

Stress can contribute to nightmares. Dreams are a child's way of dealing with the stresses that occur during the day. Therefore, stressful events and specific worries can trigger bad dreams. Sometimes, just the stresses and challenges of growing older and becoming more independent can be enough to result in a bad night or two.

Age-inappropriate material can bring on the monsters. I have had many young children tell me about the frightening and graphic movies they are allowed to rent or watch on television—sometimes with their parents! Scary books or experiences can also result in disturbed dreams. For preschool children, "magical thinking" (believing that what you think is real) results in very real concerns about monsters in the closet and crocodiles under the bed.

What Can I Do?

Find out what your child is watching. Your child could be viewing programs or reading books of which you are unaware (for instance, at someone else's house). Or perhaps you are unaware of the content of the books and TV programs that you do allow. If the material is too violent, graphic, or scary, remove it as a viewing option. Remember, the people who create shows and products for children do not always have your child's best interests in mind.

Reassure your child by letting her know that you will keep her safe. I am reminded of the story of the young boy who was in bed one night when a terrible thunderstorm arose. He called out to his father, "Dad, I'm scared. Will you come here, please?" The dad, engrossed in his television show, shouted back, "Don't worry, pal, you'll be all right. God will keep you safe." A minute later, a voice came from the bedroom a second time, "I know God will keep me safe, but I need something with skin on."

That's you. Include praying together as a part of your bedtime routine, and thank God together for keeping your family safe. You can also help prevent nighttime nervousness by keeping the door open, plugging in a nightlight, and allowing your child to have a familiar object such as a teddy bear with her. If she is scared of monsters, walk with your child around the room prior to bedtime, letting her look in the closets and under the bed, to reassure her that no monsters are hiding there.

When my children were struggling with monsters, I remember us often repeating a line from one of their favorite children's videos that stated, "God is the biggest." So, even if there were a monster (which there wasn't), we reasoned that God is the biggest, and he can beat any monster and will always look after you and keep you safe. And the fact that Daddy was close by didn't hurt either.

Help your child stay in bed. Following a bad dream, don't hesitate to spend a few minutes comforting your child, but don't get into the habit of letting her sleep with you as a way of handling the bad dreams. Instead, remind her that all children have scary dreams sometimes and that while dreams can be scary, they are not real. Assure her that she will be safe, pray together, and then help her refocus her thoughts on fun things while taking slow deep breaths and staying in her own bed.

Develop mastery over the content of bad dreams through play. If your young child has dreams about "monsters," you can play a fun game of "monsters" where your child is able to make the monster "go away." In your play, you can make the monster silly and funny rather than scary and terrifying. You can also be a monster who is friendly and makes friends with your child in play. I can't count the number of times that I was the monster and my boys either wrestled me and "pinned" me with glee or "got me" with their pretend swords. It can also be helpful to keep child-drawn pictures of the monster by your child's bed at night so that following a nightmare, your child can take a picture, tear it up, throw the monster into the garbage can, and go back to sleep.

On several occasions, I have encouraged my boys to take a scary dream and make it funny. For instance, they could imagine the monster they had just dreamed about, and then picture a banana cream pie, with lots of whipped cream, coming out of nowhere and smacking him right in the face. SPLAT! Then, a bunch of chickens start running around and it so happens that this monster is scared silly of chickens. He starts running away as fast as he can and falls through a trap door that takes him on a long, winding slide and plops him in a huge pile of green slime. So long, monster! Why not? It's their dream.

Look for signs of stress. Identify things that could be upsetting your child, as these can lead to disturbed sleep. A recent move, the loss of a loved one (or pet), family conflict, illness, a friend moving away, difficulty with school work, problems with peers, all of these can result in added stress for your child. Depending on the situation, your objective is to either reduce the stress or teach your child how to better handle it. Or both. For older children, use your problem-solving skills together (see "Solving Problems") to come up with ideas for how to do this. For all children, use the many ideas provided in this book for handling different problems, get ideas from close friends, and consult with qualified professionals as needed.

 ## How Do I Put It All Together?

The case of sleepless Susan. Ms. Jordan talked with Susan about things that she might be worrying about and was surprised to find out just how much the recent death of Curly, her pet turtle, had affected her. "Mom," Susan said, "I don't understand why God made Curly die. I miss him a lot. What will happen if I get another turtle? Will he die too?"

Ms. Jordan listened intently as Susan expressed her feelings of sadness and worry. "Sweetheart, God didn't make Curly die," she softly explained, "all animals die when their bodies stop working. I know how much you loved Curly and that you miss him a lot. I miss him too." Susan listened intently. "Y'know, that's one of the differences between animals and people," Ms. Jordan continued, "Animals aren't made to last forever, but people are. That's why God wants us all to give our lives to Jesus, so that we can live with him in heaven forever."

This turned out to be an opportunity for Ms. Jordan to remind Susan of how important it is to pray for those who don't know God. They decided to have a small memorial service for Curly to say "thanks" for all the fun they had together, and Susan drew a picture of her and Curly playing together, which she put in a special frame and kept in her room.

When talking about her nightmares, Susan mentioned that she had been scared by some of the scary movies that she had seen her older brothers watch in the den. It turned out that without their mother's knowledge, Susan's brothers had rented some scary movies and Susan had watched portions of these movies with them. Ms. Jordan spoke with Susan about things that she can do when she sees scary programs on television, such as say, "I don't like this" and walk away. She also made a mental note to pay closer attention to Susan's whereabouts and talk with her older sons about the type of movies they rented.

Ms. Jordan started to keep Susan in her own bed following a nightmare. At first, this was difficult, but she taught Susan how to calm her body down with deep breaths and think calming thoughts. (Some suggestions: "God will keep me safe." "That dream wasn't real." "Mom is just around the corner.") When Susan came to her mother's room following a bad dream, Ms. Jordan calmly walked Susan back to her own bed, and they practiced slow breathing and calm thoughts together. "C'mon honey, let's do our breaths. Nice and slow. That's good. Now let's say our thoughts together. . . ." Sometimes, they pictured the monster in a silly story that made them smile and gave Susan a sense of control over her dream. They would always end with a prayer, thanking God for keeping them safe and for helping Susan to be calm.

As Ms. Jordan left for her own room, she had Susan focus on something pleasant, like the fun things scheduled for tomorrow, and a nightlight provided just enough light to remind Susan that everything was safe. Over time, Susan adjusted to Curly's passing (and decided that she might want a bird next), and her diet of scary movies was entirely eliminated. Within a month or two, Ms. Jordan noticed the nightmares occurred less often until they eventually vanished altogether, and Susan was sleeping soundly through the night—in her own bed.

Chapter 21

Not Following Directions

The case of **"my way" Marty.** Seven-year-old Marty had one opinion about the way he wanted to do things. His way. Mr. and Mrs. Bauer agreed Marty had always been challenging; even as a toddler he threw colossal tantrums and would occasionally hold his breath when he didn't get his way. Marty no longer held his breath, but he fought his parents every day. Brushing teeth, getting dressed, turning off the television—anything could bring on a battle. Occasionally, Marty responded to his parents' requests the first or second time, but often he ignored them and just said no.

Marty's parents spanked him countless times, and felt like they had no impact; they were uncomfortable spanking him more often. Marty had also spent a lot of time in his room. Mrs. Bauer admitted that sometimes she quit arguing with Marty and did things herself because it was just easier. Nothing they tried seemed to work.

Why Does This Happen?

A difficult temperament plays a big role in understanding the behavior of some children. A person's temperament is how he is neurologically wired, his natural disposition or hereditary style of responding to the world. Some children are more intense, persistent, irritable, sensitive, and active than others. Put a few of these traits together, and you will have a very different experience with your child than your neighbors may have with theirs. Your goal must be to customize your parenting approach to best fit your child's natural characteristics.

Skills are still developing. As children learn how to control their impulses, how to express anger, how to deal with frustration, how to delay gratification, and so on, two important things are required: mistakes and time. Mistakes are necessary because we learn by making them. Time is needed because it takes time to make all of those mistakes! Don't expect your child to come fully equipped with adult-level skills. Remember that your child has had much less experience with difficult situations than you have had. Make sure you are helping him develop these important skills as effectively as possible.

Mismatched consequences often contribute to defiant behavior. Many parents of disruptive children make no consistent effort to teach or reward positive behavior. On top of that, they often give lots of extra negative parental attention (which can actually reinforce the negative behavior) right along with the negative consequences. Other times, the negative consequences are too extreme and given inconsistently. The end result is that positive behavior gets consistently ignored, and negative behavior gets routinely rewarded. This is a formula for misbehavior.

 What Can I Do?

Prevent problems by knowing your child. If your child doesn't do well on little sleep, then cut down your expectations when you know he is tired. If he doesn't do well in certain situations (such as in the grocery store), don't take him. Use forced choices (for example, "Johnny, you can read a book or play downstairs. Which would you like to do?") to allow your child some choice in age-appropriate decisions.

Make sure you get his attention before making serious requests, going out of your way to gently touch him on the shoulder and make eye contact as you speak. Remind him of the consequences for appropriate and inappropriate behavior *before* he gets into trouble to help him make the right choice. State your requests in a firm and "no-nonsense" manner so that your child knows you are serious. A little prevention can save a lot of headache.

Build your relationship. Strengthening your parent-child bond can be a helpful first step in addressing problem behavior. One way to build your relationship is to spend regular time together. Even ten or twenty minutes every couple of days can be helpful (more, of course, is even better). Do an activity your child wants to do and provide lots of positive parental attention during this time, using the Pour-It-On Technique. Respond to misbehavior by simply giving your child the choice of behaving appropriately or ending your time together. If your child continues the misbehavior, inform him that the one-on-one time is over, quickly clean up the activity, and *leave*. This way, you are not providing excessive parental attention following negative behavior. If you make this one-on-one time a regular habit, it should help build your relationship and be a building block for better behavior.

Just do it. Make a list of the various situations that typically result in oppositional behavior, such as getting in the car, brushing teeth, turning off the television, and so on. Then, using the Detour Method, identify the specific behaviors you would like your child to do in those situations, combine them into a simple plan, and teach your child how to follow the plan. For many situations, you will find the following steps, from what I affectionately call the "Just-Do-It Plan," to be helpful:

When Mom or Dad asks you to do something, then:

1. Just do it
2. If you have a question about it, ask your question respectfully
3. If the answer to your question is no, just do it

4. Talk about it with your parents later if you need to

After you explain the Just-Do-It Plan to your child, run through it together, using situations from your list of problems to practice on. Carefully show him how he would do each step (for example, "Now Marty, if I asked you to put your toys away and you wanted to just do it, what would you do? That's right. Well, what if you wanted to ask if you could play a little longer, how could you ask that question in a respectful way?").

Make the instruction brief, no more than five to ten minutes, and enjoyable. Review the plan with your child and practice together regularly, until he has learned how to use the steps in different situations. By using the Detour Method, you improve your child's skill at listening and increase the chances that he will actually listen the next time a real-life situation comes along.

Talk together about the importance of listening to Mom and Dad. During one of your family times, read Ephesians 6:1–3 and discuss why God wants children to listen to their parents. Discuss questions such as: "Why do you think God wants us to listen to our parents? What are the dangers that come from making a habit of not listening? Why is it important for all of us to listen to God? How does God feel when we listen to him and obey? How does he feel when we don't listen?"

You can also talk about how to respond to a parental request. Show your children the difference between asking a question in a respectful way and a whining or arguing way. Just for fun, have them demonstrate the different ways of asking a question (arguing, whining, complaining, respectfully, and so on), and talk about the different results each brings. Remind them that when they listen and ask questions in a respectful way, they are not only doing a super job and making you proud, they are also making God very happy.

Pour it on. Use the Pour-It-On Technique to strengthen desired behaviors. Of course, you must be *looking* for those behaviors and practicing them with your child to increase the chances of them occurring and you noticing them. When the positive behaviors occur (and they will!), *immediately* follow those behaviors with a specific verbal reward. (For example, "Johnny, I really love it when you do what I ask the *first time.* Good job!" or "That was a super job of getting your homework done right away. That's great listening pal!"). At first, use this technique as often as you can when the desired behavior occurs. Then, as the behavior starts to happen more regularly, slowly thin the specific verbal rewards out by providing them less often, but still keep them coming on a regular basis.

Use a Simple Contract. More difficult cases of noncompliance may call for a Simple Contract in addition to the Pour-It-On Technique. Your child could earn a point for each period of time (such as morning, afternoon, evening) in which he has complied with either your first or second request. If he has not listened well during that time period, he does not receive a point for that period.

You can also use a Response/Cost approach, starting out with ten points a day and losing one point for each instance of noncompliance. Tell your child that you have come up with a fun way to help him get better at listening the first time and together create a menu of fun privileges. Explain exactly how your child will earn points (such as listening to Mom and Dad), or with a Response/Cost approach, how he can lose points (by not listening to Mom and Dad). Make sure he understands that he can use his points to earn items from his menu. Practice the positive behaviors together as we have previously discussed. As your child's compliance increases, you can slowly fade the contract out.

Make the consequence fit the crime. Repeated noncompliance to parental commands or constant oppositional behavior needs to be consistently followed by effective negative consequences. Time-Out and Logical Consequences are two of the most effective consequences you have at your fingertips.

Time-Out is a Logical Consequence for noncompliance as it allows your child an opportunity to get back in control, which is obviously needed if he is choosing not to listen. The loss of a privilege can be a very good motivator once you find the right privilege to remove. Almost any privilege or preferred activity can be "logically" connected to noncompliance by explaining to your child: "Marty, fun privileges happen when you listen to Mom and Dad and treat other people respectfully. When you don't, the privileges start to go away."

It is good practice to keep the consequences immediate and usually confined to the present day, although more serious offenses may result in the loss of a privilege for a longer time. On either your second or third command, give your child a Fork-in-the-Road. (For example, "Marty, I want you to stop arguing right now. We can talk about this later if you would like. If you start to argue again, you will go right to Time-Out.") If he chooses the positive fork, tell him that he did a good job for choosing to listen. If he does not listen within five to eight seconds, then administer the negative consequence in a calm and matter-of-fact manner, without getting hooked into arguing, debating, or lecturing.

 ## How Do I Put It All Together?

The case of "my way" Marty. Mr. and Mrs. Bauer made a list of the most common problem situations and brainstormed ways to prevent these problems. For instance, they found that using a five-minute kitchen timer to signal the end of an activity helped Marty with transitions.

Other problems required more work. As it seemed that Marty's noncompliant behavior was unpredictably scattered throughout the day, they decided to teach Marty the Just-Do-It Plan. They sat down together, and Mr. Bauer said, "Marty, we want to help you learn how to get better at listening so that you won't have to go to Time-Out as much and can have more fun. Sound good? We've got a little plan that can help you listen instead of argue and get in trouble. It's called the Just-Do-It Plan. Here's how it goes. . . ."

They used the Detour Method to show Marty how to do each step of the Just-Do-It Plan, using past problem situations for examples. Mrs. Bauer practiced the plan with Marty every day for the first week and then reduced the rehearsals to twice a week for the next month. It wasn't long before Marty had memorized the Just-Do-It Plan and was able to demonstrate the steps easily in practice.

Mr. and Mrs. Bauer also made listening and treating others respectfully main themes of their family nights for a few months. They talked together about why God commands us to listen to our parents and treat others respectfully and the positive benefits that come when we do. In their nightly prayers together, they thanked God for Marty and prayed that God would help him to have a good listening day and that God would help them all to learn to listen to him better.

They also got very practical and came up with examples of respectful ways to handle a wide variety of family situations (sharing toys, getting ready for bed, choosing television channels) and conducted fun role plays to practice these behaviors.

"Okay, Marty, what would be a respectful way to handle it if you wanted to watch a certain TV show, but someone else, say Mom, was already watching another program? Let's pretend that Mom is watching TV and you show us what you would do or say."

"I don't know," Marty said, "uh, Mom, my show's going to start. Could you get off?" "Marty, if you said it like that, how do you think she'd respond?" After thinking for a moment, Marty replied, "She'd probably say no."

"Do you think the way you asked sounded very respectful?" Mrs. Bauer asked. "Um . . . I don't know," Marty said, not wanting to incriminate himself. "Well, I think there probably is a more respectful way to ask," Mr. Bauer stated. "Can you think of what that would be. . . ?" And later on, "Marty, how would you listen if Mom said that she wanted to finish watching her show and that you could watch with her or go and play in the basement? Show us what you would say or do."

Mr. and Mrs. Bauer committed themselves to using the Pour-It-On Technique whenever Marty listened and were surprised at how often he actually listened either the first or second time. When he didn't listen, they gave him a Fork-in-the-Road by either the second or third parental request: "Marty, you can turn the computer off right now, or I will turn it off and you will go to Time-Out and have no computer or video games for the rest of the day." They also were consistent with using Time-Out when it was needed.

Just for fun, they also decided to use a very simple contract where Marty started each day with five stickers and would lose one sticker each time he did not listen following his parents' second request. Saving ten stickers earned a special bike ride with Dad. Saving twenty earned lunch at a favorite fast-food restaurant. If he lost three stickers in one day, he would lose television for the day. Losing four stickers resulted in losing television and computer or video games for the day. Losing all five stickers resulted in no television and no computer or video games and early bed for that day.

Mr. and Mrs. Bauer continued reviewing the Just-Do-It Plan with Marty and were consistent with the Pour-It-On-Technique, Time-Out, and his simple contract. Mrs. Bauer really had to work at not arguing with Marty following his misbehavior and instead stick to the task of administering the Time-Out or Logical Consequences in a matter-of-fact way. Things did not turn around overnight. In fact, it took quite a while for Marty to show consistent improvement. But as Mr. and Mrs. Bauer stuck with their plan, Marty's good days eventually started to outnumber the bad ones.

Chapter 22

Separating from Parents

The case of crying Curtis. Curtis had just had his third birthday and had not yet mastered the art of being away from his mother. While he was occasionally able to make it successfully through his Sunday morning class, more often than not the appearance of another parent to tend a child could upset Curtis enough for the workers to flash his number on the "come and get your screaming child" screen in the main church auditorium.

In such cases, Ms. Burton would retrieve Curtis and walk with him up and down the halls until the service was over. At home, Curtis would scream when his mother tried quietly to sneak out the door to leave him with a babysitter. She tried different babysitters, but often ended up just sending them home as she felt guilty leaving Curtis in such a distraught state. With preschool just around the corner, Ms. Burton needed to find a solution that would help Curtis master this difficult stage.

Why Does This Happen?

Separation problems are common in young children. Between the ages of about twelve months and thirty months, your child is slowly developing the ability to hold an internal mental image of a person, even when that person is not there. This allows them to know that the person is real and still exists, even if they don't see them. Until this ability is fully developed, it can understandably be quite frightening for a young child to be separated from their parents—they haven't yet learned that Mom and Dad will always come back.

Constant rescuing delays learning. Your child needs to learn an important lesson: *Mom and Dad will always return.* If you constantly rescue your two- or three-year-old child from the perils of the church nursery, he will never get the opportunity to learn that the nursery can be fun and that Mom and Dad will indeed come back. The best way to overcome the fear is to experience the "dreaded event" enough times to realize that the feared outcome never comes. This is why helping a child move toward *remaining* in the nursery or Sunday school, for example, is the best way for him to learn that everything will be okay.

 What Can I Do?

Use familiar caretakers whenever possible. Having a wide variety of babysitters can be convenient for you but difficult for your child, who is just getting used to your absence. Use the same babysitter at the beginning, and if possible, leave your child with a trusted family friend or relative whom he already knows. Another idea is to pay the babysitter to come over once or twice to play together with you and your child for an hour or two. This sense of familiarity and safety can go a long way in soothing a child's fears.

A transitional object can be comforting for a child in a new situation. A favorite small toy, a picture of you, or any familiar object can help your child feel more secure when away from you. Not all children will require this, but for some children this can make quite a difference.

Short practices in familiar environments can help prepare a child for other separations. You want to expose your child to gradually longer periods of being away from you. You can start by getting involved in a regular play group or by getting together with other families where you are there, but your child gets used to the presence of other adults and children and to feeling safe when you are not in direct eye's view.

When in the presence of another familiar adult such as a grandparent or a close friend, you can give your child a hug and tell him that you will be back in just a minute. Then step outside (out of your child's sight) for thirty seconds, regardless of your child's reactions. Come back in and let your child know that you have returned with a big hug and positive feedback for playing nicely while you were gone. Repeat this exercise often and gradually lengthen the time you are gone. Once you have had a few shorter outings, you can easily lengthen them.

Crying is a normal reaction. I mean your child's crying, not yours. Most nursery workers, daycare workers, and teachers will tell you that many upset children stop crying and are just fine shortly after the heartsick parent leaves. This is why they typically encourage you to drop your child off and *go!* In general, I heartily agree with this advice. Your child needs to learn that tears will not save him from the situation and that, in fact, the situation is actually not all that bad. Unfortunately, some things are only learned through a few tears.

Stay with your child on some occasions. Staying with your child a few times in an unfamiliar environment such as the nursery or daycare can be helpful if you are in the early stages of this process and your child is having a *particularly* difficult time adjusting to your absence. While staying around too long will delay the learning that ultimately needs to take place, it can also help to ease the transition for an overanxious child by allowing the child to get used to the new setting in your presence.

My wife and I did nursery duty many times while our first son was learning to stay on his own; we didn't need to for our second son (although there still was some crying!). For very anxious children in daycare or preschool, you may be able to stay in the classroom quietly in the beginning to help your child grow accustomed to the new environment and people. *But at some point, you have to leave.*

Don't push too hard. While some crying is to be expected and endured in the early stages of training, it is appropriate to comfort and spend time with your upset child. I can still picture the many church services I spent walking the hallways with my young children after "getting the call" from the nursery workers that I was needed because they "missed their mommy or daddy." Sometimes, I just asked if I could be a volunteer nursery worker for the day and played with all the children there.

Remind yourself that you are not in a race and that virtually all children eventually learn to separate from their parents. Without falling into the trap of constantly rescuing your child, allow your child to learn this new skill at a pace right for him.

 ## How Do I Put It All Together?

The case of crying Curtis. Ms. Burton came up with a plan. When with other parents and children Curtis knew well, she had a friend watch Curtis, told him that she would be back in one minute, and then stepped out of sight. She started with about one minute and then gradually increased the time periods. While he cried a few times, Ms. Burton kept it up and Curtis quickly came to realize that his mom always came back and he soon stopped crying. When she came back into the house, she immediately kneeled down beside him and gave him a big hug and used the Pour-It-On Technique, "Curtis, you did a great job of playing and having fun while Mommy stepped out of the house for a minute. See, I told you I'd be right back and everything is just fine!"

Ms. Burton started leaving Curtis to play with his good friends at their house on occasion, stepping out to run an errand for about twenty or thirty minutes at a time. "I'll be back in a few minutes," she said with a smile, "you just play with Adam and Luke. Maybe I'll bring you all a little snack!"

She also decided upon one babysitter and had her over to play with Curtis on two occasions to help him become familiar with her. Then the big day came when, after about fifteen minutes of playing with the babysitter, Ms. Burton left to go out with a friend. Curtis cried for about ten minutes once he realized that she had left, but was fine after that. When she returned home an hour later, Curtis was playing happily with the babysitter. The next time, she stayed out twice as long.

At church, Ms. Burton volunteered for twice a month "helper duty" in Curtis' Sunday morning classroom. She also asked the workers to do everything possible to calm and distract Curtis before calling her and to only call if Curtis seemed extremely distraught or if his crying did not diminish with time. If she was called, Ms. Burton got permission to briefly step into the Sunday school area to comfort him (instead of taking him out). She would remain with Curtis for a few minutes to help him calm down and engage in play. Sometimes, she stayed and helped with Sunday school for the rest of the hour. Other times, she quietly left the area once Curtis had calmed down and he remained there for the rest of the service.

Ms. Burton was surprised at how well her plan worked. It seemed that all the parts of the plan worked together in a positive way. Curtis adapted well to the babysitter and within several months he had successfully learned to stay in his Sunday morning class almost all of the time. Bravo!

Chapter 23

Sharing

The case of possessive Peggy. "It's mine!" shouted seven-year-old Peggy with a vengeance, as she wrenched her well-worn Barbie doll from the little hands of her five-year-old sister, Rene. Peggy's sister had made the unfortunate mistake of picking up the Barbie after Peggy had laid it down and started playing with another doll.

Mrs. Hill had been noticing for some time that Peggy's sharing skills had been sorely lacking but had been hoping that somehow they would kick into gear. Unfortunately, the only thing getting kicked was the ill-fated victim that made the mistake of touching Peggy's toys. Mrs. Hill knew that she needed to help Peggy learn to share but wasn't sure how to go about getting it done.

Why Does This Happen?

Everybody wants something to call her own. All of us enjoy having possessions that belong to us. We also like to have some say as to if and when others use those possessions. In a child's world where parents and teachers dictate much of what they do every day and establish the rules by which they must live, the domain of their own "stuff" is one place where a child can demonstrate some power and control. Learning to give up control for the benefit of someone else is a lesson that only comes with time and the realization that sometimes giving up control works out better than holding on to it.

Naturally short-sighted thinking and the self-centered perspective of childhood account for many sharing problems. To a person whose span of life experience is still in single digits, a lot is potentially at stake when someone else grabs one of your toys. "What will happen if I share my toy?" "Will I get it back?" "Will the other person wreck it?" "What if I want to use it again (in 30 seconds) and the other person is still using it?" Rather than deal with all of those difficult questions, it can be easier just to hold on to it in the first place.

What Can I Do?

Talk about sharing together with your children. As a part of your regular family times, talk together with your children about the importance of sharing. Take turns identifying times when you have had to share and how it made the person that you shared with feel. Then make a list of times when someone shared with you and how that made you feel.

Using your child's Bible, read passages such as Luke 3:11; Luke 6:31; and Romans 12:9–13. Discuss how God wants us to treat others and what good things happen when we follow God's commands. Repeating these discussions often will help to remind your children of the importance (and benefits) of sharing in your family.

Share out loud. Make sure that *you* consistently model sharing and then *think out loud:* "Well, I guess I'm done with the computer now, so sure, you can use it!" "Sure you can play with me, which color would you like to use?" Then, quietly ask your child, "Hey, did Daddy share with you just now? How did it make you feel? Was it a friendly thing to do? See, that's how you do it!"

Thinking out loud for your child helps her to learn adaptive ways to think that will help her to share. It is like giving her a window into your mind to see the thinking and reasoning that underlie positive friendship behavior. The more often your child hears you think out loud in a positive way and gets to see how that thinking results in friendly behavior and a positive outcome, the more likely she will want to try it herself.

Make a sharing plan. Using the Detour Method, give your child a simple plan for sharing. For example, I have found the following plan to be helpful for my own children.

When someone asks to use something your child is using, she can say one of the following, in a friendly way:

1. "I'm using it right now, but you can use it later."
2. "Sure you can use it." (Then find something else to use.)
3. "Why don't we play with it together?"

Explain these three responses to your child (or come up with your own!) and practice them together, modeling exactly how they would sound and look; then have your child practice them. Practice problem "sharing" situations together, using your child's toys to make the rehearsals applicable to real-life. Make your rehearsals fun and brief and give your child lots of encouraging positive feedback. As you continue to practice these three responses, you will see your child's ability to use them naturally in real-life increase.

Don't overshare. Some basic rules of sharing that are often left unstated are that you do not have to share *everything* and you do not have to share with *everybody*. There may be a few special toys or items (that have special meaning to your child or are fragile) that your child should not have to share. After all, you don't let just anyone borrow your car, or take your laptop computer for a spring break weekend in Florida, do you? Additionally, some children can be disrespectful and destructive in their play and have a pretty high chance of breaking whatever they are playing with. Would you share a favorite toy with that child?

You need to help your child learn to identify situations when sharing is appropriate, as well as the fewer instances when it is appropriate to politely decline the request to share, put the toy in question away, and then find something else to play together. For instance, your child may not feel comfortable letting several visiting peers play with a special collector's edition doll, complete with all the detailed trimmings, that she has just been given for her birthday. But she can share other games, dolls, toys, and balls with these children.

You can also let your child know that if another child uses one of her toys in a way that could hurt someone or break the toy, that child will not be allowed to use the toy again. If another child plays too rough with one of your child's toys, your child can respectfully ask the child to play more carefully. (For instance, "Please don't throw the flashlight, it might break.") If the child continues, your child can ask for the toy back or come and get you for assistance. Knowing that she does not *always* have to share *everything* and that you will help to enforce appropriate use of her toys will help reduce your child's resistance to sharing in the long run.

Require sharing frequently; show respect always. While there may be some items that your child does not need to share, the majority of sharing problems involve situations where sharing would be the appropriate response. In these instances, you need to help your child make the mental adjustments necessary to share in an appropriate way. Help your child think through the situation appropriately so that she can choose the best sharing response for the situation (for example, "What do you think would be the best thing to do now?"). If you have rehearsed a sharing plan, now is the time to prompt your child to use it ("Peggy, how would you use your sharing plan right now?").

If needed, you can simply require her to share the toy right then ("You need to let Megan have a turn now") or set up an appropriate sharing interval ("You can have one more turn, and then it will be Megan's turn"). Sometimes, using a timer can simplify the situation, making sharing easier. For example, if your children are playing a computer game, you can set the timer for twenty minutes and then it is the other person's turn for twenty minutes.

Whatever the situation may be, you must always require your child to respond to the other person respectfully. Whether your child is handing a toy over to the other person, suggesting that they play with it together, or informing the other person that she is still using the toy right now, your child needs to learn to handle these situations respectfully. Teaching your child to respond to others respectfully in sharing situations not only helps build positive self-control and communication skills, but emphasizes the truth that people are more important than material possessions.

Be on the lookout for sharing. Attention all cars, be on the lookout for sharing children! As we have discussed, sharing is not always easy—for anyone! So, when you see your child make the effort to share and do so respectfully, take a second to let your child know that she did the right thing. A comment such as, "Hey sweetie, that was great sharing just now" (along with a little squeeze on the shoulder and a reaffirming smile) can go a long way in teaching a child that a little self-sacrifice can be a good thing.

Use Logical Consequences when a child does not share. If you have determined that it is a "sharing" situation (as opposed to a situation when it is appropriate for your child not to share), then your child has two choices: (1) Make the appropriate sharing choice and experience the positive result, or (2) not make the appropriate sharing choice and experience the negative result.

Gently prompt your child to make the appropriate choice, reminding her that sharing helps everyone to have a fun time. If a prompt doesn't work, then give your child a Fork-in-the-Road, informing her that failure to share will result in an immediate negative consequence. If your child still refuses to share or responds with some other negative behavior such as arguing or shouting, calmly and respectfully let your child know that she has just earned a negative consequence and administer it immediately.

Do your best to make the negative consequence fit the situation. If your child has refused to share a certain toy, she may lose the privilege of using that toy while the other child will be allowed to use it. If your child has repeatedly had difficulty sharing a certain item, that item may be taken out of the "play circuit" for a period of time. If your child's behavior becomes disrespectful, a Time-Out is the appropriate choice. Either way, your child learns what she needs to learn: Sharing and expressing her thoughts and feelings respectfully pays off, while refusing to share and being disrespectful to others does not.

How Do I Put It All Together?

The case of possessive Peggy. Mr. and Mrs. Hill decided that sharing was a subject that needed some attention in their family. "Well, everyone," Mr. Hill began during a family night discussion, "Mom and I have decided that a good topic that will help us all is sharing. Peggy, what do you think sharing is?"

"Well, sharing is when you let someone use your things, like your toys," Peggy answered.

"Right," said Mrs. Hill, "it's when you let somebody use something that belongs to you, or when you agree to use something together, like you share the crayons."

"Or share a hot dog, mmm-mmm," said Peggy, as they all laughed.

After reading Luke 6:31 and Romans 12:9–13, they discussed how sharing is one way of obeying God; the positive benefits of sharing; the impact that sharing has on other people; and how they feel when someone shares with them. They listed many of the times they could recall in which each of them (including Mom and Dad) had shared with another person and found that all of them had done a lot of sharing, without even realizing it.

As they talked about sharing, Mr. and Mrs. Hill helped Peggy and Rene come up with a sharing plan. "Okay, girls, here's an idea for a sharing plan. If you are using something and someone else asks to use it, you can do one of three things: (1) Say, 'I'm using it right now, but you can use it later.' Or, (2) say, 'Sure you can use it,' (then find something else to do). Or (3) say, 'Why don't we play with it together?' Now whatever one you say, you need to say it in a friendly and respectful way. What do you think?"

Peggy and her sister both thought that sounded okay. "Let's practice it a few times to see how it works," Mrs. Hill suggested. As a family, they rehearsed the plan, both during family times and when needed, "on the spot." To make their rehearsals relevant, they identified times when both girls had been slow to share and used those situations to practice sharing. They also identified times when the girls did not immediately have to share, such as when they had just opened a new birthday present, had just begun using a toy, or had a toy of special value.

Mr. and Mrs. Hill emphasized that they had to respond to the other person in a respectful way, and that they had to wait their turn (and find something else to do) when another person was using a toy they wanted to use. The Hills also did their best to "share out loud" whenever they could. ("Sweetie, I just shared part of my cookie with you, didn't I? How did that make you feel?" "Do you think that's a good way to listen to God and make friends?")

During the months that they were teaching Peggy and her sister these new sharing skills, Mr. and Mrs. Hill watched carefully for any signs that the girls were applying these skills in their daily interactions. And sure enough, the signs began to show. They saw both girls demonstrate better sharing behavior, either entirely on their own or following a parental reminder ("Peggy, use your sharing plan . . ."). Both parents made sure to give the girls lots of specific, positive feedback when they noticed this sharing behavior ("Peg, that was perfect sharing with Rene just now. That must have made her feel really good. I bet she really enjoys playing with you. Good job!"), and they could see the girls beam with pride upon knowing that they had done the right thing.

Peggy continued to occasionally earn a Time-Out and lose the privilege of using a toy due to a lack of sharing or disrespectful behavior, but Mr. and Mrs. Hill reminded themselves that this was not terrible; it was learning. And they felt comfortable that they were helping their children to learn the right lesson, namely, that with sharing, you gain far more than you give.

Chapter 24

Sibling Problems

The case of Tom and Jerry. Tom was eleven years old and his brother, Jerry, was nine. Mr. and Mrs. Vincent were growing tired of the constant name-calling, arguing, and fighting that occurred almost every time they left their two boys alone. They wanted desperately for their boys to grow to love (and even like) each other but were at a loss for how to make this happen. When squabbles occurred, they tried to listen to each side of the story, but never really knew whose version was accurate. As a result, their confidence in intervening crumbled, and they tended to rule in favor of whoever presented the most convincing case. This seemed to only increase the resentment between their boys and the sparks just got hotter.

 ## Why Does This Happen?

Close proximity. Why can a child can get along well with his friends and then be unable to play for more than thirty minutes with his sibling? Easy. Because he doesn't have to live with his friends! Friends are seen usually only for hours at a time, are novel, and hold the powerful reinforcing quality of offering peer acceptance. Siblings live together in the same house (maybe even the same room), their novelty wears off quickly, and they do not hold peer reinforcing qualities. Sharing the routine activities of everyday life provides countless more opportunities for irritation and conflict than with a peer. While living close can lead to relationships that last a lifetime, it also means that there will be some friction.

Living-together skills are still developing. No matter how old you are, living together successfully requires several complex skills, such as the ability to negotiate, solve problems, be honest, share, respectfully express feelings, and be inconvenienced. These skills take time and practice to fully develop. If you are married, you know that the lack of these skills in either you or your partner (or both!) is the culprit behind many marital spats.

If these skills are difficult for adults to practice consistently, then we shouldn't be surprised that they are difficult for our children too. Our children are early in the process of learning the most difficult (and valuable) relationship skills. Compared to our twenty, thirty-five, or fifty years of experience, they have only had six, twelve, maybe sixteen years of practice at living-together skills. When you think about it, the amazing thing is actually that your sibling problems aren't worse!

Family factors can also influence sibling relationships. Differing levels of skills, popularity, academic success, and so on, can breed feelings of inferiority and resentment in the child who ends up on the short end of the stick. Each of your children wants to feel special, competent, accepted, and loved. If a child is unhappy about some aspect of himself, a sibling becomes an easy target, both by virtue of his close proximity (close targets are easier to hit) and the fact that the sibling's success can be perceived as the other child's failure ("He's great at baseball, and I'm lousy at it"). A parent can add to sibling conflict by comparing siblings to each other. This creates a "win-lose" mentality in the family, where the success or good decisions of one child always means that the other child didn't quite measure up.

What Can I Do?

Prevent problems in the first place. Here are some helpful ideas for stopping sibling problems before they start:

- Build a positive family environment by spending regular time together as a family, doing activities you can all enjoy. Also, spend time individually with each of your children. There is no more powerful way to let them know how valued and loved they truly are. Take time to talk about issues important to your family and listen to each other's feelings and views. Reading from 1 Corinthians 13:4–7; Galatians 5:22–26; and Colossians 3:12–14, talk together about how these passages apply to your family relationships. How does God want you to treat each other? What kind of family does he want you to have? See what answers your children come up with.

- During your family times, help your kids develop "living together" guidelines for problem areas such as using the television, sharing the computer, using the bathroom in the morning, or borrowing someone else's property. These guidelines can include timetables for use, specifics about how to handle disagreements, and other general rules of engagement. Get your children involved in the solution and make the guidelines *clear* and *specific!*

- When you see trouble brewing, immediately remind all kids involved of the positive choices they can make and of the positive or negative consequences that will follow their choice to either work things out or to squabble.

Don't compare apples and oranges. Nothing can drive a wedge of resentment between two siblings faster than negative comparisons. Instead, remind yourself that your children are different; each with their own unique strengths and weaknesses. Remember, children make enough negative comparisons on their own, they don't need any help from you. Instead, address inappropriate behaviors *individually*, without making negative comparisons (no matter how tempting it may be).

Additionally, develop a habit of regularly pointing out each child's strengths and accomplishments. And don't be mistaken, all of your children have many positive qualities and skills. Find things that you can regularly give each child positive feedback about. If one child is great at soccer, then the other may be great at playing tic-tac-toe. If one does well at drawing, then the other may be excellent at telling knock-knock jokes. Regularly pointing out your children's positive skills and qualities helps them to learn that they all are good at many things and they don't have to be the best (or even good) at everything to be loved and appreciated.

Require respect. Your children don't have to always have gushy feelings about each other. In fact, you really can't make them like each other. The quality of their relationship will ultimately be determined by each of them. While providing a family environment where you model and nurture close relationships, you must also require that they treat each other with respect. Your children are much more likely to develop a close relationship if they regularly treat each other respectfully than if they do not.

Together with your children, clearly define a list of "respectful" and "disrespectful" behaviors and let them know that disrespectful behaviors are off-limits, period. Talk together as a family about the benefits of treating each other respectfully and develop immediate negative consequences for disrespectful behavior, regardless of who started what.

Teach and model good communication skills. Your children need to learn to express angry feelings in an appropriate way, instead of resorting to name-calling or put-downs when they are angry or frustrated with each other. The following sentence is a good place to start: "When _____, I feel _____, and I'd like _____."

Together with your children, pick a few common problem situations and have your kids practice using this sentence. For example, if arguing erupts when playing with their Star Wars toys because Tom always wants to use the same action figure and Jerry never gets a chance, Jerry could say, "Tom, when you always get to be Luke Skywalker and I never get a turn, I feel kind of mad because I want a turn sometimes too. I wish that we could take turns being

Luke." It might feel awkward for them the first couple of times, but it is a great way to help your children learn to identify the behavior that is bothering them, respectfully state their feelings, and suggest a positive solution. This beats the heck out of arguing and fighting. And of course, make extra sure that they see you do it too!

Teach them to solve their own problems. During calm times (not in the middle of a battle), have your children identify common problem situations and work on solving them together. This is a superb activity for a family meeting. For starters, choose an easy problem and use the problem-solving steps to guide the discussion:

S—State the problem
T—Think of solutions
E—Evaluate the solutions
P—Pick a solution
S—See if it worked

Your children should do most of the work, but you can help out with ideas when they get stuck. If you use the right ground rules and stick with the problem-solving process, you should be able to help them come up with a positive solution to even the most difficult situations. And if it's their solution, they're more likely to try to make it work. For more ideas about how to use these problem-solving steps with your children, see the section on "Solving Problems."

Teach them how to respond to sibling aggravation. It can be incredibly annoying to have a brother or sister purposely do something to get your goat. Many of us parents have forgotten how incredibly aggravating that is. When your child is being tormented by a sibling, how do you want that child to respond? This is not a particularly easy question.

Together with your children, devise a plan for how they can *respond* to sibling aggravation. The plan may include (1) asking the person to stop, (2) asking them to stop a second time (more firmly), (3) walking away, or (4) getting assistance from parents. Make it very clear that if the aggravated child uses this plan (instead of name-calling or hitting back), he or she will not get into trouble. However, the aggravated child *will* get into trouble if he or she responds negatively.

Reward positive interactions. Use the Pour-It-On Technique every time you see your children interacting positively or resolving problems creatively and effectively. Frequently point out the natural rewards of positive relating, which include not getting into trouble, having more fun, getting along better, less arguing and fighting, and earning more trust. "Guys, you both are playing great together right now! Are you having a fun time? Good. Keep up the good work!" Let your kids know how well they are doing and how much you appreciate their efforts at getting along better. You can even surprise them with an occasional unexpected reward for getting along, such as a pizza and movie night or some other fun activity.

Give negative consequences as a team. The best way to mete out negative consequences for sibling conflict is to become an equal opportunity supplier. That is, negative consequences for all.

This reduces tattling and sends the message that it is far better to solve the problem together (using those problem-solving skills) than to experience negative consequences together. The use of an immediate Time-Out for all involved along with other appropriate Logical Consequences can be very effective in reducing sibling squabbles. The only exception is when one child is an obvious offender and the other child has clearly responded appropriately. In this case, the offending child should receive immediate negative consequences while the other child should be commended for making a positive choice.

 ## How Do I Put It All Together?

The case of Tom and Jerry. Mr. and Mrs. Vincent called a family meeting to talk about the constant conflict between their boys. "Okay, boys, we've got to figure out how to get along together the way God wants us to," Mr. Vincent started, "because we want to be a family that has fun together and treats each other respectfully."

After allowing both boys a chance to air their views, they read Colossians 3:12–14 and spent time talking about what they wanted their family to be like. They targeted three of the most common problem situations (using each other's property, choosing television channels, playing basketball) and had the boys help develop guidelines to make these situations go more smoothly.

"When you want to use each other's things," Mrs. Vincent asked, "how do you boys want to handle it?"

"I don't want him using my model planes," quickly inserted Tom. "And I don't like it when he takes my new glove without asking," returned Jerry.

"Well, let's make a list of things that you can only use if you ask the other person," suggested Mrs. Vincent. "Then, let's decide what things you can use, if the other person is not using them." They ended their family time with a prayer, asking God to help them all to learn how to treat each other the way he wants them to.

They also informed the boys that certain behaviors were off limits, such as hitting, throwing things, or name-calling (such as "stupid"), regardless of who started what. With the boys' input, they devised a set of negative consequences for anyone who committed an off-limit behavior, which included an immediate Time-Out and possibly the loss of a favorite activity for the day (to be determined by parents).

The Vincents also decided that both positive and negative consequences should be given as a "team." So, they decided that any sibling arguing would be followed by one warning. If the arguing continued after the warning, whichever boy had continued arguing (or both) would serve an immediate Time-Out. If problems continued, the consequences increased for both boys equally, unless there was only one clear offender. Mr. and Mrs. Vincent taught the boys what to do if the other sibling aggravated them and they practiced together, emphasizing that making the right choices was the best way to avoid getting into trouble. "And guys," Mr. Vincent reminded them, "if we can't tell who is making the right choices, then you'll both get the negative consequences."

On the positive side, they agreed that if the boys could go three days with no conflicts in one week, they would all go out to celebrate with a fast-food dinner and a trip to the local video arcade, with each boy receiving $5 in tokens. If they could go five days in one week, they would have a special movie and pizza family night.

"Let's keep a chart right here on the fridge," Mrs. Vincent suggested, "every time we have a good "get along" day, we'll put a star on the chart. That will help you keep track of how you're doing."

To help them improve their ability to solve their own problems, Mr. Vincent took the boys to their favorite fast-food restaurant a few times during the following weeks and taught them the problem-solving steps over a hamburger and fries. Not only did this turn out to be a positive father-and-son time, but together they came up with solutions to several recent problems and the boys improved their ability to respectfully express their feelings and think of creative solutions.

While the boys were highly motivated to earn the arcade tokens, it quickly became clear that turning their behavior around would be no small task. They both regularly earned Time-Outs for arguing and lost a variety of privileges. However, Mr. and Mrs. Vincent helped each other to stay consistent with their plan. They continued problem-solving practice with the boys and gave them plenty of positive encouragement when they interacted appropriately. The main emphasis was on treating each other respectfully, positive communication, and figuring out how to solve problems instead of just arguing about them.

Eventually, the boys reduced the number of conflicts enough to earn dinner and an arcade trip. "Hooray!! I can't believe we did it!" Tom shouted with glee. With continued ups and downs and regular family meetings to come up with new ideas for handling problems, the Vincent boys were on their way towards learning how to work out many (not all) of their problems on their own and treat each other with more respect. Best of all, they were developing valuable skills that would impact their relationship for a lifetime.

Chapter 25

Stealing

The case of sticky-fingers Louie. "Mom, why can't I get some more?" whined ten-year-old Louie, bemoaning the fact that his friend Brian had just purchased another pack of the trading cards that he and all his friends were collecting. "Brian just got a really rare card, just the one I need!" exclaimed Louie. After being told by his mother that he was not getting any new cards today, Louie went back to counting and sorting his current array of cards. A couple weeks later, while Brian and Louie were playing with their cards, Louie's mother, Mrs. Olson, overheard Brian telling Louie that he had somehow lost his new rare card and was sad that couldn't find it anywhere.

Later, after Mrs. Olson ushered the boys outside to play in the yard, she took their trading books up to Louie's room and for no particular reason, casually leafed through Louie's book. Her eye caught a card sticking out from the inside pocket of the back cover and upon examining it, realized that this was the missing card that she had overheard Brian talking about. After discussing it with her husband, they asked Louie about it later that night. The immediate saucer-eyed look on his face when they asked him about the card told them that their hunch was correct.

 ## Why Does This Happen?

Acting before thinking. Raise your hand if you have never done anything stupid in your life. We have all made mistakes, and your children will make their share. A child may choose, in a split second, to forfeit his moral conviction that stealing is wrong and take something that is not his. Even though he may immediately (or soon thereafter) regret the decision and know in his heart that it was wrong, it is done. You cannot prevent your child from making his share of poor decisions, but you can ensure that he learns the *right* lessons when he makes them.

Peer pressure can play a role for some children. Proverbs 13:20 reminds us that, "He who walks with the wise grows wise, but a companion of fools suffers harm." Allowing your child to spend large amounts of time with peers who regularly engage in negative behavior has a high likelihood of causing him to gain a distorted picture of that behavior. He may subtly grow to view various negative behaviors as being glamorous, daring, exciting, and status-enhancing—all of which are the exact opposite of what God says about such behaviors.

Distant family relationships. When those all important parent-child relationships are absent, neglected, or chronically damaged, the result can be children looking for love, acceptance, and significance in all the wrong places. A lack of appropriate parental supervision is frequently found in the families of children who develop the habit of stealing. Sooner or later, that child will find himself in situations where the temptation to engage in negative behavior is substantial and, without a strong family foundation or proper supervision, the probability of holding out against such behavior becomes slim.

 ## What Can I Do?

Find out why your child made the decision to steal. Without permitting your child to shift the blame to others for his behavior or rationalize it in some way, try to understand the situation from his perspective.

What were the factors that influenced him to cross the line? Was it simply his personal desire to have the stolen item? Was it pressure from peers? Was your child stuck in an uncomfortable moment and unsure how to escape without risking peer rejection? Was it an impulsive decision or a calculated action? How does your child view his behavior now? What are the reasons for his current view? Remember, the stealing has already been done. The only thing you can do now is to make it the best learning experience possible for your child. Listening to your child's perspective will help you figure out how to do just that.

Talk about it. In addition to wanting your child to experience the right consequences as the result of his stealing, you also want him to learn to think about stealing the right way. After you have discussed the specifics about his particular stealing incident, explore your child's views about the issue of stealing in general.

What does your child think about stealing? Is there a difference between stealing something small and something big? Why is stealing wrong? What are the consequences of stealing? Do children usually get caught (sooner or later) when they steal? Is stealing okay if a person does not get caught? What does your child think God says about stealing? These discussion questions are great for a family time and will help you better understand your child's current level of moral reasoning as it applies to stealing.

Once you have explored what your child thinks about stealing, let your child know what your views are. Let your child know *why* you think stealing is wrong. Explain *why* it is important to pay for the things we buy and *why* it is wrong to take things that belong to others.

Using an age-appropriate translation, look together at Exodus 20:15; Luke 6:31; and Ephesians 4:28. Remind your child that God's commands are always designed to steer us toward things that are good for us (and others) and away from things that will harm us (or others). Share your convictions about why stealing harms both the one who steals and the one who is stolen from. God tells us not to steal because he wants us to love and respect other people and treat them the way that we would like them to treat us. Whether it seems attractive at the time or not, God clearly tells us not to take things that do not belong to us. And obeying God is *always* the right thing to do.

Build your relationship with your child. If your relationship with your child is distant or damaged in some way, then make it your job to build a bridge toward restoring that relationship. Prioritize your family and spend regular time with your child, getting involved in his life and talking about things meaningful to him. Spend regular quality time together as a family, communicating that every person in your family is important and deeply loved. Talk together about issues such as expressing love for each other, how to talk through problems, how to express frustration, and the virtue of character traits such as honesty, integrity, courage, and so on. I have seen outwardly "difficult" children sob and choke with tears, yearning for a closer relationship with their parents. Whatever you have to do, including seeking family counseling, lead the way toward restoring the relationships that God intended you to have in your family.

Examine the environment. Take a look at the factors that may have influenced your child toward stealing. Consider the friends he is spending time with and the amount of unsupervised time he has. If needed, make some drastic changes in your child's social calendar, requiring him to "take a break" from friends you think may be negatively influencing him and providing opportunities for him to get reacquainted with peers who will have a more positive influence. Make sure that you know where your child is and that he is properly supervised at all times. Remind yourself that an ounce of prevention is worth a pound of cure.

Require honesty and responsibility. One painful, but character-building lesson is to own up to our mistakes. It's not fun, but it's a necessary and restorative consequence. Have your child personally confess to and apologize for his stealing, directly to the person that he stole the item from. Whether it be a friend or a store manager, this uncomfortable experience will emotionally accent the serious and interpersonal violation of stealing. It will also give your child the experience of bringing proper closure to the incident and the satisfaction of having done the "right thing." Stay with and be supportive of your child during this conversation, letting him know that you are very proud of him for having the courage to handle this mistake the right way.

If you strongly suspect that your child has stolen on one or more occasions, but your child emphatically denies it, simply establish a "no-suspicion" rule. This means that it will be your child's responsibility to stay far away from even the suspicion that he has stolen anything. If *any* suspicions arise about an item, your child will be treated as if he has stolen the item—no questions, no investigation. Period. If your child comes home with any items that do not belong to him (without evidence that he is allowed to have the item), you will consider the items stolen and he will receive the resulting negative consequence. If anything is found to be missing around the house, he will be considered a prime suspect and receive the appropriate negative consequence. The purpose here is to take the detective work out of it and to put the responsibility and impetus on *your child* to avoid even the appearance of anything that could remotely resemble stealing. Squeaky-clean honesty is the only way out of this predicament. The "no-suspicion" rule is an unpleasant but logical consequence of stealing. If your child doesn't like it, then he can stay miles away from any suspicion of stealing and the "no-suspicion" rule will eventually be lifted.

Make the consequences fit. In addition to the important consequence of owning up to his behavior and apologizing to the person that he stole from, other consequences must be imposed.

First, your child must make restitution. He must return the item that was stolen and, if it has been damaged in any way, he should pay for the item and return both the damaged item and the new item to the proper owner. If your child does not have enough money to pay for the item, you can pay for it and your child can work off the debt by doing extra chores around the house.

If your child has taken something from a store, you can call the store manager ahead of time to let him know that your child will be coming in to return the item, pay for it if needed, and apologize.

Second, it is also appropriate for your child to lose a certain privilege or privileges for a set amount of time. The rationale is that fun privileges are the natural result of positive behavior. When your child behaves negatively, the privileges naturally must decline. Remove privileges in a way that appropriately reflects the seriousness of the incident, whether it be use of electronic devices, time with friends, telephone use, or something else. With a sense of understanding, let your child know that these consequences are the result of *his* choice to steal. However, help your child turn a mental corner by emphasizing that everyone has made poor decisions and that if he learns the right lessons from his experience, he can avoid this mistake in the future.

Come up with a plan to prevent stealing in the future. This is a very important part of your response to stealing. At some point in the future, your child will be presented with another tempting opportunity to take something that does not belong to him. Help him be prepared for this situation by planning for it ahead of time. For instance, if your child really wants a certain item, explore the appropriate options he can think of. For instance, he can ask for it for his birthday, save his money to buy it, offer to work to help pay for it, wait until he is older, or realize that he can't have everything and get used to the idea that he may not get that item.

If he is in a situation where there is peer pressure to do something that he knows is wrong (such as steal), then he can respond by saying, "I don't think this is such a good idea"; "I don't want to do this"; "Let's get out of here and do something else"; "Guys, this is wrong, I'm not going to do this"; or "I'm going home." He will also need to think about the quality of friends that would pressure him to do something wrong or illegal.

Together with your child, make up a few conceivable scenarios and have him practice responding to them the right way. Have him show you what he would think, say, and do. Review your plan as often as needed, using different practice situations, to help your child strengthen his ability to do the right thing in a difficult situation.

Teach and model contentment. Your children are constantly exposed to advertising geared toward making them discontent with their current belongings and saturating them with visions of new, ever more enticing possessions. In such a climate, it is imperative that you teach and model biblical contentment. Philippians 4:11–13 and

1 Timothy 6:8–10 remind us of the importance of separating ourselves from the material cravings of this world that reflect the emptiness of life without God. In your family times, regularly thank God for his blessings and take the time to recount them all. Help your child to consider all the blessings he has when compared to an overwhelming majority of the world.

The way you handle the temptation to covet material possessions will seep out through your daily words and actions and undeniably influence your children. How important is it for *you* to have a bigger house, a newer car, fancier clothes, or a faster computer? Let your children see you be thankfully content with the things you have. Give your children the gifts of perspective and contentment by teaching and modeling an eternal and biblical view of life for them to follow.

 ## How Do I Put It All Together?

The case of sticky-fingers Louie. Mr. and Mrs. Olson confronted Louie about the card his mother had found. "I . . . I . . . uh . . . well . . . ," Louie stammered, trying to quickly figure out what to say. Looking into the firm gaze of his parents, Louie realized that coming clean was his best option and that he really didn't want to make things worse by lying. "The card is Brian's," he confessed with a sigh, staring at the floor.

Louie explained that while at Brian's house last week, Brian had dropped the card on the floor without noticing it. When Brian stepped out to go to the bathroom, Louie had picked the card up and placed it in his card book. Louie had never showed the card to anyone and didn't know what he was going to do with it. He said that he felt bad about taking it, but didn't know how to give it back and was afraid to say anything about it.

"Lou, we're glad that you told us the truth, but stealing is a very serious thing," Mr. Olson told his son. They took the card and informed Louie that he would have to tell Brian what he had done and apologize. They also told him that there would be negative consequences for his behavior and that they would talk about it and let him know what the consequences would be.

The next day, Louie and his mother went over to Brian's house. Mrs. Olson had already let Brian's mother know what had happened and that they were coming over. Brian's mother was understanding and met them at the door. With both mothers watching and his gaze shifting back and forth from Brian to the ground, Louie explained to Brian what he had done and returned the card. He also gave Brian a brand new pack of cards that he had purchased with his own money. Louie apologized and asked Brian to forgive him. He said that he hoped they could still be friends and that he would never take something that wasn't his again. Mrs. Olson squeezed Louie's shoulder and told him he had done a good job. She thanked Brian and his mother for listening graciously and told them that if Brian would like to get together to play sometime, to please give them a call.

Later that week, Mr. Olson took some time with Louie to talk about the incident. He asked Louie how it was that a card had become more important to him than his friendship with Brian. They talked about the consequences of stealing and why God warned us not to steal. "Isn't it funny," Mr. Olson pondered, "how God always knows what is best for us."

"That's because he made us," replied Louie.

"That's right," Mr. Olson responded, "and he told us in the Bible what we should do so that we can do the right thing."

As they talked, Mr. Olson felt that Louie showed a good understanding of the issues surrounding stealing and seemed truly remorseful. "Dad, I'm just sad because Brian's not going to be my friend anymore," Louie said, his eyes filling with tears. "Well, what did you say to Brian?" Mr. Olson asked. As Louie told his father about his conversation with Brian, Mr. Olson couldn't hold back his proud, fatherly grin and he told Louie how proud he was that he had done the right thing.

Mr. and Mrs. Olson were comfortable with the friends that Louie had and did not think that any of them were having a negative influence on their son. They attributed the stealing incident to an impulsive poor decision. After talking together, they informed Louie that in addition to apologizing to Brian, returning the card, and buying him a new pack of cards, Louie would lose the privilege of using his trading cards for one month. They both felt that this was an appropriate set of consequences and while unhappy about it, Louie did not complain.

To Louie's delight, Brian eventually did call and the boys played with something other than trading cards for a while. Brian's mother told Mrs. Olson how impressed she was with how they had handled this situation and reaffirmed that she liked Louie very much.

In their family times, they talked together about being satisfied with what you have and how to handle it when you are tempted to disobey God. Mrs. Olson pointed out how both kids and grownups can be tempted to steal or do other wrong things, and they came up with examples of things to think, say, and do that would help a person handle those situations the right way. As time went on, Mr. and Mrs. Olson felt comfortable that Louie had learned the right lesson through his experience and had become better prepared to handle things the right way the next time the temptation to steal came along.

Chapter 26

Talking About Difficult Subjects (Sex, Drugs, Alcohol, Smoking)

The case of risky Rebecca. Rebecca was a ten-year-old girl who was going on twenty-one and showing all the signs of preadolescence. Her parents were becoming concerned about some of the music her friends were listening to and the types of movies some of them were talking about. While Rebecca had many positive friends whose parents enforced appropriate boundaries, there were other friends who had much more freedom than Mr. and Mrs. Weeks were comfortable with and they knew that this was starting to influence Rebecca.

However, Rebecca's parents were not just paying attention to her attitudes toward music and movies, they were also aware that underneath those issues loomed the larger issues of sex, drugs, alcohol, and smoking. They decided that it was high time to head things off at the pass and talk about these important subjects.

Why Does This Happen?

We have to learn our own lessons. Sometimes we are smart enough to learn a lesson just from watching another person make a mistake and experience the unfortunate consequences of a bad decision. More often, however, we insist on going through the pain of our own mistakes before the truth finally hits home. As parents, we don't want our children to experience painful mistakes although we know in our hearts that this is an unavoidable part of growing up. And while we cannot prevent our children from making mistakes or shield them from the resulting painful lessons, we can teach our children to think clearly and do everything in our power to help them avoid mistakes that are particularly costly and devastating.

A limited perspective. Preadolescence is a time of transition. Your child is walking across the bridge between being a child and becoming a full-fledged teenager. This brings with it a myriad of important and sometimes difficult subjects that need to be discussed at increasingly younger ages.

However, it is important to remember that your child's reasoning abilities are still developing and her reservoir of experience is limited. You have the benefit of your own experiences, your observations of others' experiences over the years, and the chance to see the long-term results of certain lifestyles and choices. Your ten-year-old child has only a ten-year-old version of these things. She is thinking these issues through for possibly the first time. You must teach her how to think right.

Poor communication can make talking about difficult subjects even more difficult, or flat out impossible. When relationships have been repeatedly hurt and meaningful communication or quality family time are not regular occurrences, talking about such subjects can be difficult. A family communication tune-up or serious overhaul may be needed to restore broken relationships and learn new ways of talking and going through life together.

A job left undone. Some parents relinquish their job of discussing these topics with their children, waiting instead for teachers or church leaders to take care of it. However, this teaching and discussion is most effectively done by parents. Why? Because you are the guide your child instinctively looks to for clues about what is important in life and how to answer life's tough questions. While certain teachers, church leaders, and family members may prove to be valuable allies in the effort to teach your child crucial lessons about life and values, don't forget that you are the main teacher that God has placed in your child's life. And that classroom is too important to be absent from.

 ## What Can I Do?

Talk about it sooner rather than later. In our media-rich and value-poor society, children are being exposed to these issues far earlier than when we were kids. As such, effective education about sex, drugs, alcohol, and smoking does not begin when children are teenagers, it starts when your children are in the elementary and pre-teen years.

Early messages about sex include proper definitions of and boundaries around "private parts"; appropriate privacy and modesty modeled and required at home; and age-appropriate discussion of "where babies come from," explaining that God designed babies to come from moms and dads who are married.

Early messages about drugs, alcohol, and smoking include teaching the simple facts that cigarettes and drugs hurt your body or brain and can kill you. God gave us the gift of life and wants us to take good care of our bodies. Many people die each year because of drug, alcohol, and cigarette use and while the Bible says that some use of alcohol for grown-ups may be acceptable at times, using too much can really hurt your body. All three (drugs, alcohol, and cigarettes) can be addictive, which means that it can be really hard to stop once you have gotten into the habit of using them. Some grown-ups spend their whole lives trying to stop using them and are never successful. While more detailed discussion of these topics will need to occur somewhere between the ages of ten and twelve for most children, these later discussions will be more effective if they are built on a foundation of having heard the right messages many times before.

Know your stuff. Discussion about sex, drugs, alcohol, or smoking is sometimes considered difficult because parents are not sure how to go about it. One place to start is to know your stuff.

One wonderful series of books designed for several different age-levels, written by Stanton and Brenna Jones, can help you teach your child about sex over the years. The first book in the series is entitled *The Story of Me* and is written for children aged three through five.

Focus on the Family has a very helpful selection of resource materials that parents can use to brush up on their facts about substance abuse and read or watch with their pre-teen or teenage child (see www.family.org). The National Institute on Drug Abuse (www.nida.nih.gov) and the National Clearinghouse for Alcohol and Drug Information (www.health.org) also offer a nice array of factual information for parents and children on a wide variety of substances. Using these and other quality resources, prepare yourself to talk informatively and intelligently with your child about these important subjects. If you want to be a good teacher, then do your homework.

Accent the issue. While your child should see and hear correct messages about these issues woven into the fabric of everyday family life, accent the importance of these issues by scheduling a special time for an in-depth discussion during the pre-teen years.

With regard to sex, this discussion can be more effective with the same-sex parent and can be worked into a special parent-child time that "launches" your child into adolescence. The "memory value" and significance of this time can be heightened by adding elements that communicate the importance of this transition, such as making it a parent-child overnight event. However you choose to conduct your initial discussion, remember to keep the conversation open-ended. There will be plenty of need for more dialogue on these issues down the road.

Be all ears. Begin your discussion by listening to your child's views on these important issues. Ask your child what she knows about the issue you are discussing, where she has learned it from, and just how that issue impacts her life.

Then follow up with questions that will help her think through the issue clearly. How has her relationship with God impacted her thinking? What does she think about how the issue is portrayed in music, television, and the movies? How do her friends handle the issue? What pressures has she encountered? How has she responded to those pressures?

As you listen, be understanding and supportive. Your child is learning how you will respond if she is honest and open with you. Your response now may dictate whether your child will be honest with you in the future, when she may need you even more.

Review the facts. Prior to talking with you, your child's main source of information may be the misinformation gleaned from uninformed peers. Whether reading through a pamphlet together, watching a video, looking at portions of a book, or a combination of these approaches, discuss the facts about the issue you are talking about, using the resources that you have consulted.

If you have done your homework, you should be able to present the issue as a parent who is not only armed with your own experience and opinions, but also with a good grasp of the facts and realities of the issue, many of which may be new to your child. Your preparation and the use of credible resources will help your child to view your opinion as a well-informed one, and she will be grateful that you have taken the time to help her get the straight story on important life issues.

Take a look at the book. As you want your child to learn to think through these important issues from an intelligent Christian perspective, make sure to discuss what the Bible says about them.

While the resources you use can help with this, you and your child can examine relevant passages on your own. For example, Genesis 1:27–28; Ephesians 5:3; and 1 Thessalonians 4:3–8 set the stage for understanding God's design for sex within marriage and include commands to avoid sexual impurity.

Verses that shed light on a biblical view of substance use include Luke 21:34; Romans 13:11–14; 1 Corinthians 6:10, 19; Galatians 5:19–21; and Ephesians 5:18. First Corinthians 6:19 advocates taking care of our bodies and keeping them pure as temples of the Holy Spirit.

Either individually or during a family time, and using a child-friendly translation, select a few of these passages and talk about God's design and plans for us. Ask your child why she thinks God commands us to do (or not to do) certain things? What are the benefits of obeying God (regardless of what others do) and the negative consequences of disobeying him? Helping your child to accurately think through these questions will help her learn how to approach important life issues from a Christian perspective.

Make your convictions clear. As you listen to your child's views and review the facts about these important issues, make sure that you share your own views and the reasons for them. It is not enough for your child to know that you think that sex outside of marriage and drug use are wrong. Your child will learn more if she understands *why* you hold these views. Share with your child why *you* think it is wise to follow God's commands and communicate your positive expectations that your child will make good decisions on these important issues.

Look for positive examples. As you move through the late childhood and preadolescent years, be on the lookout for examples of people who have been brave enough to stand out from the crowd. You will find examples in the Bible, history, current real-life, and fictional movie or cartoon characters. Jesus, Paul, Esther, and many other biblical persons are great examples of obeying God and doing what is right, regardless of the popular opinion of their day. When you see an example, point it out to your child and discuss the benefits of being strong and courageous in obedience to God.

Take immediate action if your child has shown any signs of inappropriate sexual activity, substance use, or cigarette use. In addition to the suggestions listed above, you should contact a qualified therapist who can help you and your family work through these issues. Specialized treatment for some problems, such as substance abuse, may be necessary. The therapist can help your child find more appropriate ways to handle the challenges of preadolescence, help you set and enforce firm limits around these behaviors, and help your family address important relationship issues.

How Do I Put It All Together?

The case of risky Rebecca. Mr. and Mrs. Weeks decided to take a tag-team approach. Mr. Weeks began doing the homework on issues of drugs, alcohol, and smoking while Mrs. Weeks prepared for a discussion of sex and the changes that occur during the teen years. They told Rebecca that they were going to have a special night of talking about important things together and to choose her favorite restaurant for dinner next Saturday. After a fun, scrumptuous meal, they came back home and talked about drugs, alcohol, and smoking.

"Becky," Mr. Weeks began, "since you're getting older, we need to talk about some very important things with you. So, for starters, let's talk about drinking and drugs. What do you know about alcohol and drugs?"

They found that, outside of the general idea that drugs and drinking are bad for you, Rebecca did not know many details. Mr. and Mrs. Weeks explained a few basic details about the negative effects of drugs, alcohol, and cigarettes and showed Rebecca some of the resources they had gathered that outlined the facts.

"Honey," Mrs. Weeks said, "it's important for us to think about what God says about drinking and drugs. So, let's take a look." They used Rebecca's Bible to look at selected verses together and discussed God's view about doing things that will impair your thinking or hurt your body. As they talked, Mr. and Mrs. Weeks not only listened intently to Rebecca's thoughts, but also shared their views about drugs, alcohol, and smoking and the negative effects that they had seen in people who had engaged in these behaviors. The evening was a positive one and Rebecca felt honored that her parents had gone to all this work just for her.

The next Saturday, Mrs. Weeks took Rebecca for the afternoon and they discussed the facts about sex and the physical and hormonal changes that Rebecca would experience over the next few years. "Susie Johnson has already started growing those," Rebecca joked, referring to her thirteen-year-old friend from church. Mrs. Weeks explained God's plan for marriage and babies and discussed how it made so much sense. Then they talked about what happens when people get sex and marriage out of order. When her mother described sexually transmitted diseases Rebecca reacted with a "Yuck, that's gross." They also shared a moment of sadness as they considered how many babies are aborted each year by their teenage mothers.

Mrs. Weeks' preparation was evident, and this discussion turned out to be a memorable bonding time for Rebecca and her mother. Over the following months, Mr. and Mrs. Weeks made sure to point out examples from the Bible, real life, and movies, of persons who had made wise choices in these important areas. They were also able to highlight many examples of those who had made poor choices and contrasted the results.

While the challenges of adolescence were still around the corner, Mr. and Mrs. Weeks felt that they were off to a good start in staying connected with their daughter and beginning a dialogue on these important issues. They had given Rebecca a very real head start by opening the door of communication, arming her with the facts, and helping her learn to think through these important issues from a Christian perspective.

Chapter 27

Talking Disrespectfully

The case of sassy Sara. Mr. and Mrs. Maxwell were astounded when their eleven-year-old "angel" started talking back to them like a seventeen-year-old juvenile delinquent. "You don't love me!" "You are so unfair!"

At first, Sara's parents were so shocked they didn't know what to do. Mr. Maxwell's immediate urge was to give Sara a good paddling, but a little voice in the back of his head told him that such a move would probably end up backfiring. Instead, he told her that she was "grounded," which usually meant the loss of a couple privileges for a day or two. Sara would occasionally reduce her grounding through good behavior but then would earn another one shortly after.

Mrs. Maxwell had always had difficulty with her temper and often responded to Sara's cutting comments with a few heated, emotional words of her own. Sometimes, Sara and her mother would engage in a shouting match that would cause Mr. Maxwell to wave his hands in despair and leave the room.

Why Does This Happen?

Preadolescence. Enough said. This is an awkward time of life for a child who is beginning the process of becoming a young teenager. Everything begins to change. Growth spurts, menstruation, changes in body proportions, increase in sex hormones, dissatisfaction with physical appearance, increased moodiness, feeling self-conscious, ideas and tastes that are different than yours, peers becoming even more important, increased social pressure, and a greater desire for autonomy and independence. This is quite a list. And while reasonable behavioral limits need to be maintained, it is also a time when mom and dad need to have an extra dose of patience.

Child see, child do. You reap what you sow. If Mom and Dad have sown years of poor communication habits, those bad habits will bear fruit. Do you talk respectfully to your children and to other family members? Remember, your children learn more from what they see and hear you do than from the best lecture you can muster.

Peer influences can have an effect on how your child talks to you. Kids pick up the darndest things at school, preschool, parks, friend's houses, and yes, even Sunday school. Trying out something that someone else said is a very common childhood behavior, simply because most of us are natural born imitators. This is part of how we learn social behavior. This is even more true as kids get older and the power of peer pressure increases.

 What Can I Do?

Keep your thoughts on track. It can be shocking to hear your child suddenly unleash words that are intended to be hurtful. However, you must keep in mind that all preadolescents have their disrespectful moments. Remind yourself that your child needs to learn how to express angry feelings more respectfully and make it your goal to teach her the right lesson.

Show them how it is done. It is futile to expect your children to speak respectfully if you do not do the same yourself. Take a close look at how you communicate with your children and spouse when you are angry and make sure that you are leading by setting a positive example.

Talk together about the behavior. During a positive time, have a discussion with your child about talking to other people. Let her know that feeling frustrated or upset is a normal emotion and that it can be more difficult to talk respectfully in those situations.

Make up some scenarios (for instance, "Heather's mother told her to come inside and she didn't want to, so she told her mother, 'No!' in a really rude way") and have your child identify how the various people in the scenario might be feeling. Then discuss situations where your child has spoken disrespectfully to someone and have her identify how the other person probably felt. Explore how your child thinks God wants us to treat others, even when we are mad, and think together about why this might be so, using Philippians 2:14–15 and James 1:19–20 as a biblical starting point. Try to make these discussions fun and interactive so that your child will get the most out of them.

Teach them what to do. Building on the previous step, make a list of the most frequent situations in which your child speaks disrespectfully. Using the Detour Method, decide *exactly* what you would like your child to think, say, or do in those situations. In other words, help her come up with a plan for how to better handle the situations that prompt disrespectful behavior. With older children, have them be involved in the development of the plan.

For instance, when she doesn't get her way about something, your child's plan might be to:

1. Think, "I can't always do everything I want"
2. Say, "Okay, Mom (or Dad)"
3. Do what I was asked
4. If I have a question about the situation, I must ask it respectfully

As you go through each problem situation, identify the types of words, tone of voice, and so on, that you would like your child to use. Then, practice these situations together, making your rehearsals short and enjoyable. You can model the positive behav-

iors by pretending that you are your child and let her play you—
she'll probably enjoy that.

In a role play, pretend to speak disrespectfully to her (as she
has done in the past), have her tell you how it feels to be spoken
to this way, and let her decide what negative consequences she
would give you. Then, model the replacement behavior and have
her point out the natural rewards that follow. Make sure to switch
roles and have her practice the behaviors. Practice the replacement behavior in different problem situations, providing plenty of
specific verbal rewards as you go! See the section on "Expressing
Angry Feelings" for more ideas.

Catch your child being respectful. As always, you want to help
your child come to the conclusion that making the effort to obey
God and treat others respectfully pays off, both in the short-term
and in the long-term. You can do this by watching for your child to
speak respectfully on *any* occasion and especially during times when
she has been disrespectful in the past. When your child speaks in a
respectful or self-controlled manner, use the Pour-It-On Technique
and immediately follow this behavior with a specific verbal reward.

Additionally, you can use natural rewards by frequently pointing out the connection between respectful behavior and the natural rewards that follow (for instance, more positive interactions
with others, less Time-Outs, more privileges, knowing that her
choices are pleasing God) and by surprising her with a special
privilege (renting a fun movie, a special activity with Mom, having a sleepover with a friend) just because she has worked so hard
at treating others respectfully.

Clearly define "disrespectful" talk. As you are going to be
using negative consequences for disrespectful behavior, make sure
that your child knows how to *avoid* those consequences. Let your
child know *exactly* the type of words, phrases, tone of voice, and
so on that signal disrespect. Make sure that your expectations are
reasonable and that you allow your child some room for expressing frustration in a less than perfect way.

**Use negative consequences for clearly disrespectful
behavior.** An immediate Time-Out is an appropriate choice for
this type of misbehavior. If your child is in the habit of speaking

disrespectfully several times a day, you can link various privileges to respectful talking by removing them for repeated instances of disrespectful talking.

For example, in addition to an immediate Time-Out, your child could experience thirty minutes of room restriction for three instances of clear disrespect in a day, the loss of television and other electronic games for four instances, and an hour of early bed for five instances. When your child begins to talk mildly disrespectful, give her a Fork-in-the-Road to help her change her course and avoid the negative consequences that are lurking just around the bend.

Apologize when appropriate. This applies to both you and your children. If anyone speaks in a demeaning or disrespectful way to another, an apology is in order. While you cannot force a genuine apology, it is easier if apologizing is taught and modeled from a young age and held as a general family expectation when one person is disrespectful or hurtful in any way to another. One does not necessarily need to apologize for feeling angry, in fact, the angry feelings may be quite understandable. However, expressing those feelings in a disrespectful or hurtful manner damages relationships and an apology can help to heal this hurt. And don't forget, forgiveness should be waiting on the other end.

 ## How Do I Put It All Together?

The case of sassy Sara. Sara's parents sat down to discuss this issue and develop a plan. They pinpointed the types of situations that usually triggered Sara's disrespectful talk and discussed other ways that Sara could express her thoughts, possible negative consequences, and ways of strengthening her positive behavior.

They scheduled a "family meeting" to discuss the situation with Sara. "Sara," Mr. Maxwell started, "we want to be a family where everybody treats everybody respectfully. All the time." "And that means everyone," Mrs. Maxwell chimed in, "including your father and me. So honey, let's talk about how we can all do that."

They started off by talking about how important each person in their family is to each other and to God and how the only way to make things work is to treat each other respectfully. Mr. and Mrs.

Maxwell made sure to point out that this family rule applied to them as much as it did to Sara. They shared their concerns about the way Sara had been talking lately and listened attentively to Sara's point of view. "Well, you guys don't ever let me do anything," Sara complained. "Well, honey," Mr. Maxwell replied, skillfully keeping the discussion on track, "we'd be happy to talk about some of the rules if you want, that would be fine. But our main concern right now is *how* we talk about things, even if we disagree or feel frustrated."

Together, they discussed situations where Sara had frequently been disrespectful and made a list of ideas for how Sara could handle the situations more respectfully. Mr. and Mrs. Maxwell helped Sara choose a few of these ideas and turn them into a plan that she could use. Sara's plan included reminding herself that God wants her to treat others respectfully, making all comments or asking questions in a respectful way, and accepting her parents' decision about the issue. If she needed to, they could talk about it in more detail at a later time.

During the next several weeks, both Mr. and Mrs. Maxwell spent time with Sara, practicing how she could use her plan and using past "disrespectful" situations for rehearsal. They always ended their practice sessions with a prayer that God would help them all learn how to be more respectful to each other.

"Now this is more like it," Sara commented when Mrs. Maxwell suggested that Sara receive a special privilege following four consecutive days of respectful behavior. While Sara was not thrilled about it, she understood that Time-Out and removal of privileges were fitting negative consequences for talking disrespectfully. Sara appreciated it when Mr. and Mrs. Maxwell agreed to give Sara more freedom in how she handled her homework and chores, as this was one of her chief complaints. Mrs. Maxwell also apologized to Sara for her own angry outbursts in the past and told Sara that she, too, would work hard at being more respectful.

When using the Pour-It-On Technique (for instance, "Sara, that was a very respectful way of asking your question. I really appreciate that."), Mr. and Mrs. Maxwell were actually surprised at how often Sara did talk respectfully (had they not noticed before?). Despite all their planning, Sara earned her fair share of

Time-Outs and lost several privileges for being disrespectful during the first few months. Mrs. Maxwell had to work particularly hard to keep a "matter-of-fact" attitude when Sara was disrespectful and to break the habit of responding to Sara in an emotionally charged way.

However, this time Sara's parents were together in their plan, and they consistently used the Fork-in-the-Road and followed through with the negative consequences Sara earned. In their family times, they continued to discuss their progress, address additional concerns, and pray together that God would help them all learn to be respectful to each other. As needed, they revised the negative consequences that Sara received for being disrespectful and the special privileges she could earn (such as having sleepovers) for longer periods of consistent respectful behavior. These meetings gave Sara the opportunity to regularly share her thoughts and feelings, which she enjoyed. With perseverance, Sara eventually did earn her special privilege and soon was working for longer periods of respectful behavior. Before long, the tide began to change and while Sara remained a normal preadolescent, she was learning to handle the challenges of preadolescence in a much more respectful way.

Chapter 28

Temper Tantrums

The case of Tony the typhoon. Three-year-old Tony was a generally happy child. Except for when he didn't get his way. He had refined the art of screaming and "throwing a fit" to perfection. Because of her own unpleasant family background, Ms. Wood did not want to impose too much discipline on Tony. Instead, she wanted to nurture him and help him to have a happy childhood. As a result, when push turned to shove, she usually allowed Tony to have his way. When she didn't, Tony would throw a colossal tantrum and Ms. Wood would respond by trying to comfort and reason with him. This seldom seemed to help, however, and with preschool not too far away, Ms. Wood was starting to wonder if she should be doing something different.

 ## Why Does This Happen?

Many lessons are being learned during this important stage of life. Your child is experiencing a normal and predictable collision between his natural desire to do things on his own timetable and the reality that this cannot always happen. Here are a few of the important lessons that your child is learning during these preschool years: He is not the center of the universe. He can't do or get everything he wants. Sometimes he has to wait. Someone else is looking after him and is in charge.

These can be tough lessons for a three-year-old, but they must be learned. If they are not learned, behavior like Tony's is bound to be the result. At a deeper level, these lessons are actually comforting realities—just think how frightening it would be to be a three-year-old and the strongest person you know!

Are you expecting too much? Noncompliance and tantrums can be prompted by a parent over-taxing a young child's ability to respond correctly. Are you asking too much, requiring flawless behavior (even when he is tired), or expecting him to make abrupt changes without giving a warning or using a warm-down routine (for example, "Tony, we are going to leave in just a minute")? If so, then these expectations are setting you and your child up for frustration and battles that could have easily been avoided.

Ineffective responses to tantrums can help to maintain tantrum behavior. For example, following a tantrum by providing extra attention, using an ineffective Time-Out procedure, or giving in to your child's demands results in your child learning that throwing a tantrum works. Conversely, you want him to learn that making an effort to talk nicely, controlling his angry feelings, and listening to Mom and Dad pay off, and that negative behaviors do not.

Your child's temperament may contribute to tantrums. Some children find it much more difficult than others to regain control once they have become angry. For these temperamentally difficult children, prolonged tantrums may happen with some frequency and the parents' job will not be an easy one. The process of learning how to regulate their emotions will take time and may require professional intervention.

What Can I Do?

Try to prevent tantrums whenever it is possible. If your child has difficulty with transitions, then give several advance warnings or use a timer before switching activities ("Hey pal, when the timer goes off it will be time to put the toys away. Do you understand?"). If your child gets grouchy around afternoon nap-time, don't take him on an extended grocery store trip in the afternoon. Instead of just saying no to your child, offer him another alternative ("Johnny, I don't want you to drum on this pan, but you can drum on this box"). Finally, use "forced choices" whenever possible ("Would you like to play downstairs or outside?"), so as not to overtax your child with too many options. If you can prevent even a few tantrums, it will be worth it.

Use the Detour Method. As your child gets older, you will be able to teach him simple steps for handling situations that lead to tantrums. Taking a deep breath, counting to three or five, saying, "Okay, Mom (or Dad)," asking a question in a nice voice, playing with something else—these are all possible steps you can use. Develop a simple two- or three-step plan and practice it together. For younger children, keep your plan as simple as possible and your rehearsals short and fun.

Watch carefully for appropriate behavior. Using the Pour-It-On Technique, be on the lookout for instances when your child controls himself in a situation that has led to tantrums in the past. When this happens, *immediately* follow this behavior with a specific verbal reward ("Tony, you did a great job of using your calm words just now! I'm really proud of you. Give me five!"). Your child has just begun to move in the right direction! He is learning what you are teaching him!

You should also use this technique when you are ignoring your child during a tantrum. Out of the corner of your eye, be watching for your child to start to calm down and regain control of himself. When this happens, immediately *turn on* the parental attention, letting him know that he is *now* doing a good job at listening, calming down, and so on. I have seen this happen with mothers and angry young children in my therapy sessions many times, and it is fascinating to watch how these children respond to the wise use of parental attention.

Whenever possible, ignore. I mean really ignore. Don't say anything, don't even look at your child—just leave! The lesson is this: Inappropriate behavior gets followed by the immediate *withdrawal* of *all* parental attention. A preschool-age tantrum is one of the all-time classic situations for ignoring. Make sure your child is safe and simply walk away. One warning: If your child has learned that tantrums usually pay off, then you should expect the tantrums to grow worse when you ignore before they get better. It will take a few times for your child to realize that the rules have changed and that tantrums no longer work.

Use Time-Out. If your child follows you around with a "walking tantrum," or continues his tantrum past the point you are comfortable ignoring (excessive screaming, throwing things), simply give him a Fork-in-the-Road. Give him five to eight ten seconds to respond and escort him quickly to Time-Out if he chooses to continue to throw a tantrum. The key is to stay calm and to provide as little parental attention as possible during this exchange.

 ## How Do I Put It All Together?

The case of Tony the typhoon. Ms. Wood realized that she was not doing her son any favors by allowing him to call the shots. She decided to do some things differently right from the beginning. For starters, she began to give Tony two clear choices when preparing meals and when offering him options for playtime. "Tony, would you like a peanut butter sandwich or ham and cheese?" she asked at lunch time, knowing that Tony liked both types of sandwiches.

"I don't want any," Tony shot back. "I want some crackers."

Without losing a beat, Ms. Wood continued, "Tony, you can have some crackers after you eat your sandwich. Now which would you like, peanut butter or ham and cheese? You decide, or I'll pick one for you."

When Tony did throw a tantrum, Ms. Wood decided to ignore him. This was a challenge, because Tony had plenty of tantrum experience and did not give up easily. The first time his mother ignored him, Tony was initially caught off-guard. However, he quickly recovered and escalated his tantrum to new heights. Ms. Wood resolved herself to stick with her plan and simply walked into another room, leaving Tony there putting on a show for the walls to see. When Tony began to calm down (about fifteen minutes later), Ms. Wood immediately went back in to give him positive feedback for calming down. The minute Tony saw his mother, he went right back into his tantrum—and she turned and went right back into the other room. Eventually, Tony got tired and calmed down, and Ms. Wood was able to give him positive attention for this. This sequence happened more than a few times and eventually, to Ms. Wood's amazement, Tony's tantrums began to shorten.

On occasions when ignoring was not possible, Ms. Wood used Time-Out. She simply gave Tony a choice to listen and say his feelings in a calm way or to choose a Time-Out. "Tony, I can tell you're a little frustrated. You need to listen and say your words in a calm way or you will choose a Time-Out." When he chose the latter, she matter-of-factly ushered him to the Time-Out spot, set the timer, and left. Once in Time-Out, Tony cried and shouted, but rarely extended the Time-Out beyond fifteen minutes.

Ms. Wood also became very skilled at using the Detour Method and Pour-It-On Technique. She taught Tony that when she asks him to do something, he needs to say, "Okay, Mom" and do it, instead of throwing a tantrum. They also worked on expressing feelings in a respectful way, such as saying, "I feel kind of frustrated right now." Whenever Ms. Wood saw Tony do this, she immediately gave him a big hug and said, "Tony, you stayed calm and did what I asked you the first time! Great job!" Tony was surprised the first time she did this, but was soon eagerly anticipating this positive attention from his mother when he listened.

It took lots of perseverance for Ms. Wood to get Tony's tantrums under control, especially at the beginning. But this was to be expected, because Tony had learned several years that tantrums and shouting were effective ways of getting what he wanted. However, as the result of his mother's consistency, Tony began to learn that tantrums did not pay off and that listening and staying calm were much better alternatives. He still continued to throw the occasional three-year-old tantrum, but now Ms. Wood felt much more confident about her ability to handle them effectively.

Chapter 29

Time-Out Troubles

The case of stubborn Samantha. "Get back over there!" bellowed Mrs. Gooden, like a drill sergeant at basic training. Five-year-old Samantha, who had just left her Time-Out spot for the third time in the last minute and a half, looked directly back at her mother and shouted, "No!" before taking off down the hallway.

"You little brat!" Mrs. Gooden said to herself, just loudly enough for everyone in the room to hear. Samantha rounded the corner into her bedroom. "Okay, then, you just stay in there!" Mrs. Gooden victoriously stated as Samantha sat on her bed, wondering what would happen next. As Mrs. Gooden slammed the door shut, she bemoaned the fact that Time-Out just didn't work with her child.

 ## Why Does This Happen?

They think it will pay off. Children learn more than you think they do. If a child routinely behaves negatively, you should ask yourself where the payoff is for her. When a child behaves negatively in

Time-Out and the result is getting Mom or Dad all flustered, receiving additional parental attention, or moving to a better Time-Out spot, then the child learns that her negative behavior works. In fact, it works quite well.

The Time-Out spot is ineffective. The lesson behind Time-Out is this: Negative behavior results in the immediate loss of all forms of positive reinforcement. This means that the choice of a Time-Out spot is very important, as it must be as *un*reinforcing as possible for your child to be maximally effective. If you are using the kitchen, a bedroom, or your family room for Time-Out, ask yourself what there is for your child to see or do or hear in that spot. Perhaps your child can look at books, play with toys, hear the television or radio, watch you fume around the house, do annoying things to get your attention, and so on. Remember, the more entertaining it is for your child, the less effective the Time-Out experience will be.

A difficult temperament makes Time-Out more difficult to manage for some children. Face it, children are not at their best when they earn a Time-Out. They have just gotten in trouble for an inappropriate behavior and are likely feeling angry—at themselves or at someone else. Or both. It is at exactly this moment that some children have a particularly difficult time holding it together. Shifting gears from a current activity to accepting an immediate negative consequence when one is feeling frustrated and angry is not especially easy for anyone, much less a child with a challenging temperament. For these children, your skills at administering Time-Out will need to be in tip-top shape. And even then, you'll run into some rough waters.

What Can I Do?

Build your relationship during the positive times. If you have a child who earns more than her share of negative consequences, you can turn the tide by making sure to build some positive time into your schedule. Spend at least five or ten minutes each day in a positive activity with your child. Make it even longer when you can. Finding an activity that is enjoyable *for your child* will help it to be a positive experience for both of you. Pour on the specific verbal rewards for positive behavior and enjoy your time together.

Increasing the frequency of positive parent-child interactions is an important first step to turning negative behavior around.

Keep your thoughts on track. If your thinking is off-track, the rest of you is sure to become derailed at some point. Children are not the only ones who fall into negative thinking traps; adults can rack up the frequent flyer miles as well. Thoughts such as, "Time-Out will never work with my child!" or "I cannot believe how much of a *brat* he is!" or "He *never* listens to *anything* I say!" are so common and destructive that they should have their own "WANTED" posters at the post office.

Instead of letting your emotions get beat up by this onslaught of negative and inaccurate thinking, get grounded in reality. As Romans 12:2; 2 Corinthians 10:5; and Philippians 4:8 encourage us, make every thought that flows through your cerebral cortex obedient to Christ, choosing to think only things that are biblical and true. For instance, try these thoughts on for size:

"God will help me to handle this the right way."
"I need to be consistent."
"Lots of kids who had trouble with Time-Out have learned how to do it properly."
"I need to make this the best learning experience for _____ that I can."
"Remember, _____ is learning right now from how I act."
"If I need to, I can always get some help to learn how to handle this situation the best way."

Keeping your thoughts on track will help you handle difficult Time-Out situations as effectively as possible. And when your child is misbehaving, this is just what she needs.

Stay focused on the job at hand. When your child has behaved negatively enough to earn a Time-Out, your job is to effectively administer the Time-Out. That's it. It is not to lecture, teach a lesson, or anything else—you can do those things *later* (not the lecturing, of course). Some children are quite skilled at getting parents sidetracked on some other issue, or caught up in arguing about the fairness of the Time-Out. And some parents fall for it every time.

Like a pitbull locked onto a juicy steak, stick to the task of administering the Time-Out. Remember, you call the shots. And you have determined that your child should have a Time-Out. Once your child has earned a Time-Out, the *only* appropriate thing she can do is to go to Time-Out. The reward for appropriate Time-Out behavior is a short Time-Out. Inappropriate Time-Out behavior must not result in getting your attention or postponing the Time-Out, but must result in making the Time-Out longer, or adding additional negative consequences for your child. Every time.

Review your Time-Out procedure. The purpose of Time-Out is to help your child get "back in control" and make better choices when she is displaying inappropriate behavior. Make sure that you have chosen an appropriate Time-Out spot that has nothing fun to do, see, hear, or play with. You get the idea. The three criteria for an effective Time-Out spot are (1) boring, (2) safe, and (3) easy for you to monitor.

Your child will earn a Time-Out in one of two ways: automatic or gradual. If your child has displayed an extremely inappropriate behavior, then inform your child that she has earned a Time-Out and administer it immediately. This is an "automatic" Time-Out, as your child's behavior was inappropriate enough to automatically earn a Time-Out. If your child is beginning to behave slightly inappropriately, then give her a Fork-in-the-Road, outlining two clear choices: to either behave appropriately or to choose a Time-Out. (Here's an example: "Sammy, you need to give that toy back to your brother right now. If you don't, I will give him the toy and you will go right to Time-Out."). If she chooses to behave appropriately, then let her know that she has made a good choice. If she continues the inappropriate behavior, inform her that she has chosen a Time-Out and administer it immediately. This is a "gradual" Time-Out, as your child gradually worked her way into it.

Start Time-Out with a minimum of three minutes. If your child displays appropriate Time-Out behavior (calm hands, calm feet, calm mouth), then the result will be a short Time-Out. For each instance of inappropriate Time-Out behavior, such as leaving the Time-Out spot, shouting out, or hitting the wall, inform your child in a matter-of-fact way that she has just earned one extra minute as the result of that behavior.

After you have informed your child of this, don't stick around to talk about it, just leave. The Time-Out can last up to approximately thirty minutes, if your child's behavior warrants that much additional time. If the Time-Out has lasted that long, walk into the Time-Out area and let your child know that Time-Out has now come to an end, and, because she has chosen not to complete Time-Out properly, she has lost a certain privilege for the rest of the day. This could be no television for the rest of the day or thirty minutes early to bed.

If your child refuses to go to Time-Out, providing mild physical assistance by guiding your child by the arm is effective for some children. For those who respond to physical guidance by throwing their entire body to the ground and insisting that you drag them to Time-Out, do not take the bait and get into a wrestling match. This is, of course, what your child is hoping for.

Simply inform her that she needs to be on her way to Time-Out by the count of three or she will choose the loss of a privilege (of your choice) for the rest of the day. By the count of three, your child will either be on her way to Time-Out or will have just chosen a negative consequence that will be *far worse* than a short, three minute Time-Out. If she heads to Time-Out by the count of three, fine. If not, simply inform her of the consequence that she has earned and walk away, leaving your child to deal with the fact that she was not able to hook you into a power struggle and that she just made a *very* poor choice.

If you respond with Time-Out immediately following the negative behavior, are consistent with your Time-Out procedure, and administer the Time-Out in a matter-of-fact way, you should find Time-Out to be an effective negative consequence.

Walk through it with your child. It is very helpful to walk through the Time-Out procedure with your children when first introducing Time-Out or when your Time-Out routine needs a brush-up. In the spirit of the Detour Method, you want to teach your child how to do Time-Out the right way, so that she can have a short Time-Out every time (if that were possible!). Emphasizing the purpose of Time-Out as an opportunity for your child to get back in control so she can make better choices and have a good day, walk through each step of the procedure. Make sure your child knows exactly what behaviors will earn an "automatic" Time-Out and how to recognize a Fork-in-the-Road, which offers one final choice between listening and choosing a Time-Out.

Practice how to go to Time-Out quickly and quietly, so that the Time-Out is not made longer and to avoid the addition of another negative consequence. Rehearse how to have calm hands, calm feet, and a calm mouth in Time-Out. Contrast the happy consequences that come from a short Time-Out (feeling happy, having more fun, getting to come out sooner) with the sad consequences that result from a long Time-Out (feeling sad, having less fun, having to spend more time in Time-Out). A little practice can go a long way toward a successful Time-Out.

Accent the positive. It may sound backwards to give your child positive feedback for her positive Time-Out behavior (after all, she's in trouble, isn't she?), but don't be fooled by that mistake in logic. If you want your child's appropriate Time-Out behavior to happen more often, then make sure to point it out when it happens.

If your child has been having fifteen-minute Time-Outs with regularity and then one day does a five-minute Time-Out, make sure that you let her know what a great job she did at getting back in control so *quickly!* Point out the benefits of her positive choice, give her a big smile, and help her come to the conclusion that she made a very good choice.

 ## How Do I Put It All Together?

The case of stubborn Samantha. Mrs. Gooden realized that her Time-Out procedure needed a face-lift. After determining the changes that she needed to make, she sat down with Samantha and talked about Time-Out as being something that happens when she doesn't listen in order to help her get back in control and make a better choice next time.

"Sam," Mrs. Gooden started, "when you are arguing and not listening, are you making a good choice?" Samantha answered no.

"Well, we're going to do Time-Out a little differently now, to help you get back in control when you start to argue, so that you won't get in as much trouble. Does that sound like a good idea?" Samantha said, "Okay," thinking that not getting in as much trouble sounded good.

They reviewed exactly how it would work when Samantha chose a Time-Out and where the Time-Out spot would be (in the downstairs bathroom). Mrs. Gooden sat down in the Time-Out spot and showed Samantha exactly how she could have a short Time-Out by keeping calm hands, calm feet, and a calm mouth. "See, sweetheart, that's how you keep your Time-Out short. Calm feet, calm hands, and a calm mouth. Now, you try it." She then had Samantha practice these behaviors, and they contrasted this with behaviors that would result in a long Time-Out and talked about what would happen if Samantha made her Time-Out too long.

To help Samantha learn her "short Time-Out plan," Mrs. Gooden made a colorful poster for the bathroom wall that showed pictures of calm hands, calm feet, and a calm mouth with an arrow pointing to a picture of a smiling girl who was no longer on Time-Out. They rehearsed the new plan several times, keeping the rehearsals positive and short, and Samantha quickly learned the new Time-Out rules.

Mrs. Gooden did some proactive thinking by writing down a few sentences for herself and placing them on the refrigerator for emergency viewing. She wrote, "It will take Sammy a while to learn to do Time-Out right, so I must stick with it," and "Sammy is learning from how I act—set the right example!"

Not surprisingly, Mrs. Gooden's prediction was not far off the mark. It did take Samantha a while to change the old Time-Out habits that had become second nature. However, Mrs. Gooden was serious about her resolve to be consistent and to set a healthy example for her young daughter.

When Samantha left her Time-Out, she was promptly escorted back and informed that she had just made her Time-Out longer. "Sammy, because you walked out of Time-Out, you now have an extra minute. Now, stay in there and remember your calm feet, calm hands, and calm mouth." No sirens, no chases, no sky-rocketing emotions. Just matter-of-fact consequences.

While Mrs. Gooden's patience got stretched to its limit a few times and Samantha took many Time-Outs to their full thirty minutes, something was different now. Samantha's negative Time-Out behavior did not pay off anymore. Instead, it always made things worse for her, with a longer Time-Out, and if it went too long, the loss of another privilege.

Another funny thing began to happen as well. Samantha noticed that her mother was not getting red in the face anymore and was no longer calling her bad names under her breath. Instead, her mother was staying calmer and Samantha was not able to make her mad like she used to. Over the next few months, Samantha learned that negative Time-Out behavior just wasn't as fun as it had been in the past and it only made things worse for one person: her. With a little time and the right kind of experiences, Samantha eventually learned that short Time-Outs were much better than long ones.

Part 2

Common Peer Problems

God designed us as social beings. We're created to have relationships with other people. Some children are naturally gregarious and establish relationships with their peers easily. Others are more shy, impulsive, or even aggressive, and have difficulty effectively interacting with other children. But all children learn. And what they learn in their social interactions will shape their self-concept, influence the development of their social skills, and play a large role in determining the social niche they carve out for themselves.

The social world of children, like a tropical rainforest, is filled with beauty and potential and danger all at once. Fun experiences, wonderful friendships, and lifetime memories are being made during the childhood years. At the same time, many children learn what it is like to be teased and to feel left out. Our job as adults is to equip our children to handle both the ups and downs of social life and still come out on top. We want them to learn to interact with peers positively and confidently while effectively handling the difficult times that life is sure to provide.

Children need different kinds of assistance as they learn to navigate their social world. Some need help overcoming their social anxiety. Others need to learn not to run roughshod over others' feelings. Still others need to learn how to handle it when things don't go their way. In this section, I have included several of the most common social problems that children experience. You will have to tailor your responses to best fit your child's needs. You will learn how to influence your child's thoughts and expectations, improve your child's skills at handling various situations, and teach your child to cope effectively with the frustrations that social situations can bring. As you teach your child to approach the social demands of life with an optimistic attitude rooted in biblical thinking, you will help your child blossom into that unique person that God created him or her to be.

Chapter 30

Being Left Out

The case of the last pick. Tonesia was a nine-year-old girl who got along well with other children and always seemed to have a couple of friends. However, Mr. and Mrs. Williams had become aware that Tonesia was sometimes left out of peer activities.

Tonesia had told them that she had been picked last a number of times in softball and volleyball games at school. There had also been times when one of her friends paired up with another girl for a classroom activity, leaving Tonesia without a partner. Tonesia was starting to react to these instances by getting mad at the other children and adopting a negative attitude toward them. Her parents had noticed this and wanted to help Tonesia learn a better way to handle these situations.

Why Does This Happen?

It happens to everyone. I doubt that there is a single person alive who on occasion has not felt left out. When I have looked carefully in both school and work situations, I have been amazed to see "popular" people walking by themselves, sitting for a time with no one to talk to, or even eating alone on occasion. While it is true that some children are at risk for being left out more often than others, it happens to us all and a person's response to being left out will have a strong influence on how often this will happen in the future.

Negative thinking traps play a big role in determining a person's response to being left out. A person can attribute being left out to a perceived negative quality in themselves, such as not being likeable, or as being different from others in some negative way. They can also attribute it to a perceived negative quality or attitude in others, such as, "They're all stuck up" or "She must not like me." While these types of thoughts occasionally can be accurate, they often are not. If a child develops a pattern of responding to difficult situations by misattributing the cause of them, her style of thinking will quickly become part of the problem.

A child's self-esteem will influence her response to being left out. If a child has developed a strong sense of competence and confidence in herself, she may be less likely to be left out in the first place. But, when those occasions do happen, a confident child will be more prone to attribute them to neutral factors (she might think, "Jenny is sitting with Aspen today; maybe she didn't see me over here") and then to respond in a positive manner (walking over to join Jenny and Aspen).

On the other hand, a child with low self-esteem and little self-confidence will be more likely to assume that the instance of being left out is due to something negative about her, which will make it more difficult to respond in an effective and pro-social way.

 ## What Can I Do?

Correct negative thinking. If you suspect that your child has fallen into one or more negative thinking traps, gently help her out of them. Talk together about her experiences of being left out and find out why she thinks this has happened. Does she attribute it to herself ("There must be something wrong with me"), others ("They're just mean"), or neutral factors ("Maybe they didn't notice me"). Has she fallen into any of the negative thinking traps discussed in the glossary?

If you find that your child's thinking is overly negative or inaccurate in any way, ask her if there is another way of looking at the situation. There are probably ways of viewing the situation that she has not considered. Examine the evidence together for her thoughts and if the evidence falls short, help her come up with alternative ways of thinking about the situation that provide a more balanced view.

Use the Detour Method. Your child needs to learn how to effectively respond to being left out. Her response will consist of how she thinks and how she behaves. Using the Detour Method, devise a plan together, consisting of things to think, say, and do, that your child can use when she feels left out. Depending on the circumstances that tend to accompany her feeling left out, come up with a few thoughts that your child can immediately think when she feels this way. For younger children, have them remember only one or two thoughts; older children can memorize four or five different thoughts. Sample thoughts include:

"Even if I get picked last, I can still have fun and play good."
"Instead of sitting alone, I can find someone new to talk to."
"It's fine to be alone sometimes."

Once you have developed a list of thoughts, then think of how your child can respond to the common situations. Examples include playing the game with a friendly attitude (even if picked last), finding another friend to play with, attempting to meet a new friend, joining another activity, or finding something to do independently.

Put your plan together in a simple "step-by-step" format, allowing your child to have as much input as possible into the plan. For example, if your child finds herself alone at lunchtime at school, she can:

1. Think, "You can't sit with your friends every time."
2. Find someone who looks friendly to sit by.
3. Say, "Hi," or start a conversation with the new person you are sitting next to.
4. When done with lunch, find your friends or get some homework done.

Next, practice the plan together by role-playing the various situations in which your child tends to feel left out. Take turns being your child in the role-plays, so your child has the opportunity to see you perform the steps. Ask her how she thinks the steps would work and what the likely outcome might be from using them. Provide lots of positive feedback and encouragement as you practice, building your child's sense of mastery and confidence in this situation. Regularly review the steps and rehearse them as necessary. When your child responds to being left out in a self-defeating manner, find a time to talk about the situation and explore how your child could have responded more effectively and practice those thinking and behavioral steps. Remember, your child is learning a new (and difficult) skill—and learning usually takes time.

Use the Pour-It-On Technique. Be on the lookout for situations when you see your child use her steps or when she tells you that she responded to a situation in a positive manner. In the beginning, you may have to look for even small signs of progress. When this happens, ask her to tell you all about it and teach her to identify the thoughts and behaviors that helped her to handle the situation successfully. Use your specific verbal rewards to let her know how proud you are about her effort and about the fact that she is learning an important new skill.

Build self-esteem. Your child will be better able to withstand the difficult social situations that come along from time to time if she has a strong sense of confidence and competence. This, in turn, will have a positive effect on her self-esteem, or how she thinks she "measures up." Help your child to build this type of confidence by promoting positive and biblical thinking and doing what you can to help your child develop skills that will positively affect her experiences in family, social, and academic areas. Review the suggestions under "Poor Grades" for more specific ideas about how to build your child's self-esteem.

 How Do I Put It All Together?

The case of the last pick. Mr. and Mrs. Williams decided to talk with Tonesia about some of the situations in which she had felt left out. "No one picks me in gym," Tonesia began, "and yesterday, Annette was talking to Maria and acted like I wasn't even there!"

"Well, honey, Annette is one of your good friends," Mrs. Williams replied, "do you think she would do that on purpose?"

"I don't know," said Tonesia, "but she did."

"Tonesia, about gym class," Mr. Williams wondered out loud, "you're good at sports, so I don't understand why you would get picked last all the time. Did you get picked last today?"

Tonesia thought for a moment, "Well, today wasn't so bad," she said, "but that's because Lauren was picking and she likes me."

Mr. and Mrs. Williams listened as Tonesia shared her view that other children did not like her very much and her corresponding feelings of dejection. After Tonesia had shared her feelings, Mrs. Williams reminded her that everyone feels left out sometimes.

"Even King David felt left out," said Mrs. Williams. "When Israel was going to fight the Philistines, he wanted to help, but they told him that he couldn't. He had to stay and look after the sheep. All his brothers got to go, but he had to stay home. But eventually God gave him his chance," she continued, "and what did he do?"

"Is that when he beat Goliath?" asked Tonesia. Mrs. Williams smiled and said yes.

"He went in there and did a better job than all of the regular soldiers and won the battle, even though he got picked last."

With a little help, Tonesia was able to generate other possible reasons why she was picked last or why her friend sat with someone else. "Tonesia, why do you think that a person might get picked last for a sport?" asked Mrs. Williams. Tonesia said the person must not be any good at the sport.

"But sweetheart, you are good at sports, so that couldn't apply to you. What are some other reasons why a person could get picked last?" asked Mr. Williams.

"I don't know," said Tonesia, drawing a blank. Mrs. Williams suggested that people sometimes pick their best friends or the people they think are the best players. "Yeah, that's the problem," Tonesia said sourly.

"So, someone might pick their best friends, just like you might pick Lisa and Megan, right?" "Well, maybe," replied Tonesia.

"Well then, that means that sometimes you can get picked last just because people are picking their best friends and that even good players get picked last sometimes," Mr. Williams summarized. "And," Mrs. Williams added with a smile, "could it be that the harder you play and the friendlier you are, the more likely you are to get picked earlier next time?"

"Maybe that would work," said Tonesia.

During family times over the next few months, Mr. and Mrs. Williams made up different practice scenarios and had Tonesia practice coming up with different ways to view and respond to the situations. They identified a couple thoughts that Tonesia could use ("I can find someone else to play with" and "Even if I get picked last, I can still play hard") and behaviors that she could do. In their nightly prayers together, they thanked God for the friends he had given all of them, and asked God to help them be good friends to the people he had put in their lives.

Tonesia practiced using her new plan and her parents gave her plenty of encouragement as she worked at handling difficult social situations in a positive manner. In situations where she didn't respond well, Tonesia discussed it with her parents and they talked about how she could have handled it differently.

One day, Tonesia came home beaming and proudly exclaimed, "I was picked second for softball today!" As Tonesia improved her skill at handling it when she felt left out, she started feeling left out less often and became aware that other children felt left out sometimes too. As time passed, Tonesia eventually learned that feeling left out happens to everyone and, most importantly, that she could handle it.

Chapter 31

Bullying Others

The case of big bad Ben. Eleven-year-old Ben was a big boy. He was not a fast runner and was an average student who struggled a little with reading. But he was big. And strong.

Quite by accident, Ben had discovered that his size and strength could get him something that he had not been able to attain otherwise: the respect of other children. Or, at least, what looked like respect but was actually more along the lines of fear. Ben had learned that if he used his size to intimidate other children, or intimidated them verbally by teasing, they backed down and his social status increased with a certain group of "rough and tumble" kids. Some social status was certainly better than no social status, so Ben kept it up.

 ## Why Does This Happen?

Like parent, like child. While not all bullying children have aggressive or intimidating parents, it is not surprising when one does. If a parent's daily behavior teaches that the best way to solve problems is to raise his or her voice, use hurtful or disparaging words, and overpower with size, then it should not come as a surprise that the young child who sees this behavior hundreds of times will imitate it.

Aggressive behavior comes more naturally to some children than to others. As a part of their neurological temperament, these children are far more susceptible to responding to frustrating situations with easily-triggered anger and aggressive behavior than those more even-tempered.

Social reinforcement can play a role for some children. If bullying or teasing behavior result in increased peer social status, a child views this behavior as a quick way of gaining peer status and acceptance. While it will ultimately be self-defeating for the child, it can initially be interpreted as a social niche bringing with it a certain amount of power and safety (albeit at the expense of others).

A lack of positive guidance is a major culprit for some children. While some children have poor male role models at home, others have none. As such, they take their cues from their peers, television shows, professional athletes, and movies they may see. While there are some positive role models to be found, there is an abundance that are far from desirable which paint the picture of a "real man" (or "real woman") as tough, explosive, and indifferent to the feelings of others.

 ## What Can I Do?

Model respect for others. The best way to learn something is to see someone else do it. Not once, but hundreds, even thousands, of times. Don't be afraid to show appropriate signs of frustration or even anger around your child. But show your child how to be frustrated and angry and *respectful* at the same time. Let your child see that angry feelings can be expressed in a way that does not violate, attack, or intimidate another person. Allow your child the privilege of seeing you respond to a frustrating situation by appropriately expressing your feelings and then actively looking for positive solutions. Give your child the gift of a good model.

Regulate the input. Pay attention to with whom your child is spending time and what types of media he is watching. Make no doubt about it, children are influenced by their peers and by the words and actions of their favorite characters. If your child is spending time with children who display or encourage negative behavior, discontinue those contacts. For friends whose behavior is more "borderline," allow them to play only within the context of close parental supervision. If the child in question behaves inappropriately under your supervision, call his parents and have him go home.

Alternatively, help your child to choose friendships and encourage contact with children who are fun, respectful kids that will have a positive impact on your child. Regarding television and movies, limit your child's viewing time and make sure that the content of what he is watching is healthy and appropriate. In general, fill his mind and life with good things and good relationships and you'll have a better chance of getting good results.

Develop empathy and perspective-taking skills. Discuss the impact of bullying behaviors on others. Using instances of your child's behavior or fictional scenarios, think together with your child about how a child might feel after being bullied or teased. Consider feelings like being embarrassed, scared, nervous, angry, and humiliated. Talk together about what it means to your child to hurt other people with his words or actions. Ask him if he has ever realized that this is what happens when he bullies and teases. Remind him that everybody whom God has made is valuable and important to God. Then ask your child what God might think or feel when people he loves get hurt. How would your child like it if an older or bigger child were to do this to him?

You also can talk about how other people view bullying or teasing behavior. If some other kids see someone bullying or teasing another child, what do they think about that? What do they think about the child who is doing the bullying or teasing? It may help your child to realize that adults and most children do not respect or admire the bully or teaser; instead, they view that person as being mean and not the kind of person that they want to be friends with. Have these discussions as often as needed, using current situations as examples to help your child understand these important lessons.

Teach your child how to be strong. It is important for your child to learn how to be a strong young boy or girl. Being strong does not mean hurting or bullying others, it means respecting and standing up for yourself while respecting others at the same time.

In Luke 6:31, Jesus instructs us to, "Do to others as you would have them do to you." Proverbs 24:5 tells us that, "A wise man has great power, and a man of knowledge increases strength." Lashing out with verbally or physically hurtful behavior does not display strength; it actually shows a lack of real strength. Real strength is the ability to control yourself and handle a situation the way that God wants you to.

Ask your child which is more useful, a strong, muscular bull that is wild and out of control, or a strong, muscular horse that has been tamed and can use its brain and muscle in a productive way? Real strength was powerfully demonstrated by Jesus in Matthew 26:51–54, when he could have easily defended himself but chose instead to obey his Father.

Pick a few situations that often provoke your child to bully or tease others and talk together about how he can respond to these situations in a way that obeys God and shows respect for both himself and the other person. If your child has difficulty identifying appropriately strong solutions, this may be part of the problem. Once you have helped your child identify some appropriate responses, then practice them together, role-playing how your child would actually say or do them. This helps him visualize how it would actually look and sound responding this new way and to get an impression of what the result might be. Regularly review and practice these behaviors to help your child build the habit of thinking and responding to others in a way that is *truly* strong.

Teach and reward friendship behaviors. There are many ways to make friends, such as sharing, taking turns, smiling, asking someone to play, starting conversations, negotiating play activities, letting others go first, handling it when you don't get your way, and so on.

If your child is trying to gain peer acceptance and social status in a negative and self-defeating way (by bullying or teasing), teach him how to make friends the right way. Choose a few "friendship behaviors" and talk about them with your child. For instance, you can discuss how he responds when someone asks him to play, what he thinks of the person who asks him to play, how often he asks someone else to play, what another person might think of him if he asked that person to play, and how skilled he is at asking someone to play.

If you find that your child is uncomfortable or unskilled at a certain friendship behavior, then break the behavior down into simple chronological steps and practice it together. For example, asking someone to play may include: (1) choosing someone to ask, (2) picking the right time, (3) deciding what to say, and (4) asking the person to play in a friendly way (for example, with a friendly voice and a smile).

Secondly, when you see your child display positive friendship behaviors with friends or siblings, make sure to use the Pour-It-On Technique to help him realize what a good choice he has just made. The more often your child exhibits positive friendship behaviors and comes to the conclusion that they were a good thing to do, the more often he will want to do them. The more often he does them, the better he gets at doing them. The better he gets at doing them, the more of a positive impact they have on other children as your child learns how to get peer attention and make friends the right way.

Show no tolerance for hurtful behavior, words, or attitudes. Serious offenses will result in automatic negative consequences, which may include Time-Out and loss of privileges. Requiring your child to respond with a written or verbal apology following more serious offenses is also appropriate.

Gradual offenses, such as when your child demonstrates milder forms of inappropriate behavior, should result in an immediate Fork-in-the-Road, giving your child a choice to either correct the behavior or experience an immediate negative consequence. You can later review the situation with your child and help him to identify how he could have handled it more appropriately. The goal is to help your child have the experience that making a choice to bully or tease someone just doesn't pay off. Ever.

Get additional help if you need to. A continued pattern of trying to solve problems and gain attention in ways that violate the rights of others is an issue of significant concern. If your child displays such a pattern or has been involved in serious violations of others' rights, consult with a qualified mental health professional to help you and your child get on the right track.

How Do I Put It All Together?

The case of big bad Ben. Ben's parents became aware that Ben was bullying and teasing other children. Mr. and Mrs. LeVan decided to address this problem with Ben right away. They both felt that they modeled appropriate behavior at home and that Ben's diet of television and movies was not excessive nor did it contain inappropriate content. However, Ben had often been teased and made fun of in the past due to his size and they suspected that he was responding in kind.

"Ben, we've got to talk about how you treat other kids," Mr. LeVan told his son. "We've heard that sometimes you bully kids around, or tease them at school," Mrs. LeVan continued, "and I know that you know that's not right. Can you tell us what's going on?"

The LeVans listened carefully to Ben's version of why he engaged in these behaviors. As it turned out, Ben felt rejected by his peers and related, "At least if they don't like me, they'll be afraid of me."

Mr. LeVan decided to start spending some extra time with Ben and teaching him how to make friends more effectively. He and Ben decided to have breakfast together on Saturdays and talk about how to make friends and treat others respectfully. They started their own "Breakfast Club."

During these meetings over the next several weeks, Ben and his dad ate breakfast and discussed how it feels to have someone pick on you or call you names and what other kids think of people who do such things. Ben was able to admit that what he was doing was wrong, but seemed truly unable to figure out how to make friends in a more productive way.

As Ben liked football and admired athletes who were strong and agile, Mr. LeVan encouraged Ben to learn how to be strong.

"Ben, who do you think came up with the idea of being strong?" asked Mr. LeVan. Ben didn't have an answer.

"God did," Mr. LeVan explained. "God wants us to be strong. He wants you to be strong. Remember, he told Joshua to be strong and courageous. Moses had to be strong to stand up to Pharaoh. David had to be strong and brave to defeat Goliath. Think about how strong Jesus was, not with muscles, but in obeying God. And he defeated the biggest enemy of all, Satan, so that we could have our sins forgiven. And through the years, there have been thousands of men and women who have obeyed God and risked their lives to tell people about Jesus. Being a Christian isn't for wimps. It's for people who are strong. And God said that he'll teach us how to be strong—the right way."

They talked at length about different kinds of strength: intellectual strength, physical strength, inner strength (self-control), and strength in obeying God. Ben and his father made a list of things that Ben could do to be strong in each of these areas and become a strong boy who obeyed God, respected himself, and respected others. They identified situations that had provoked Ben to tease or talk rudely to others in the past and practiced how to handle these situations in a strong, wise, and respectful way. They ended their breakfast times with a prayer that God would help both Ben and his father become all that God wanted them to be.

Ben and his dad also identified friendship behaviors that would help Ben become better friends with the children he knew and meet new kids to become friends with. They came up with practical steps for starting conversations, joining in, and handling it when kids want to play something different than what he wanted to play. Ben and his dad rehearsed these behaviors together and Ben slowly improved his ability to do these important friendship behaviors. Ben and his parents also talked about what sports or clubs Ben might want to join as a way to meet new friends. Ben expressed an interest in football and in an art class that was offered at his school and plans were made for him to enroll in each.

Mr. and Mrs. LeVan made it a point to watch for Ben to display positive peer behavior and they gave him plenty of specific positive verbal feedback when they saw him exhibit one of his friendship behaviors. They also made it clear to Ben that they would not accept any behavior that was hurtful or disrespectful to another person. Ben was told that he would experience immediate Time-Outs and could lose privileges such as electronic games, television, and playing with friends, as a way of helping him learn that treating people respectfully is always the best thing to do.

Ben and his dad worked hard on friendship behaviors for several months. While Ben showed improvement, his transition was far more gradual than sudden. During the next year, Ben slowly improved his skill at starting conversations and playing cooperatively and developed two new positive friendships. He also got better at responding with self-control and even humor to situations that had caused him to tease and bully others in the past. As Ben's social skills improved, his self-image and social confidence improved right along with them. Over time, Mr. and Mrs. LeVan were excited to watch their son learn to handle the challenges of growing up in a way that was truly strong.

Chapter 32

Butting In

The case of "jump-in" Jenny. Jenny was a six-year-old girl who was beginning to jump right into social situations, sometimes at the expense of tact or timing. Her mother, Ms. Bradley, admitted that she had been the same way as a little girl. Even as an adult she had to watch her own tendency to act a little headstrong at times.

Jenny's tendency to jump in was starting to cause problems with her friends. Ms. Bradley was noticing that certain friends were not calling as often as they had before. When Jenny's friends did come over, Ms. Bradley observed that while there were many periods of positive playtime, Jenny's habit of butting into conversations and abruptly joining established activities was starting to annoy her friends. Jenny didn't seem to notice. Ms. Bradley knew that Jenny needed to learn a different way of joining activities if she wanted to keep her current friends and continue to make new ones.

Why Does This Happen?

Poor impulse control plays a role for some children. Whether it is a temperamental tendency or the result of Attention Deficit/Hyperactivity Disorder, some children are just prone to impulsively acting without taking the time to stop to think about the appropriate method for joining an activity. If you are concerned that your child may have a significant problem with impulsivity, talk to your pediatrician or a qualified child therapist.

Increased anxiety in social situations can cause a child to behave in an awkward or socially inappropriate way. These children may have difficulty making friends or lack social confidence, and may worry about how peers will perceive them. Consequently, their heightened sense of anxiety makes it difficult for them to handle social situations with ease and contributes to the presence of repeated social mistakes.

They need to learn. Due to various circumstances, some children have been exposed to an abundance of inappropriate social behavior. Others find it difficult to "catch on" to the unwritten social guidelines that govern our interpersonal behavior. As a result, they often break social rules, fail to notice the nonverbal communication of others, annoy their peers, and unwittingly alienate themselves from potential friends. Some children may not even realize that they are contributing to their social problems. These children will need plenty of guidance and encouragement as they learn to be attentive to social guidelines and to the effect that their behavior has on others. Many of them will benefit from explicit training in social skills from a qualified therapist.

 What Can I Do?

Break it into steps. A behavior like joining in can be more easily taught if it is broken into several steps that can be taught, discussed, and practiced. While there is not one magic set of steps, here is an example of how you can break this behavior into steps: (1) Decide if it is a good time to join; (2) join in a friendly way; (3) see if it worked.

Once deciding upon your steps, you will need to discuss the specifics. For instance, how do you know if it is a good time to join an activity? What would tell you that it is or is not a good time to join? What constitutes joining in a friendly way? How can you tell if you have done a good job at joining? How do you know if you have not done a good job? What do you do if your attempt to join is not responded to favorably?

As you can see, these are valuable questions that will help you and your child to really think through the steps in a practical way and will prepare the way for productive rehearsal.

Practice together. Once you have developed the steps for joining in, you can begin to practice them together. Have your child identify several situations where she could join in with others and role-play the situations together, taking turns using the steps. As you use the steps, have your child watch for them and point out the specific ways that you decided that it was a good time, or joined in a friendly way, and so on.

Provide plenty of positive feedback as your child rehearses the steps, and have her identify the specific ways she thought about and completed the steps. Another good method is to videotape the rehearsal, if you are able to. Watch the tape together and have your child point out the steps and look for areas to improve on. As always, make the rehearsals brief and enjoyable. Practice with your child enough for her to learn the steps well, and discuss and rehearse situations that she continues to have trouble with.

Take small steps. One way to help your child learn to use her steps successfully in more difficult situations is to help her use them in less challenging situations. Be creative and talk with your child about "safe" situations where she can practice her steps to build her skill and confidence. Inviting a close friend over to the house; attending a youth group function; playing with cousins when relatives visit, all of these could be comfortable opportunities for your child to practice her skills.

For example, if she had a couple of friends over to play, she could excuse herself for a moment (perhaps for a trip to the bathroom) and then come back and use her steps to join the activity or discussion. Or if at a larger youth activity, she could make it a goal to use her steps two times in an evening by actively looking for an ongoing activity or discussion and then joining in. Following these real-life rehearsals, review how she did and practice the situations as needed, providing plenty of positive encouragement. Help your child to build her skill at a level that she is comfortable with without going too fast.

Use the Pour-It-On Technique. While joining in may be easy for you as an adult, it can be very challenging for your child. As such, make sure to provide lots of encouragement and positive feedback as your child works at learning this new social skill. There are bound to be failures and disappointments along the way and your child may occasionally get discouraged or want to quit. Without turning it into a battle of wills, encourage your child to keep trying (in safe situations!). Express an undying confidence that your child *can* learn this skill, and pour on the specific verbal rewards whenever you see your child perform even one of the steps or make an effort to do so.

 ## How Do I Put It All Together?

The case of "jump-in" Jenny. Ms. Bradley did not suspect that Jenny had a significant attention problem as she was able to concentrate on school work and homework without difficulty and did not appear excessively impulsive or fidgety. She decided to discuss the topic of joining in with Jenny by asking her about it in the "third person."

"Jenny," she asked, "if a girl wanted to join some of her friends in an activity that they were already playing, what would be the best way to do that?"

"I don't know, just jump right in," said Jenny.

Ms. Bradley was not surprised. "Well, Jenny, if she joins in at the wrong time, she could interrupt the other girls, and that might make them kind of frustrated. How could that girl tell if it is a good time to join in?" With her mother's help, Jenny was able to identify ways of knowing when to join in and when to wait, and how to join in a friendly way.

They also talked about how other people feel when someone joins an activity in an abrupt or inconsiderate way. "Sweetheart, when kids are talking or playing a game and someone bursts right into the middle of it at the wrong time, how do the other kids feel?"

"They feel mad?" Jenny answered.

"Yes, they do. They wish the other person would have been more considerate and would have waited for the right time to join in."

As they talked, Ms. Bradley reminded Jenny about situations in the past where she had not waited for a good time or had not joined in a considerate way. Jenny for the first time realized that she had been inconsiderate in these instances. They discussed how Jenny could have handled the situations differently by picking a good time and joining in a friendly way, and Ms. Bradley gave Jenny plenty of positive feedback for her participation in their discussion and for her good ideas.

Jenny and her mother discussed this topic over the next week and came up with a simple plan for Jenny to use when joining an activity. Their plan was for Jenny to wait for a good time (for instance, when no one else is talking), join in a friendly way (asking, "Can I play?" with a smile), and see how it worked (asking herself, "Did I pick a good time and use a friendly voice?").

Just for fun, they practiced the plan together a few times and Jenny thought it was funny when her mother kept on making obvious mistakes during their rehearsal. Ms. Bradley suggested that Jenny do a "secret practice" the next time her friends came to visit and agreed to give her a "thumbs up" sign when she observed Jenny use her plan properly. Jenny thought that this was a great idea. When her friends came to visit, Ms. Bradley looked for an opportune moment to remind Jenny to use her plan. She flashed a thumbs up sign along with the proudest grin on the planet when she saw Jenny use her plan to join her friends in an appropriate way and then glance up to see if her mother had noticed.

Over the next few months, Ms. Bradley made sure that she and Jenny spent time practicing how to join into lots of different situations. She continued to watch for opportunities to give Jenny positive feedback whenever she saw her use her plan to join in with her friends. When she noticed Jenny make a mistake, they later discussed it and practiced how Jenny could do it differently next time. Soon, Jenny improved her skill at noticing her own mistakes and even self-corrected them at times. As Jenny continued to use her plan, she eventually became very skilled at joining in, and Ms. Bradley felt proud that her daughter had learned a valuable social skill.

Chapter 33

Getting Teased

The case of the bumbled pass. Carl was an eight-year-old boy who had never been too coordinated or athletically inclined. He had been occasionally teased in the past for wearing glasses, but his recent dropped pass during a football game in gym class gave the resident teasers some fresh ammunition.

"Oops, I pulled a Carl!" one of the boys exclaimed, as he pretended to clumsily drop the football. "Why don't you guys shut up!" Carl stammered in a desperate attempt to say something in his defense. The offending boys just continued to laugh, knowing that they had upset Carl.

Through the halls during the following week, Carl could occasionally hear a whisper, "Don't pull a Carl," followed by snickers of laughter. Carl would immediately look around with a scowl and see the same three or four boys, elated with themselves that they had gotten a reaction out of Carl. Carl shared these events with his parents, who felt heartbroken at the fact that their son was being teased by his peers. Mr. and Mrs. Knapp knew that they needed to help their son handle this situation more effectively.

Why Does This Happen?

Kids can be cruel. If you have forgotten this fact, volunteer as an aide at your local elementary or junior high school for a few weeks. I am regularly astounded at the way that children can hurt each other—especially those who are different in a way that makes them vulnerable to teasing. Having graduated to the workplace, many of us no longer encounter this type of behavior and can easily forget that our children live in a world that often plays by a much meaner set of rules.

A lack of social skills often plays a role in sustaining this type of teasing. While almost everyone has been teased on at least one occasion, children who are regularly teased often lack either strong coping skills or strong social skills. This means that the way they respond to teasing serves only to invite more of it and they may not have developed their skills at establishing positive relationships. These children often end up by themselves and make perfect targets for those who wish to take aim.

 ## What Can I Do?

Talk with your child. If your child is being teased by his peers, take the time to really listen to how he feels. As he describes his feelings, picture how you would feel if you were in his shoes, or if your coworkers were treating you in the same manner. Empathize with your child and help him put his feelings into words, remembering that peer relationships are becoming more important as he gets older.

At the same time, try to discover what may have caused the teasing to happen. Sometimes, another child may have been trying to get a laugh at your child's expense. Other times, the teaser is a bully who indiscriminately teases many different children. In some cases, something about your child or his behavior may have prompted the teasing. If you can figure out what may have caused it, you will be in a much better position to help your child prevent it or effectively respond to it.

Correct negative thinking. A child who is regularly teased is certainly at risk for falling into several negative thinking traps. While your child may have all sorts of ability and potential, this fact will be easily obscured in his mind behind the more painfully "visible" reality that he is low on the social totem pole. If you see your child falling prey to negative thinking and beginning to develop a negative self-view, talk with him about his feelings and the thoughts that lie behind them. It is quite likely that your child is overlooking areas of strength and accomplishment and falsely concluding that he is "stupid" or that something is wrong with him. Using the questions provided in the Glossary to correct negative thinking traps, help your child identify other ways of thinking about himself—ones that are positive and true.

If your child is being teased as the result of a learning problem or physical condition of which he is well aware, it will not help to pretend that this is not the case. Gently and honestly acknowledge the situation, but then help your child learn to place it in a proper perspective.

"Johnny, I know some kids have teased you about being short. We both know that you're a little shorter than most of your friends, just like I have a lot of friends who are taller than me. I know that sometimes it's hard to feel different, but Johnny, everyone's body is different. Just think of your friends. Some of them are taller, shorter, wider, or skinnier. Can you think of people that are any of those? And the thing is, anyone can be smart, a good athlete, funny, and have lots of friends regardless of their size. Can you think of any examples? Johnny, God loves you just the way you are, and so do I. People don't decide to be your friend because of a few vertical inches, they like you because of the kind of friend you are inside."

If the issue is regarding physical appearance, unwaveringly affirm your child that he is a handsome young boy (or she is a beautiful young girl) with a great smile and a wonderful personality and the ability to be a great friend. If you really want to drive the point home, spend a few hours together at your local mall. Sit down at the food court with a paper and pencil, have a soda, and watch all the people go by. Make a list of all the ways in which people are different—and get ready for a long list! Different noses, eyes, hair color, heights, body sizes, skills, abilities, and so on. Discuss the fact that different does not mean bad, it just means different, and people with all kinds of differences still have plenty of good friends!

In short, you want to help your child remember who he is. He was created by God and is destined for great things of eternal significance. Believing anything less is falling prey to thoughts that will rob him of his true potential! Romans 8:31–39 and Psalm 139 remind us of the value that God has graciously placed on us. Remind your child, over and over, that he is special and important to God, and that God has a wonderful and exciting plan for his life.

Build coping skills. Responding to teasing is a difficult task—for anyone. I often ask parents how they would handle a similar situation if it happened in their workplace and a quick answer is not often forthcoming. While a witty or humorous comeback is probably one of the most effective ways to quickly squelch teasing, these can be difficult to come up with on the spot. In addition, children who are frequently teased are often not verbally agile enough to do that. More common responses to teasing that can be quite helpful include:

- Ignore the teasing
- Walk away
- Make a neutral "disarming" comment such as "Everybody makes mistakes"; "I did my best"; "I'll get it next time"; "Win some, lose some"; "It works for me"
- Get involved in another activity
- Express your feelings in an appropriate way
- Go talk to someone else
- Talk to a friend about it
- Talk to a parent or teacher about it

Discuss these options with your child and choose three or four that will work for him in the teasing situations that he most often encounters. Think about *exactly* how your child will do these steps and place them in chronological order. For example, a plan might include ignoring, then making a neutral disarming comment, then walking away. Once you have your list, rehearse the steps together, taking turns being the teaser and the "teasee." This will allow your child to learn by watching you use the steps. It will give him valuable practice at using his steps when under verbal attack, and will give you a chance to see how well your child can put the plan into effect.

As your child learns to complete the steps successfully, have him identify the probable outcome of using them. Remind him that it will be more difficult when he is really being teased and provide plenty of positive feedback as he becomes more comfortable and natural with his steps. When teasing occurs, review your child's response together and discuss how he was able to use his steps or practice how he could have used them more effectively.

Develop a plan for building friendships. An old sports adage touts that the best defense is a good offense. We want to incorporate that idea here by not only helping your child learn to respond effectively to teasing, but to also help him develop the skills that will lead to more positive peer relationships. The more time he spends with positive friends, the more difficult a target he is for those who would tease. See "Learning to Make Friends" for more ideas on how to do this.

Build self-confidence. If your child experiences a lack of skill in a certain area that regularly invites teasing, such as playing sports in gym class, make the time to help him improve his skills in this area. Practice shooting free-throws together, play football with a small "nerf" football that is easy to catch, go for a bike ride together, or have fun hitting and catching a softball. Your child can improve his physical coordination and confidence by participating in an individualized sport, such as martial arts, where learning at your own pace is more easily done and a respectful atmosphere is strongly encouraged.

Find other activities that your child is interested in, such as music, science, scouting, art, and so on, and participate in them together. While it is not important that your child turn into the school's star athlete or star musician, helping to improve his basic physical skills and sense of competence in an encouraging environment can do a lot for his self-confidence and can reduce the opportunities for peer teasing.

Get involved. If you have attempted the above ideas and have given them time to work and your child is still being regularly targeted as a verbal dartboard, or if the teasing is particularly vicious, it is time to take some action. Talk to the teasing children's teacher or parents and let them know what is going on. Together as reasonable adults find a way to enforce appropriate behavior and make school a safe place for all children. Let the teacher or parents talk with the offending children about the seriousness of their behavior and implement negative consequences as needed.

 ## How Do I Put It All Together?

The case of the bumbled pass. "Hey buddy, you look sad. What's going on?" Mr. Knapp asked at dinner after noticing the dejected look on Carl's face. "I'm getting teased again," Carl moaned, "and there's nothing I can do to stop it."

Carl's parents sat down with him and listened as Carl talked about feeling really embarrassed and angry about being teased by this group of peers. His parents then suggested that while it may be hard to stop the boys from teasing, they can help Carl handle it the smartest way possible.

Mr. and Mrs. Knapp wanted first to make sure that Carl was not falling into any negative thinking traps. They asked him why he thought the boys were teasing him. Carl said he had seen these boys tease other kids as well and thought that they just enjoyed making fun of others. "Carl, that means that they want to make fun of anyone they can—not just you," Mrs. Knapp was quick to point out. "So, they'll make fun of whoever is easiest to tease," she concluded. "Let's make sure that it is not you anymore."

Carl also identified that playing sports was not something he was really good at and that most of the other children were better than he was at football. Mr. Knapp offered to help Carl learn how to throw and catch a football and Carl's eyes lighted up with excitement at the idea of practicing with his dad.

Next, they examined together exactly how Carl was responding to the teasing and discovered that he was giving the boys exactly what they wanted—an immediate reaction of frustration. Together, they made a list of all the possible ways that Carl could respond to the teasing and decided to come up with a plan. The plan included making a disarming comment ("There's always next time"), ignoring it (by walking away), finding someone else to talk to, and getting involved in another activity. They also decided that it would be helpful for Carl to tell himself, "God will help me handle this the right way" and "They'll stop sooner or later if I use my plan" when they teased him.

While Mr. and Mrs. Knapp knew that the teasing could get a little worse before it got better, they also agreed to talk to Carl's teacher if it started to get out of hand. During the next several months, Carl and his parents practiced this plan together many times and Carl became very good at making disarming comments and walking away. They also made it a point to regularly remind Carl of how special he is to them and to God.

"Carl," his father would often say just before turning the lights out at bedtime, "do you know what a great boy you are? I love you so much. I'm so proud of how you're doing at school and with friends, and how you're handling it when those kids give you a hard time, because I know that can be tough sometimes. God's got great plans in store for you, pal, and I'm excited to watch them happen."

The final part of their plan was for Carl to focus on making new friends and on getting more involved with the friends he already had. Carl asked if he could join a scouting club as several of his school friends were involved and Mr. and Mrs. Knapp thought that it would be a good opportunity to learn new things, build self-confidence, and make new friends.

While some of the boys at school continued to tease Carl, they soon discovered that something was different. Carl was not as easy of a target as he used to be. Instead of responding to their comments in the manner they had come to expect, Carl began to ignore them and just walk away. Once, when getting teased about missing a shot during basketball in gym class, Carl turned and replied with a smile, "I'm just warming up" as he ran down court with his team. The teasers were not quite sure how to respond when they couldn't make Carl frustrated. They tried even harder, but Carl was often able to walk away and find someone else to talk to. This was not easy for Carl and his frustration seeped through from time to time. But more often than not, he felt like he was handling these situations better than he had in the past. While the boys still teased Carl on occasion, the teasing slowly became less frequent as he learned how to become a more difficult target.

Chapter 34

Handling Peer Pressure

The case of the right fit. Abby was a twelve-year-old girl who wanted to fit in with her friends. As a result, it became very important for her to dress the same, like the same things, and listen to the same music as her peers. Mr. and Mrs. Martinez grew concerned, however, when Abby seemed to become overly worried about what her friends thought and wanted to avoid being different from them in any way. They knew how important peer acceptance was for a preadolescent girl, but wanted to make sure that Abby's individual personality didn't get lost in the shuffle.

 ## Why Does This Happen?

Peer acceptance is important to children. It is particularly meaningful during the preadolescent and teenage years. Reminiscing about your own childhood should bring back memories of how much you did not want to be different from your peers. Because God designed us to be social beings, fitting in with and being part of a group helps us to feel safe, accepted, and like we "belong" in our social world. The alternative, feeling like you don't fit into any group, is a pretty lonely place to be and most of us work hard to avoid it.

The growing independence that accompanies the preteen and teen years also plays a role here. It is natural for children to differentiate themselves from their parents by making their own decisions and trying out different styles and fads. Again, most of us did the same thing when we were in their shoes. Remember, the desire for gradually gaining more independence is not negative; it's how God designed your child. These important years are full of valuable learning experiences that will help prepare your child for the decisions and challenges of adulthood.

Trying out new things is how we all learn. Did you ever listen to music or wear any clothes that your parents were not particularly crazy about? I remember the intense *need* to have holes in the knees of my jeans when I was in the sixth grade. For some reason, my need for this type of apparel is now gone and I realize that I can be accepted with or without air-conditioned jeans. But my parents gave me the gift of being able to learn this lesson for myself. One year it is a specific style of jeans, the next it is a certain music group, hair style, or ear rings, and the list goes on.

Trying on different "hats" is how children learn who they are and just how and where they fit in. It is a necessary, not an optional, part of learning. While there will be some hats that will not be allowed into the closet, your child's hat closet should have a good assortment of different ways she can express and discover her unique individuality.

What Can I Do?

Listen first and talk second. When your child is in the throws of the tumultuous waters of preadolescence, you need to stay as connected as possible. You can do this by spending time listening to your child about the details of her world. Her new friends, her recently lost best friends, the music that "everybody" is listening to, the new styles, what Jason did, what Sarah said, and so much more.

Walk a mental mile in her shoes for a while first, then begin to explore her thoughts and feelings about the particular issues that you are concerned about. This may take a bit more time than just getting right to the main issue, but any gardener will tell you that preparing the soil before you plant your seed will help you get a better flower in the end.

Correct negative thinking traps. While your child may be correctly tuned into the sometimes brutal social realities of the preadolescent world, she may have fallen into some negative thinking traps along the way. As you discuss the particular issues you are concerned about, such as her choices regarding music or clothing, discover what she really thinks about the issue at hand. "Why do you want to wear that certain dress or pair of shoes?" "What do you think your friends will think if you don't wear them?" "What would *you* think if a girl in your class didn't have the latest style of clothing?"

As you explore her thoughts, expectations, and fears together, keep your eyes open for magnification, mind reading, and other forms of negative thinking traps that may be fueling her worries. Gently and gradually help her bring a balance to her thinking, remembering that she has not had the benefit of the additional years and experience that you have had.

Encourage principle-driven decisions. As you talk with your child, bring up the issue of how decisions should be made about various issues, such as music or clothing. Do we do things just because we see them on television? Or because some other child is doing them? There are so many thousands of children at thousands of schools across the country doing different things, how can you choose which thing to do?

Make a list of positive reasons to do things, such as doing things that help us obey God, learn things, respect others, accomplish goals, make friends, and have fun. What if something meets one of these criteria but fails another, such as being fun but disobeying God? Should she do it, or should *all* of the criteria be met?

Allow your child to wrestle with these issues as she confronts the reality of needing to be strong enough to make difficult choices. Emphasize the importance of obeying God and doing what is right and the benefits that come from such choices. Remind her how God repeatedly commanded the children of Israel to follow his commands and be different from the neighboring countries so their faith would not be weakened and they would not stumble and fall. I once saw a poster at a high school that read, "What is popular is not always right and what is right is not always popular." Help your child develop the habit of thinking through her decisions in a way that is driven by biblical principles, not by the current thinking or fads of the day.

Look at the big picture. Parents sometimes forget to look at the big picture of how their child is doing. Take a look at the big areas of your child's life: her relationship with God, her behavior at home, her effort at school, the quality of her friendships, her view of herself and sense of self-confidence. If your child is doing well in the big areas, then she is showing you that she is learning how to make positive decisions where it really counts. Sit back, take a deep calming breath, and remind yourself that your child is doing well.

When a child is making good decisions in the big areas, one logical reward is a bit more freedom in the smaller areas, because chances are that your child will continue to make good decisions there as well. However, when a child consistently makes poor decisions in the big areas, then a more watchful eye is needed, as poor decisions are likely to be made in the smaller areas as well. Good decisions result in more freedom. Bad decisions result in less.

Turn decisions into learning experiences. As you walk that balancing act of providing parental guidance while still giving your child the ability to make certain decisions for herself, use those decisions as experiences for your child to learn from.

For example, if you buy her a certain type of clothing because "all my friends have got one," revisit the issue a few months down the road. How important was it for her to have that piece of clothing? Maybe it was really fun for her to have it. Fair enough, we all enjoy getting fun things sometimes. However, did it vastly improve her friendships? Did it make her smarter and more popular? Now that some time has passed, what does she think would have happened if she would not have bought it? Would she really have lost all of her friendships and have become a social train wreck? Does she know of any girls from school, church, sports, or other clubs who do not have this item of clothing? Have they become social outcasts because they do not have that item, or do they still have friends? Helping your child to reflect on her past decisions and experiences can help her to put things in better perspective the next time around.

Maintain firm and reasonable boundaries. While there will be some items of clothing, jewelry, music, or movies that you will allow your child to have, there will be others that you will not. After you have listened to your child's views, respectfully share your own thoughts about how certain types of clothing and entertainment are appropriate and some are inappropriate and why. While respecting your child's right to think things through on her own and encouraging her to make principle-driven decisions, calmly but firmly remind her of the fact that the ability to make certain types of decisions *gradually* increases with age and responsibility.

This means that there may be certain types of things that she will want to do, buy, and wear that she will simply not be allowed to. There are negotiables and there are non-negotiables. And you must wisely decide what items and issues fall into which category. You are the parent, and you must provide strong and healthy leadership for your child. Don't ever forget that in this world of shifting and waning values, your child *needs* your guidance more than ever.

Finally, remind your child that one of the things you are looking for is for her to be able to *not* get her way and handle it respectfully and maturely. This shows you that she is learning to make good decisions—that she can have things not go her way and still be respectful and make the best out of the situation.

How Do I Put It All Together?

The case of the right fit. Mr. and Mrs. Martinez knew that Abby was a girl who was making many good decisions in the big areas of her life, so they were not too worried about things. However, they wanted her to learn how to balance her efforts to make friends with confidence in being herself.

They decided to talk with Abby about their observations that she seemed to be more concerned about fitting in with her friends than they had seen in the past. "But Mom," Abby exclaimed, "if you don't fit in with the right group, nobody will have anything to do with you!" Abby explained that she had seen girls in her school be very mean to those who didn't fit in. In fact, Abby was becoming hesitant to talk to certain "outcast" girls because she was afraid that she might be made fun of if she did.

"Honey," Mrs. Martinez asked, "is that really how God wants you to treat other people? When Jesus was here, who did he hang out with? Was it just the popular people or was it all sorts of different people?"

"All sorts of people?" Abby replied, unsure if her answer was correct. "Yes," said Mrs. Martinez. "Jesus spent time with people who were rich, poor, sick, and some who didn't have any friends at all. He showed them how much God loves them. How do you think God wants you to treat people at your school?"

"He wants me to be friendly to everyone, I guess," Abby said hesitantly. As they talked, Abby admitted that it wasn't right to just try to be friends with the popular girls. She understood that God did not want her to treat others like that, but she was still afraid of what would happen if she strayed from the whims of the popular girls. Mr. and Mrs. Martinez gently challenged Abby to think about just what would happen if she treated others the way that she really wanted to and the way that God wanted her to.

"Abby," Mr. Martinez asked, "what do you think would happen if you stood up for someone who was getting teased by saying, 'Hey guys, she's okay, leave her alone.'" Abby admitted that she hadn't thought about it. "Or what if you didn't try to wear everything that the other girls wear, what is the worst thing that would happen?"

"They wouldn't like me anymore," Abby answered.

"They wouldn't like you just because you don't have a certain pair of jeans?" Mr. Martinez asked, incredulously. "And these are your friends?" Mr. and Mrs. Martinez encouraged Abby to examine her worries. Would she really lose her *good* friends? If she lost a friend or two by just being a good friend and obeying God, does she lose or does she really win? And would she really lose friends, or end up gaining real friends?

Abby pondered the things her parents had said. Not too long after, Abby overheard some popular girls making fun of another girl's new dress during lunch break. She knew in her heart that this was not the kind of person she wanted to be. If that was what being popular meant, then maybe being popular was not what she wanted. Abby knew Jesus would be a friend to that girl with the new dress, even if others made fun of him for it. Later that day, Abby went up to that girl and said, "Hi. Hey, I like your dress, it's nice." The girl smiled at Abby and said, "Thanks." Abby's heart leaped inside her, she knew that she had done the right thing.

Over the next few weeks, Abby continued to talk with her parents about the kind of friends she wanted to have. "Let's start from the beginning," suggested Mrs. Martinez. "What kind of girl do *you* want to be?" Abby decided that she wanted to be a girl who obeyed God, worked hard at school, was respectful to everyone in her class, had good friends, and had lots of fun. If she did that, Abby reasoned, she would be the right kind of friend and make the right kind of friends. If a few kids didn't like her, so what. Mr. and Mrs. Martinez told Abby that they were proud of her for coming to that conclusion and that God was proud of her too.

They continued to check in with Abby over the following months as to how things were going. Mrs. Martinez encouraged Abby to invite some of the other girls over to play and Abby discovered that she really liked one girl in particular that she had never gotten to know before.

Abby told her parents that she was much happier with her decision to be herself and was finding that she was still friends with some of the popular girls after all. Abby's parents let her pick fun clothes that they felt were appropriate, giving her room to express her personality through her clothing choices. There were a few music groups that Abby liked but was not allowed to purchase their CDs, and they talked together about the reasons for this. With a little effort, Abby was able to find several other groups she was able to listen to that she liked just as much. While Abby occasionally felt frustrated with the limits that came with being twelve years old, she was much happier with the person that she was becoming and with the *good* friends that she was making.

Chapter 35

Learning to Make Friends

The case of hesitant Holly. While ten-year-old Holly had a few friends and enjoyed playing with them, she was shy and had always had difficulty meeting new kids. Her parents, Mr. and Mrs. Endicott, were both rather gregarious by nature and had tried to get Holly involved in every activity that you can imagine. However, it seemed that the more they tried to push Holly to get involved, the more she shied away. Now they were starting to become upset that she was not fitting into the "Endicott mold." Mr. and Mrs. Endicott desperately wanted Holly to be able to be comfortable around other people and knew that they needed to handle the situation more effectively.

Why Does This Happen?

It doesn't always come naturally. Some children are naturally outgoing and enjoy being the life of any party. Others prefer playing with one or two familiar friends and are slower to warm up in unfamiliar situations. Whether due to a genetic influence, biological factors (such as articulation difficulties or a soft voice), family learning (parents who are reserved, for instance), or a combination of factors, some children simply find that too much social interaction feels uncomfortable.

Mismatched expectations can make things more difficult for children. If parents are expecting their shy or quiet children to be extroverted and exude social boldness, then they are setting everybody up for disappointment. These children are bound to feel the pressure to be something that they are not. They are going to leave social situations feeling as if they have disappointed their parents and failed at being what they were supposed to be. This only makes these children more hesitant to go out and try again and will lead to a fragile or damaged sense of self-esteem.

A lack of skill in social situations can increase a child's level of anxiety. Children who have not developed a strong sense of social competence enter into social situations with a heightened sense of anxiety and a confidence level that is easily shaken. Their increased anxiety level makes it more difficult for them to relate easily and naturally with others, which increases their chances of behaving awkwardly with their peers. Anticipating that things will go poorly, they will tend to shy away from these uncomfortable situations. Unfortunately, as a result they end up avoiding the very situations that, if handled properly, will build their social confidence.

 ## What Can I Do?

Accept your children as they are. Not every person is going to be a social magnet. Nor does every person need to be. Differences in temperaments and natural dispositions are not bad; in fact, they are wonderful! Look around and you will see the richness of the different types of people God has created. People can be socially satisfied, spiritually growing, and personally fulfilled with any temperament. God has called you to be an encouraging and nurturing parent to *your* children, whatever their temperament may be. So love and accept your children as they are and help them develop into the wonderful and unique persons God has created them to be.

Talk with your child about her social interactions. Allow your child to tell you what parts of social interaction feel easy and what parts feel difficult or overwhelming. Try to discover how nervous your child feels and exactly what situations trigger that anxiety. If your child's social anxiety is too high, you may need to consult with a child therapist to help your child learn to overcome those very real and crippling feelings of fear. As you talk together, remind her that God will help her to be brave and that with practice, talking to other kids can get easier.

Observe your child with other children. See if you can spot the particular areas of social difficulty that your child experiences. Does she greet other children properly? Can she join an ongoing activity with ease? Can she play cooperatively with other children? Are there behaviors that your child does or fails to do that cause moments of social awkwardness? If you can identify some of the social behaviors or situations your child struggles with, you will be in a much better position to help your child overcome them.

Teach pro-social skills. Your child may be lacking in skills that will help her to effectively handle certain situations. Friendship skills like introducing yourself, greeting another person, joining into an activity, beginning or ending a conversation, sharing, and negotiating can be difficult for some children.

If you find that your child needs help in a particular social skill area, use the Detour Method to break the skill into simple steps. For example, greeting another person may involve deciding who you want to greet; looking at them (in the face or eyes); and saying "Hi" in a friendly way (with a smile). Starting a conversation may begin with choosing a person to talk to; deciding what to say (make a comment or ask a question); and saying it in a friendly way (with a smile). Negotiating could include asking the other person what they would like to do; stating what you would like to do; and deciding to take turns, compromise, or come up with another activity.

Once you have devised your steps, discuss them with your child, making sure to cover all the necessary details, such as how to decide what to say or how to say it in a friendly way. Then, practice the steps together, taking turns using them in "real-life" practice situations. This will allow your child to see you perform the steps and will allow you to observe your child using them as well. Continue to have regular practice sessions until your child becomes comfortable using the steps. If you have difficulty identifying particular social skills to work on, breaking them into steps, teaching them to your child, or if your child is having a hard time learning the skills, consult with a qualified child therapist for assistance.

Safe practice. Once your child has begun to learn some of the basic friendship skills, you can help her build confidence by setting up some safe situations in which she can practice. Visiting relatives, playing with siblings or parents, having close friends over to the house, an upcoming birthday party with good friends—any of these can be a great practice situation.

Decide together on the situation and on what your child will practice. Perhaps your child will practice greeting her grandmother and starting a conversation with her grandfather. Or maybe she will work on sharing with a close friend who comes over for an hour on Saturday. The idea is to help your child build both her skill and confidence at her own speed—so be careful not to push too hard or too fast. If your child is very hesitant to practice even in a safe situation, you may need more rehearsal or a safer practice situation.

When your child practices her skills, provide lots of encouragement and find several positive things to point out about her efforts. Ask your child to evaluate her use of the skill during her practice, having her point out things she did well and things that she could improve in. Slowly decrease the "safety level" of the practices so that your child gradually can get used to using her new skills in more challenging situations such as attending a birthday party, playing with more than one friend, going to Sunday school or a youth group, or attending a sports event.

Promote areas of strength. One way to build social and personal confidence is to help your child develop areas of strength that can be turned into peer activities or that will allow your child to meet new friends in a comfortable setting. This could include skills in a sport (soccer, swimming, baseball, karate), an outdoor activity (fishing, biking, working with animals), organized groups (scouts, school clubs), or other areas (photography, computers, cooking, sewing). If your child feels confident in her swimming skills, for example, she may feel more at ease when interacting with peers on the swim team than when interacting in less confident situations. This confidence can facilitate the development of friendships with peers who have a common interest and provide wonderful growth opportunities for your child.

Pour it on. As you rehearse social skills with your child, watch for times your child makes attempts to use her new skills in real-life settings. Then make sure to reinforce her efforts by giving specific verbal rewards (for example, "Holly, you did a great job looking right at her and asking her to play in a friendly way! Good for you!"). Even if she makes a mistake, let your comments be positive and encouraging, setting the stage for success the next time around.

How Do I Put It All Together?

The case of hesitant Holly. The first thing that Mr. and Mrs. Endicott did was to adjust their expectations for their daughter, realizing that God did not intend her to be a carbon-copy of them. Then, they asked Holly how she felt about her social relationships. After dinner one night, Mrs. Endicott brought up the subject.

"Holly, we know that sometimes you feel a little nervous around other kids. Like when Michael and Sally came over the other day and you didn't really talk to them much. You know what I mean?"

Holly nodded, and Mrs. Endicott replied, "Well, that doesn't sound like very much fun to feel that nervous. When do you feel the most nervous around other kids?"

"Well," Holly thought out loud, "it's mostly when I meet someone I don't know very well, or if someone comes over that I wasn't expecting, like when Sally and Mike came over. If I'm playing with someone I know, like Kelly, I feel fine."

Holly and her parents discussed how there are lots of times when we have to meet new kids, like at school, church, and in the neighborhood. "Holly, we can practice how to meet new kids, just like you practice your piano lessons," Mrs. Endicott said. "And the more you practice, the better you get at it."

Together, they identified simple steps for introducing herself and starting a conversation with a new person. Holly and her mother practiced these steps together over the next several weeks and Holly found that with practice she was able to perform them quite easily. Once she had learned the steps, Holly used them to start conversations with friends she was already comfortable with while her mother watched.

When she felt ready, Holly decided to practice her skills at a birthday party she had been invited to. Instead of just talking to her friends, Holly decided to be brave and introduced herself to a girl she didn't know. She picked a girl that looked friendly, walked up to her and said, "Hi, my name's Holly," with nervousness in her voice. "My name's Anna," the girl replied. Then, motioning to the girl standing next to her, Anna asked, "Do you know Debbie?" Before she knew what had happened, Holly had met two new girls. After the party, she was thrilled at how well she had done and couldn't wait to tell her mother that she had made two new friends.

As Holly's confidence began to grow, she got involved in a dance class that one of her friends was in. Holly loved the class, enjoyed her friend, and was able to meet a couple other girls. Mr. and Mrs. Endicott did not push Holly to move faster than she was comfortable with and continued to be sensitive to the fact that their daughter needed more time and encouragement in social areas than did some children. While Holly never became the "life of the party," she gradually improved her ability to make new friends and was happy being the girl that God had made her to be.

Chapter 36

Poor Sportsmanship

The case of "must-win" Matt. Matt was a very athletic and competitive ten-year-old boy. He seemed to have gotten his fierce desire to win from his dad, a die-hard sports fanatic who specialized in professional, college, and high school sports. When Matt played baseball or soccer, he played to win—second place did not exist for him.

When he was younger, Mrs. Peterson thought his strong desire to win was cute; Mr. Peterson still seemed to think that it was part of being a "champion." More recently, however, Mrs. Peterson had noticed Matt displaying a negative attitude when his team was getting the worst of it during a game. "This stinks!" Matt would complain with a scowl. His countenance would become sullen, his comments critical and sarcastic, and his behavior anything but sportsmanlike. Matt's frustration at losing had recently caused the soccer coach to make him sit on the sidelines, as he was becoming more of a negative distraction than a positive contributor to the team. Matt even shoved a player on the opposing team two weeks ago. Both Mr. and Mrs. Peterson were beginning to realize their little "champion" was in danger of self-destructing.

 ## Why Does This Happen?

Who wants to lose? Let's be real. Most kids would want to win a game, if given a choice. In fact, whether playing kick-ball, soccer, checkers, or Monopoly, they are usually trying to win. However, while losing is not as much fun as winning, it is something that all of us need to learn to do. Why? Because we'll do it countless times. And as is the case with many of the important lessons of life, handling it right doesn't always come naturally.

How do you handle it? If a child displays negative behavior, such as poor sportsmanship, your responses are extremely important. If you have not spent the time to actively teach your child how to handle these situations positively, then in effect you are asking him to do a difficult behavior without giving him the instruction he needs to learn how to do it. The longer the negative behaviors continue, the more they become habitual, or automatic, for your child. And the more difficult they are to change.

Temperamental tendencies can contribute to poor sportsmanship. Some children seem to be almost totally unaware of the impact they have on others. While they may have many wonderful qualities, these children will require consistent parental involvement and may take longer to develop appropriate social and "perspective-taking" skills.

 ## What Can I Do?

Set the right example. The best lessons are taught at home. Give your child the gift of a healthy example to follow. You will play hundreds of games together and be involved in thousands of informal play activities during the many years you spend together. Your child will have many opportunities to see you win, lose, and get frustrated. Let him see you handle each situation in a way that treats others with respect, keeps things in perspective, and values the relationship more than the activity.

Teach sportsmanship skills. Through "on the spot" redirection and planned rehearsals, teach your child how to respond to losing the right way. First, help your child identify one or two things that he can tell himself when he finds that he is losing a game or activity. He can tell himself, "I'm not winning right now, but if I keep trying, maybe I can catch up"; "Everyone loses sometimes; it's no big deal"; or, "I lost this time, but it was still fun playing."

Second, he needs to learn what to say to the person who is winning or has just beaten him at the game. Phrases such as, "Good game," "Nice shot," and "Good move" work very well.

Third, there are certain actions that go along with good sportsmanship. They include sticking with it and finishing the game, making encouraging comments, and occasional slaps on the back and "high fives."

Fourth, help your child identify the results of sportsmanlike behavior. Talk together about the effect that good sportsmanship has on other people and the impact that poor sportsmanship makes. Point out how God wants us to do everything in a way that honors him (Colossians 3:17), and that the way we play a game is one way of showing people the difference God makes in our life. Ask your child which is more important: winning a game of basketball or making friends and treating people the way God wants us to. Spend time together role-playing and practicing these thoughts, words, and actions in different scenarios. Purposely practice them when you play a game of checkers, wrestle, or shoot baskets. Help your child remember that he can lose a game and still win a friend.

Talk to the coach. While some coaches can be wonderful influences on their players, other coaches can be a major part of the problem. Whether coaching a five-year-old in T-ball or a major high school sport, some coaches embody the very attitude you are teaching your child *not* to have. Share your concerns with the coach about your child's unsportsmanlike behavior and try to enlist him or her as an ally in positively influencing your child. If you determine that your child's coach is a part of the problem, talk with the appropriate personnel (league board of directors or principal) about getting a new coach. Or consider moving your child to a new team. Sports involvement should have a positive influence on your child, not a negative one.

Look for positive models. Whether in professional level sports or on your child's soccer team, look for examples of people who exhibit a good attitude whether winning or losing, play hard until the last second, congratulate the winning players, and play respectfully even when others do not. If you point out examples of this when you see them, you will help your child realize that many people are sportsmanlike and are respected and liked better for it.

Watch out for negative thinking traps. One of the reasons that children behave negatively is that they are thinking negatively. As you work with your child on his sportsmanship skills, find out what types of thoughts fuel the unsportsmanlike behavior. If he is thinking, "I never win," or "Our team is terrible," then poor sportsmanlike behavior is probably just around the corner. Once you identify some of these negative thoughts, help your child examine them, looking together for the evidence for such thoughts to see if they are really true. Consider, for example, the following questions:

- Is it true that your child *never* wins at anything?
- Think about the thousands of soccer, baseball, football, basketball games that were played this week at school and in organized leagues across the country. How many of those kids lost a game this week?
- Does that mean that they are bad at their sport? Does it mean they didn't have fun?
- Even if your child's team is not the best this year, is it possible for your child to still improve his skill? Can he still have fun if he loses?
- Did current professional sports stars always win every game when they were kids? Do they win every game now?

With guiding questions such as these, gently help your child to examine his negative thoughts and come up with thoughts that are true and balanced. Yes, his team may not be the best this year, but he can still make friends, play his best, improve his skill, and have fun. If your child can learn to keep his thoughts on track, then his actions will not be far behind.

Think out loud. One way to take advantage of the teaching power of modeling is to not only model positive behavior but positive and accurate thinking as well. This means that when you lose a game or find a situation or person to be frustrating, think out loud so that your child can benefit from hearing your thoughts. This is like giving him a secret telescope into your mind so that he can see how positive and accurate thinking is done when it counts. So, when you are losing at a game, let your child hear you say with a smile, "Well, you're beating me, but I'm not giving up." And when your child beats you at a game, let him hear you say, "Well, good game. That was fun. Maybe I'll get you next time," or "Congratulations, you got me. You're pretty good at that." The more he hears how you think, the more he will be able to think that way too.

Watch for progress. As you teach your child how to think and respond to difficult game situations, keep your radar on the lookout for instances when your child uses the skills you are teaching him. When you see him make an encouraging comment to a teammate or to a player on the opposing team, when you see him hang in there when he is losing, or when you see him try his very best, make sure to let him know that you are proud of him. Beam brighter than a neon sign as you squeeze him on the shoulder, saying something like, "Buddy, that's the way to hang in there"; "Now, that's the kind of attitude that makes you fun to play with"; or, "You keep that up and you might just turn this thing around." Then continue to watch your child make important steps toward developing the kind of attitude and character that will make him a winner where it really counts.

The right consequences must follow instances of poor sportsmanship. If your child displays inappropriate game behavior, you know that his thinking has gone off track. Give him an immediate reminder that will help him put things back into proper perspective and remind him of the importance of treating others respectfully. Reminders may include, "Hey, don't give up"; "Let's just have fun playing together; don't worry about who wins or loses"; "It's just a game; sometimes you win, sometimes you lose"; or, "Focus on having fun and doing your best. Then we'll have a great time."

If your child continues with poor sportsmanlike comments or behavior, give him a Fork-in-the-Road—a clear choice between choosing to handle things differently or losing the privilege of continuing in the game. For instance, you might say, "Matt, you need to be able to be a good sport even if you're losing or we'll have to stop the game." Continued negative behavior should then result in your child either taking a break from the game, discontinuing the game altogether, or serving an immediate Time-Out.

 ## How Do I Put It All Together?

The case of "must-win" Matt. Mr. and Mrs. Peterson realized that Matt was becoming anything but a champion. Deciding he needed to take a primary role in reshaping Matt's competitive attitude, Mr. Peterson took Matt out to dinner and a movie one night and they talked about Matt's overzealousness for winning. Mr. Peterson tried to get a feel for what Matt was thinking when he felt particularly angry about losing. He wanted to see if Matt was falling into any negative thinking traps. As it turned out, Matt was: "I hate losing," and "If I lose, then I'm no good at soccer," were thoughts that frequently came to his mind when losing a game. Gently, Mr. Peterson encouraged Matt to examine these thoughts, to see if there was any other way to look at things.

"What if you played basketball as good as Michael Jordan?" Mr. Peterson asked. "That would be cool," Matt responded, trying to visualize how he would handle all the fame and money.

"Y'know, you would still have to learn how to handle losing, wouldn't you?" Mr. Peterson asked. Matt slowly returned from his daydream.

Mr. Peterson continued. "Sure. The last I heard, Michael Jordan and the Chicago Bulls didn't win every game they played. They lost many games to other good teams, in spite of all the talent they had. Isn't that right?"

"Okay," Matt said, "I get your point." Mr. Peterson asked him what the point was. "That even the best players and teams lose sometimes," Matt stated, "no matter how good they are."

As they talked, Matt's dad reinforced the importance of having fun as well as playing hard. He reminded Matt of how important a positive attitude is toward turning a game around, encouraging other teammates, and building friendships that will last far after the game is over. They made a list of athletes who demonstrated good sportsmanship, including children from Matt's own team as well as professional sports figures, and talked about the positive results of being a good sport.

On the nights before Matt's games, he and his father began to pray that God would help Matt to do his best and to play in a way that would help others come to know about God. Matt started to wear a special wrist band to help him remember that he wanted to honor God in everything he did.

Mr. Peterson spoke with Matt's coach about encouraging Matt to demonstrate a positive attitude during practices and games. The coach was more than happy to do this, as he agreed Matt's potential as an effective team leader was being hampered by his negative attitude.

In order to give Matt some concrete skills to help him improve his sportsmanship habits, Matt and his dad spent time working on things that Matt could think, say, and do when losing at a game or sporting event. For example, Matt decided that he could think, "The best way to help my team is to keep a good attitude"; or "No one wins every game; I'll just do my best and have fun." He also reminded himself that God wants him to always try his best and treat others respectfully, whether he is winning or losing. He and his father practiced making encouraging and congratulatory comments, such as, "Good job!" and "Nice game," and giving "high fives" or a friendly slap on the shoulder as a way of being friendly to another player.

Mr. Peterson also started paying closer attention to the example that he was setting when playing "one-on-one" basketball with Matt or even a game of checkers. He even made sure that he lost on occasion and "thought out loud" as a way to model positive thinking for his son, flashing an encouraging grin and saying, "Good game!" and "Well, that was fun. I'll get you next time!"

Mr. and Mrs. Peterson both watched closely for signs of Matt showing a considerate, positive, or sportsmanlike attitude in any competitive activity. As soon as they saw any sign of this attitude, they immediately gave Matt a squeeze on the shoulder and told him, "Matt, you did a great job being a good sport. That makes you a fun guy to play with." If Matt began to display a negative attitude or behavior, they reminded him of a better way to think about the situation. If the negative behavior continued, Matt was given an immediate Fork-in-the-Road, "Matt, you need to work on being a good sport right now like we practiced, or you will have to stop playing and maybe even go to Time-Out."

While Mr. Peterson's time and investment and the encouragement from both of his parents did have a positive effect on Matt, his unsportsmanlike habits did not change overnight. His coach continued to make him sit on the sidelines on occasions when his attitude became too negative. He earned some Time-Outs at home for poor sportsmanship as well. However, as Matt and his dad continued to work on different ways of keeping things in perspective, Matt slowly began to see that being a good sport, in a board game or a soccer game, not only improved his chances of coming back to win but was a great way to obey God and have a lot more fun, all at the same time.

Chapter 37

Solving Problems

The case of "act now, think later" **Michael.** Michael was a very self-confident and athletic twelve-year-old boy. He was good at sports and had gained a reputation for being a strong competitor. However, Michael often made decisions without thinking them through, and got into a fair amount of hot water because of it.

When one of his friends suggested they fill a peer's gym locker with shaving cream, Michael was there without giving any thought to the potential consequences. When his parents told him that he had to get his homework or chores done before he could play with his friends, he would spout off comments about them being unfair and grudgingly drag his homework out, not realizing that his slow approach was costing him his free time.

Mr. and Mrs. Long had observed that Michael often didn't consider the end result of his actions. Instead, he made a quick decision and then stuck with it, no matter how self-defeating it was. While Michael's ability to make quick, reflexive decisions was a great asset for him on the sports field, his "act now, think later" style of decision-making was starting to cost him too many penalty yards in real life.

 ## Why Does This Happen?

No time to think. Children who are naturally impulsive often run into problems with their decision-making skills. This is not because they do not have the ability to make well thought-out decisions. They simply do not take the time. It is not uncommon for these children to get into the "habit" of responding to situations in a reflexive manner and to speak or behave in a way that quickly aggravates the situation and causes it to become much worse than it needed to be.

A lack of instruction. Some children do not use effective problem-solving skills because they have never been taught to do so. Being slow to speak and quick to consider effective ways of responding to a situation are not traits that come naturally to us all. I'm not even sure that they come naturally to most of us! Many children need to learn these valuable skills and experience the short- and long-term benefits of using them on a daily basis.

What they see is what they learn. The problem-solving skills that you model for your child will have a huge impact on the problem-solving skills that he develops. If your child sees you react to the problems of daily living in an impulsive, thoughtless, or irrational way year after year, this will impede his development of sound problem-solving skills.

On the other hand, if your child is able to see you approach the challenges of life in a balanced manner, he will be able to learn not only from your consistent example, but also from seeing the positive results that will tend to follow your problem-solving efforts. While good problem-solving on your part does not guarantee that your child will automatically follow suit, it sure improves the odds.

 ## What Can I Do?

Model good problem-solving for your children. Life presents parents with many opportunities for modeling problem-solving skills for their children. We must choose whether we will model effective or ineffective problem-solving skills. Responding to stresses at work, appliance breakdowns, car problems, marital disagreements, difficult child behavior, financial stress, inconsiderate neighbors, household duties, traffic jams, relatives that drop in at the last minute—the list could go on and on. Make sure that your children see you handle the problems of life in a wise and godly manner, one that you would like them to emulate. They probably will.

Teach problem-solving skills. The Bible teaches us that thinking before we speak is a profitable habit (Proverbs 29:20; James 1:19). One practical way to help your child build this habit is to teach him a simple set of problem-solving steps. Below are the problem-solving steps that I frequently use with children and families, followed by an explanation of each step. As you can see, the first letters of the problem-solving steps conveniently spell the words "STEPS" to aid with memorization:

S–State the problem
T–Think of solutions
E–Evaluate the solutions
P–Pick a solution
S–See if it worked

State the problem. Stating the problem is helpful in narrowing it down and making it more manageable. Thinking, "I can't stand having a brother!" does not help your child solve her sibling problem. Conversely, thinking, "I don't like it when Johnny makes fun of me in front of my friends," helps her focus on the situation and begins to lead her toward a solution. When these steps are used in a family setting, each member gets an opportunity to state the problem from his or her perspective. A sentence that can help your child to briefly and clearly state the problem is, "When _____ happens, I feel _____ and I would like _____."

Think of solutions. The next step is to think of solutions, at least four or five. I sometimes have families think of eight to twelve possible solutions for a problem and have never yet been disappointed in their ability to do so. The key is to be creative and to entertain any solution, including both positive and negative solutions. (Another word for this is brainstorming.) Think of helpful guidelines, ways to prevent the problem, uses of positive and negative consequences, compromises, how to use positive communication, and so on. Children choose a poor solution for their problem mainly because they haven't taken the time to think of other ways to handle it.

Evaluate the solutions. Once your child has a list of solutions, they can then be evaluated. Your child can consider the pros and cons, the likely outcome, and give each solution a "+" or "-" rating and then explain why. Some solutions are obviously poor while others may seem to solve the problem but actually only postpone it and result in greater problems in the future. Still other solutions sound harder but work out better in the long run. The important aspect of this step is that each solution is carefully and realistically evaluated as to how well it will solve the problem.

Pick a solution. Your child must then pick a solution or a combination of solutions he thinks will be the most effective approach to the problem. It is important to specify exactly what will be needed for the solution to be implemented. In your mind, picture the solution being attempted and see if you can think of any potential problems with the solution that may have been missed. If needed, figure out a way to prevent these problems by altering the solution or adding another one to it. If your child is having difficulty arriving at an effective solution, he can go back to Step 2, take a break and come back to the problem-solving process at a later time, or do some "research" to get some ideas from other credible sources (parents, friends, friends' parents, teachers, books, and so on). Once your child has chosen a solution, then he will need to specify when it will be put into effect.

See if it worked. The last step is to make sure that your child develops the habit of learning from his problem-solving work. Every problem-solving attempt is an experiment—either the chosen solution will be effective or it will not. If the solution was effective, then your child should remember this for the future. If the solution was not effective, then your child should not repeat it in the future but instead should find a better solution next time. This step can be put into action by setting a date to review the solution and to determine how effective it was.

Discuss these problem-solving steps with your child, writing them out and explaining them in simple terms. As a general rule, reserve these steps for children eight or older, as younger children will likely have a difficult time understanding them and will profit more from the concrete guidance of the Detour Method. For the purpose of instruction, it can be helpful to work through an easier problem together, so that your child can see how the steps work. Use the acrostic "STEPS" to help your child remember each step of the process. As always, keep your instruction lively and positive.

Practice together. Once your child has learned the problem-solving steps, begin to apply them together to the social, school, and family problems your child may face. Having to do homework instead of playing with friends, solving peer problems, tackling a difficult class, getting along with a challenging teacher, or resolving family conflicts are just a few examples of situations where good problem-solving skills can come in handy.

During a positive time, pick a situation and together work through the steps, making a list of the solutions that your child thinks of and his evaluations of them. Offer as much assistance as needed to help your child effectively think through the problem. For instance, if your child often gets mad when asked to do his homework, your problem-solving practice might look like this:

State the problem: "I feel mad because homework is so boring and I don't want to do it right now."

Think of solutions:

1. Refuse to do my homework.
2. Shout and throw a fit.
3. Throw my books out the window.
4. Say what I think in a respectful way.
5. Ask if I can do my homework later.
6. Just do it and get it over with.

Evaluate the solutions:

1. Minus: I'll get in trouble, go to Time-Out, have to do my homework anyway, and if don't do it, I'll get a bad grade.
2. Minus: I'll go to Time-Out, lose privileges, treat my parents disrespectfully, and I'll still have to do my homework.
3. Minus: I'll have to buy new books if they get damaged.
4. Plus: I'll tell my parents what I think. Maybe they'd listen and we can talk about it.
5. Plus: I can explain why I would like to play now and do my homework after dinner. If I make sense, they might let me do it.
6. Plus: Probably the best thing to do. Just get it done and then I can play later.

Pick a solution: I choose:

1. Say what I think in a respectful way.
2. Just do it and get it over with.

See if it worked: Do my plan every day for one week. Review how my plan has worked with dad on Saturday.

You may find that you and your child will evaluate the solutions differently—this is to be expected. Help your child to clearly think through the reasons for his evaluation. This is what learning is all about. Encourage your child to decide on a solution and talk together about what will be needed for this solution to work and the likely consequences that will follow.

Set a review date for one or two weeks later to talk about how well the solution is working. You can also use these steps together as a family by having regular family meetings where you work through family problems together in this format. If you do this, have everyone take turns offering solutions and then evaluations. Make it your job to keep everybody on topic, encourage comments to be brief and to the point, and enforce rules of respectful communication.

Review mistakes together as they occur in everyday life. Whether done in family meetings or just one on one with your child, talk about situations that were not handled well. Have your child practice using the problem-solving steps to think of other ways that he could have solved the problem. As you do this, your child will become more proficient in his use of the steps and you will be turning negative situations into positive learning experiences.

Reward good problem-solving. If you would like your child to engage in effective problem-solving more often, then make sure you reward his efforts to do so whenever you can. This does not mean dropping him a five-dollar bill every time he looks like he is thinking about how to solve a problem. Instead, make good use of the Pour-It-On Technique and natural rewards. Let your child know that you notice and appreciate his efforts to think about positive solutions before he acts. When you are able to, make sure that natural rewards follow good problem-solving efforts. As effective problem-solving is going to naturally bring in positive results, make sure to point out this connection to help your child realize that good problem-solving pays off.

Use negative consequences. Just as the use of good problem-solving skills should result in positive consequences, a failure to effectively problem-solve should result in negative consequences. Many times, these negative consequences will occur naturally, such as when your child shouts at a friend and the friend decides to go home. However, there will be times when your child chooses a poor solution regarding his behavior at home, at school, or with peers that will need to be followed by a negative consequence that you provide. The purpose is to reinforce the idea that good problem-solving pays off and poor problem-solving does not. Depending on the negative behavior your child has displayed, you can use a combination of Time-Out, Logical or Natural Consequences, and Response/Cost.

 ## How Do I Put It All Together?

The case of "act now, think later" Michael. Mr. and Mrs. Long took Michael out for some ice cream and initiated a discussion about solving problems. "Michael, we know you're a smart boy and you love God very much, and we're very proud of you," began Mr. Long. "But sometimes, you don't take time to think before you do things, and it gets you into trouble. Do you know what I mean?"

"I think so," Michael said wryly.

"Well, pal, we want to help you learn how to think before you act, so you can avoid some of those troubles. Sound like a good idea?"

"That wouldn't be too bad," Michael said with a grin, "if it could help me get to stay out with my friends longer."

Mr. and Mrs. Long made sure not to be critical of Michael and kept a positive tone to the conversation. They discussed the benefit of making good decisions and how poor decisions can quickly make a situation worse. Without launching into a sermon, Mrs. Long paraphrased Proverbs 3:13–15, 21–24, emphasizing the value of wisdom and good decision-making, and they talked together about why God places such importance on gaining wisdom. "Why do you think that God wants us to be wise?" asked Mr. Long. Michael correctly responded that being wise helps you to do what's right and stay away from stuff that's wrong.

Michael's parents then introduced him to the problem-solving steps, which Mr. Long had already printed out on a sheet of paper. Michael seemed to understand them fairly well and they worked through a problem of Michael's choice (his little sister bugging him) as an example. Michael's parents told him that using these steps for problems at home, school, and with friends could be a tool to help him make the type of good decisions that God wanted him to. They made an agreement to use the steps as a family when problems came up and agreed to talk more about using the steps later.

Within the next few weeks, Mr. Long took some time with Michael and they went over the problem-solving steps a few more times, practicing them on problems from school, home, and with friends. Michael initially had difficulty coming up with more than two or three solutions to a problem but soon got the hang of it with his father's help.

"Okay, so if Tony wants to joke around in class again, what are your options. See how many solutions you can think of."

"Well," began Michael, "I could mess around like usual, or maybe punch him. There's two." Mr. Long rolled his eyes and asked for more. "I could ignore him, or tell him to knock it off," Michael continued.

"How could you prevent the problem?" asked Mr. Long, pushing Michael to think more creatively.

"I could talk to him before class and tell him that I don't want to get in trouble again, so we've got to cool it."

"Not bad," smiled Mr. Long. They also talked about the benefits of good problem-solving (such as having fun with friends, good grades, obeying God, privileges at home, fun family activities) and the negative consequences that often follow poor problem-solving. The Longs did their best to take time with Michael whenever he made a poor or hasty decision and to review the decision with him, helping him to come to a better solution by using his steps. They found that when Michael just took the time to stop and think, his decisions were usually quite good.

Mr. and Mrs. Long made sure to consistently use the Pour-It-On Technique when they noticed Michael stopping to think instead of just reacting to a situation. "Hey, Mike, I can tell that you're thinking about what to do right now. Good job, keep it up." They also made sure that appropriate negative consequences followed situations where Michael made poor decisions about homework, home responsibilities, or getting along with his sister.

Michael's parents knew that learning to make good decisions was a process that would take time and continued their efforts to teach, model, and encourage good problem-solving skills with all of their children. As the months passed by, they noticed that Michael was stopping to think before acting more often and that his decisions with friends, at school, and at home were beginning to show the tell-tale signs of good problem-solving.

Part 3

Common Classroom Problems

During the thirteen years from kindergarten to high school graduation, our children spend most of their days, five days a week, in one place. School. And, in case you have forgotten, school is not a walk in the park. Do you remember struggling with reading, grammar, math, or social studies? Getting strict Miss Thompson instead of fun-loving Mrs. Smith? Having all your classes assign homework on the same day?

In spite of its difficulties, or perhaps because of them, school provides the learning ground for many important lessons. In order to succeed at school, children must learn to work hard, to stay organized, and to stick with tasks that are tedious and difficult. Their skills at reading, math, writing, and reasoning are developing in leaps and bounds.

And all of this happens within the daily context of being surrounded by the people whose opinions of you begin to matter a great deal: your peers.

Your child must fight through some noteworthy challenges to succeed at school. For starters, all children enter with their unique set of strengths and weaknesses. These abilities cause academic tasks to be easier for some and harder for others. Add to that the element of peer pressure and comparisons about who is the smartest, the best athlete, the best looking, and so on. Then, add some wonderful teachers who are custom-made for your child, and others who are far from a perfect fit. Finally, throw in academic demands that get tougher every year, requiring more homework and responsibility. And your job is to help your child not just survive, but thrive and grow in this environment.

To help you with this formidable task, I have included a few of the most common classroom problems that children experience. As you encourage, guide, and pray with your child every day, you will find that she has what it takes to make it. But your diamond in the rough may need a little polishing before she begins to shine. Take advantage of all the resources at your disposal, including your spouse, friends, your child's teachers, and other school personnel — the principal, counselor, school psychologist. Be an advocate for your child; help create the best classroom environment for her. Help your child learn the valuable life-shaping lessons of hard work, self-discipline, and perseverance. And most importantly, teach your child to think accurately about herself, seeing herself as God's wonderful handiwork, designed for eternal significance. And he always gets an A-plus on his projects.

Disrupting Class

The case of joking José. Even though José had just turned eleven, he was on his way toward winning the "Most Likely to be a Comedian" award. His willingness to daringly "push the limits" in class was earning him big status points with his peer group. However, his joking and mischievousness were beginning to get him into trouble at school. He was starting to lose recess privileges with regularity and to earn detentions for repeated classroom disruptions. His teacher had just called his parents to set up a parent-teacher conference. Mr. and Mrs. Sanchez were concerned about this, as José had never had any behavior problems in school before. They wanted to address this problem before it got any worse.

 ## Why Does This Happen?

Peer acceptance carries a lot of weight during the preteen and teenage years. If a child discovers that a certain type of behavior gets rewarded with increased peer status, it will become powerfully appealing. The problem is that peer acceptance can reward behaviors deemed acceptable by peers—but not by the rest of society. Therefore, help your child to remember to work toward pleasing God rather than peers, and to gain peer acceptance through appropriate behaviors and not through self-defeating ones.

Learning problems can also contribute to disruptive behavior. This is true particularly if they are significant or have not been detected. If a child cannot understand the work, easily gets lost or confused, or is able to complete it only at a slow and grueling pace, he might be tempted to do something (anything!) other than his work. While this is not an excuse for disruptive school behavior, remember that the academic expectations of school can be much more frustrating and difficult to achieve for some children than for others.

Other factors can contribute to disruptive school behavior. Examples of such factors are Attention-Deficit/Hyperactivity Disorder (ADHD), oppositional behavior, depression, and significant family problems. If you suspect that any of these factors may be playing a role in your child's disruptive behavior, your best move is to consult with a mental health professional right away.

 ## What Can I Do?

Talk with your child about his behavior at school. Without accusing (this will only make your child defensive), tell your child that you have become aware that there has been some inappropriate behavior at school and would like him to tell you what has been going on. This gives you a chance to see how well your child takes responsibility for his own behavior and may help you to become aware of other factors that have contributed to the behavior, some of which the teacher may not even be aware of (after all, they can't see everything!). Before you try to solve a problem, gathering information from your child's point of view is always a good place to start.

Talk with the teacher. Unless you regularly volunteer as an aide at your child's school (or have a video recorder secretly placed in your child's classroom), you have no way of knowing what is really going on except for the report you get from your child and from the teacher. So don't lose out on half of your information by neglecting to talk with your child's teacher. Most teachers I have talked with want to keep parents updated and discuss ways to help with the child's behavior.

Ask the teacher *specific* questions about the disruptive behavior, such as how often it happens, where and when it usually happens, are other children regularly involved, what has been the teacher's immediate response to the behavior, and have there been positive or negative consequences used at school to address the behavior. It can also be nice to ask the teacher to point out any positive behaviors or attributes that he or she has noticed in your child, just to balance things out. It is possible that something as simple as changing your child's seating arrangement will squelch the problem. A teacher-family conference could also have a big influence on your child's behavior. If needed, you and the teacher can put together a plan that will help your child learn to make better decisions in the classroom.

Use problem-solving skills with your child. After you have discussed the behavior with your child, talk together about what your child thinks about the situation. Perhaps he doesn't like the teacher, likes being funny, gets bored, finds the work hard, wants others to like him, and so on. Try to see the situation from your child's perspective and help him use the right "feeling words" (frustrated, angry, bored, nervous, confused, etc.) to describe how he feels.

Help your child think of other ways he can respond to the situation that will help him reach his goal. His goal might be to have fun and make friends while still being respectful to the teacher and following class rules. Another child's goal might be to respond the right way when the work is difficult or boring. Once your child has identified possible solutions, discuss the likely outcomes that each solution would bring. Then have him pick the solution or solutions that he thinks would be the most productive and explain exactly how he could put these solutions into action.

To really put his plan to the test, practice it together a few times (with you pretending to be another child or the teacher) and see how your child does at his new plan. If you do your best to make the practice realistic, this type of rehearsal can highlight potential problems with the plan, give you ideas for improving the plan, and will help your child begin to get used to solving problems in a more adaptive way.

Decide for your child to try this plan for a certain amount of time such as a week, and check with him to see how the plan is going. Continue having "problem-solving" discussions together, helping your child to gradually improve his skill at handling situations more effectively and making better decisions. See "Solving Problems" for more details.

Use a daily behavior sheet. There's nothing like a little accountability to help improve a behavior and at the very least, keep accurate records. Use a daily behavior sheet like the ones I have provided at the end of this book or, after talking with the teacher, you can customize one specifically for your child.

Ask your child's teacher to rate your child every day on the "target behaviors" that you have decided to work on. Examples of positive target behaviors include asking permission to get out of your seat, asking questions during class discussions, getting class work done on time, following the teacher's instructions, exhibiting appropriate work-time behavior (completing assignments without talking or messing around), exhibiting appropriate play-time behavior (appropriate play without fighting or aggressive behavior), following class rules, and so on.

The daily behavior sheet needs to be completed and sent home every day with your child. Negative consequences can be earned if your child fails to get the daily behavior sheet completed and signed or for repeatedly forgetting to bring it home. Using a daily behavior sheet will help you get accurate, specific, daily information about your child's school behavior and can be used to determine your child's school and home privileges. Occasionally, just the act of keeping a daily behavior sheet will have a positive influence on your child's behavior.

Devise a simple contract, using Natural Rewards and Logical Consequences. If you have begun to use a daily behavior sheet, this is rather easy to do. For example, if you are working on exhibiting good work-time behavior and using a daily behavior sheet that assigns a Great, Fair, or Poor rating each period, you can determine what a reasonable daily report should be (such as a combination of Great or Fair ratings). You can decide that your child will get certain after-school and evening privileges only if he receives a reasonable daily report. If he receives an exceptional report (for instance, three Great ratings), a special privilege can be earned that day or bonus points can be given that can add up to a special privilege when a certain number is reached (such as five bonus points = a fun activity with Dad, or a family ice cream outing). It is also possible to use certain activities at school as immediate rewards (such as extra computer time) if the teacher desires. If your child receives one Poor rating, certain privileges will be lost for the day. If he receives two Poor ratings, additional privileges will be lost.

You can also use a daily behavior sheet that assigns a numerical value to the teacher rating (Excellent = 4, Good = 3, etc.), and simply use the number value as points for your simple contract. Points can be accumulated to earn items from your child's reward menu and failing to earn a reasonable number of points each day can result in negative consequences for the day.

Pour it on. Even if you use a simple contract, make sure to use the Pour-It-On Technique when your child behaves appropriately at school. And, as you are not at school to give social rewards *immediately* following the desired behaviors, ask your teacher to be on the lookout for positive behavior and to give positive, *specific*, verbal feedback to your child whenever possible.

Get additional assistance. On occasion, disruptive school behavior may be related to a lack of social or problem-solving skills, emotional upset, academic difficulties, or some other significant issue. If a lack of social skills, anger-management problems, attention problems, or any other psychological or emotional issues are suspected, an immediate consultation with a mental health professional is warranted. If you are concerned that your child may have a learning disorder or other academic or ability deficits, talk to your teacher and the school principal. In many cases, the school will help by thoroughly evaluating your child to see if additional academic resources are needed.

How Do I Put It All Together?

The case of joking José. Mr. and Mrs. Sanchez sat down to talk with José about his school behavior. "José, let's talk about what's going on at school. We've talked with Mrs. Wagner on the phone . . ." Mrs. Sanchez started out.

"Oh no," groaned José painfully, "you talked with her?"

"Yes we did," continued Mr. Sanchez, "and she says she likes you a lot, which we can understand. But, you're really disrupting the class, and we've got to figure out what's going on."

"Nothing is going on," explained José, trying to get this situation under control. "I'm not doing anything and neither are my friends. She always picks on us. You should see what everybody else is doing!" José raised his voice to make his final point, "She's so mean!"

"Why do you think this is happening?" Mrs. Sanchez asked.

"I told you," exclaimed José, "she's mean!" Mr. Sanchez said calmly that he was glad José had some thoughts about the issue because he would be able to tell them to Mrs. Wagner when they all got together for a conference.

José's jaw dropped. "You've got to be kidding! Not a conference!"

They weren't kidding. Mr. and Mrs. Sanchez had spoken with José's teacher and their discussion revealed that José was frequently talking during work time and that his non-stop sense of humor was beginning to disrupt the class. The following week, José attended the parent-teacher conference with his parents and they started by making special note of his positive attributes and behavior. Mrs. Wagner told José she really enjoyed his humor and wit, but explained that there were times when his behavior made it hard for her to teach and for others to do their work. The teacher assured Mr. and Mrs. Sanchez that she had no concerns about José's academic ability and was sure that they could find a solution to this problem.

For starters, they decided to rearrange the classroom seats, so that José and a few other boys would be less likely to get themselves in hot water. They also decided to use a daily behavior sheet to help with José's behavior. The target behaviors that they chose were: (1) listening attentively during class discussion (eye contact with teacher, asking questions, no talking to others); and (2) appropriate class work behavior (completing assignments, no talking or joking around during work time). José's teacher would record a "check" on his daily behavior sheet when he completed each target behavior for each class subject (there were six daily subjects), for a total of six checks possible for each target behavior. As such, twelve total checks could be earned each day. Mrs. Wagner estimated that José's current behavior would earn between seven and twelve checks a day.

Following the meeting, Mr. and Mrs. Sanchez took José out to a favorite fast-food restaurant to discuss the class situation. They developed a menu of extra privileges José could earn with his points by getting eleven or twelve checks on his daily behavior sheet. They also decided on daily privileges he would lose for getting fewer checks on his behavior sheet. The plan looked like this:

- Twelve checks = standard privileges and five points toward a menu item.
- Eleven checks = standard privileges and three points toward a menu item.
- Ten checks = loss of television for the day.
- Nine checks = loss of television and video/computer games for the day.
- Eight checks = loss of television, video/computer games, playing with friends for the day.
- Seven or less checks = loss of television, video/computer games, playing with friends, and one extra homework assignment for the day.

Over the next few weeks, Mr. and Mrs. Sanchez spent time with José, helping him to identify ways to have fun with friends at school and use his sense of humor without getting into trouble. They considered a variety of classroom behaviors such as joking during class, throwing spit wads, talking quietly with permission, and saving jokes for recess. Then they discussed the likely outcomes of each behavior. José agreed that quietly talking and joking with his friends after his work was done or just waiting until lunch time was the best idea. They also discussed the importance of being respectful to his teacher and the importance of honoring God with his classroom behavior. They agreed to check in together every Saturday for the next month to discuss José's progress.

The combination of moving his desk, using a daily behavior sheet, and helping him use his problem-solving steps worked well for José. During the first month, he had more than a few days of earning only seven or eight checks and did not enjoy the loss of privileges and extra homework that consistently followed. Most of the time, however, José earned most of his checks and even earned a few perfect days.

Before the year was over, with the help of regular problem-solving discussions with his parents, José began to earn eleven and twelve checks most of the time. He soon developed the habit of making his funny comments quietly during appropriate times and saving the rest of his humor until lunch.

Chapter 39

Not Paying Attention

The case of distractible David. Nine-year-old David had always found it difficult to pay attention when things got boring. Although he got fairly good grades, his teacher felt David could do much better if he could just maintain his attention for longer periods of time.

At a recent parent-teacher conference, the teacher told Mr. and Mrs. Eaton that David was a very pleasant and likeable young boy. However, he was also very distractible, disorganized, and inattentive in class. The teacher frequently had to repeat her instructions for David and his work was often messy because he had rushed through it.

At home, David often resisted doing his homework, had trouble following through with chores, and forgot what he was supposed to do when he was asked to do more than one thing at a time. Some of David's past teachers had also mentioned that David might have an attention problem and David's parents were starting to wonder if maybe they were right.

Why Does This Happen?

You don't catch ADHD. Attention-Deficit/Hyperactivity Disorder (ADHD) is a neurological disorder that approximately 5 percent of children are born with it. Current research strongly suggests that ADHD is passed on genetically. While children with ADHD can display symptoms in different ways, they characteristically have difficulty with some combination of inattention, impulsivity, or hyperactivity.

Learning difficulties can masquerade as attention problems. If a child has a learning disorder, the academic struggle that this causes could be misinterpreted as a problem with attention, when in fact the child is simply lost, confused, or frustrated with the work. This is particularly possible if the child's learning problem has not been identified. While a child can have a learning disorder *along with* ADHD, it is also possible that for some children with academic deficits, their "off-task" behavior is largely a result of academic difficulty and frustration. For these children, an evaluation for a possible learning disorder will need to be a part of the ADHD evaluation.

Other significant issues can result in a decreased ability to concentrate. Such issues include anxiety, depression, or significant family problems. Sometimes, the boredom of intellectually gifted children faced with unchallenging work can look like inattentiveness. Much less commonly, there can be a medical problem that results in difficulties with attention and concentration. Some children may have slightly more difficulty with attention and organization than is considered "average," but may not be severe enough to warrant an ADHD diagnosis. As such, an evaluation for ADHD needs to carefully consider these other factors and make sure that the apparent attention problems cannot be attributed to another disorder or situation.

 What Can I Do?

Talk to school personnel. This includes your child's teacher, the guidance counselor, school psychologist, and whoever else might be able to give you helpful information about your child's school behavior. Find out what concerns they have and what factors they think may be contributing to the behavior in question. A school psychologist will often be willing to talk to your child's teachers, observe your child in the classroom, and have the teachers complete a behavioral checklist in order to gather preliminary information about the possibility of ADHD. Information from the school is crucial because this is a setting where problems with attention, impulsivity, and overactivity can often be readily observed.

Get an evaluation. If you or your child's teachers have serious concerns about the possibility of an ADHD condition for your child, the next step is to get an ADHD evaluation. This can begin with your pediatrician, but is often completed by a mental health professional who is experienced with ADHD evaluations.

While professionals will conduct the assessment in different ways, components of a thorough assessment include a physical evaluation, an interview with the parents, an interview with the child, obtaining information from teachers, a review of past school records, and parent- and teacher-completed behavioral checklists. Computerized testing and additional emotional, intellectual, or achievement testing may also be helpful or even necessary in some cases. The evaluation should conclude with a clear discussion of the results providing evidence for or against the diagnosis of ADHD for your child, identification of other factors that may be contributing to your child's behavior, and recommendations about effective treatment options.

Learn about ADHD. If the evaluation indicates that your child has ADHD, you will need to become well educated about the nature of ADHD and the various methods for addressing ADHD-related behavior at home and at school. It can also be very helpful to start learning about ADHD during the initial stages of the evaluation to help better understand your child's behavior and know what behaviors to look for. A national organization such as C.H.A.D.D. (Children and Adults with Attention Deficit Disorder, www.chadd.org) can be a source of up-to-date information and research and can help you get involved with local support groups.

Research has found that a multimodal treatment is most effective for helping ADHD children. Primary treatments include teaching parents how to implement effective preventative and behavioral strategies for home and school behaviors, and the use of medication. Both treatments have been found to be very effective with ADHD children. Interventions that help improve a child's skills in other important areas, such as anger-management, problem-solving, and building social and organizational skills, are also often very useful. In many instances, family therapy can provide a helpful setting for working through difficult issues. If your child has ADHD, make sure that you are working with a mental health professional who is knowledgeable about ADHD and can help you develop an effective treatment plan for your child.

Modify the home environment. Children with ADHD respond better in environments that are clear and structured. Here are some ideas to help you get things at home going in the right direction:

Rules and instructions need to be clear, brief, and to the point. ADHD children often forget multi-task instructions and get off track with even the most familiar routines. Physical reminders, such as sign and notes posted in strategic areas, can help children remember (and most importantly, follow) daily home rules.

Write a short list when giving tasks and chores to your child. This reduces the chance of failure, increases the chance of success, and helps your child learn a good way of organizing himself.

Routines are very helpful for an ADHD child. A regular time for meals, getting up, homework, going to bed, and so on, will bring a needed sense of structure and consistency to the schedule.

Immediate consequences, for both positive and negative behavior, are needed for an ADHD child. This will increase the impact of the consequence on the behavior and will help your child become more aware of and learn to regulate his or her behavior more effectively.

Make every effort to strengthen your child's positive behavior. There are many ways that you can teach and reward positive behavior to help your child learn better ways of completing tasks, listening, and getting along with others. Relying primarily on negative consequences to improve your child's behavior will create an extremely negative family environment and is not effective with ADHD children. Negative consequences are necessary, but are far more effective when used in an atmosphere that provides plenty of positive feedback and actively rewards positive behavior.

Realistic expectations are a must. While always expecting the best from your child and consistently holding your child accountable for his behavior, do not expect your ADHD child to "be just like other kids." The ADHD child will have a unique set of struggles and challenges that will require special understanding and loving patience from you. Remember regularly to point out your child's strengths and communicate that you appreciate his hard work. Make extra sure he knows that God created him as a capable and valuable young person through whom he wants to do great things. And he will.

Modify the classroom environment. There are several things that the teacher can do in the classroom to help a child increase his on-task behavior. These modifications are often formalized in what is known as a 504 Plan. For children with learning problems as well as ADHD, all of the necessary modifications can be included in your child's Individualized Educational Plan (IEP). For ADHD children who do not require an IEP, a 504 plan is used. You can initiate a 504 plan by talking to your child's principal or school psychologist. Modifications often included in a 504 plan are:

- Break assignments down into smaller tasks.
- Allow as much "hands-on" work as possible.
- Use ample positive verbal reinforcement for on-task behavior.
- Identify nonverbal "cues" that the teacher can use to provide your child with feedback concerning positive and negative behaviors.
- Use a teacher-initialed assignment notebook to keep track of daily homework.
- Allow your child to use a non-distracting object, such as a "squeeze-ball" to manage his need for excess motor movement.
- Tape 3-by-5 desk cards containing steps for various classroom procedures (such as getting out of seat, asking a question) to your child's desk or notebooks.

- Place your child's desk in a position that allows good eye contact with the teacher and minimizes distractions.
- Use an in-class behavioral program to increase the frequency of selected appropriate or "on-task" target behaviors. Such a program should be designed by a behavioral clinical psychologist or the school psychologist.
- Reduce the amount of daily homework, particularly written work.
- Use your child as a classroom helper as often as possible as a way of providing positive motor movement, adding novelty to the class day, and increasing a sense of positive classroom contribution.
- Allow additional time on tests.

Build organizational skills. Children with ADHD often forget to bring materials home and lose important papers because of their poor organizational skills. The teacher can give you valuable tips on how to help your child organize his notebook, such as with color coding, special folders for homework and finished work, and zippered pouches for pencils and pens. They also can allow your child to use an assignment notebook for writing down homework assignments. Some ADHD children benefit from a daily check-in time with the teacher at the end of the day to ensure that the assignment notebook is complete and that all the materials needed for the evening's homework have been gathered.

Teach and strengthen the positives. These children are at risk for having more negative interactions at school, home, and with peers, and thus arriving at negative and false conclusions about themselves. You must lead the effort in helping your child to develop a positive and accurate self-view by helping him learn to interact effectively with his environment.

One way to do this is to actively teach and strengthen positive behavior. You will undoubtedly use (and re-use) the Detour Method and problem-solving steps with your child to help him learn how to handle difficult situations and to get in the habit of stopping and thinking about his actions—before doing them.

The Pour-It-On Technique will need to become second nature to you as you become a consistent source of positive reinforcement for your child. From time to time, or perhaps consistently, you will find yourself using a Simple Contract in order to more specifically and effectively address certain home and school behaviors. Your child will have a better chance of developing positive habits and skills if you get in the habit of regularly teaching and strengthening them.

Build islands of competence. Children with ADHD can be talented and gifted in many ways. Help your child find his areas of giftedness and encourage him to develop them. Some ADHD children are talented at sports, chess, art, building things, and just about anything else you can think of. As your child's ADHD will result in some guaranteed frustration, it is very important that you put extra effort into helping him develop areas of strength that he can feel good about.

Use negative consequences to weaken inappropriate behavior. Again, you will find yourself using all of your discipline tools at different times. Time-Out, Natural and Logical Consequences, and the Response/Cost approach can be very effective with ADHD children. When verbal reprimands, Fork-in-the-Road, or loss of privileges are needed, they should be given immediately following the inappropriate behavior. Such comments should always be given in a firm yet calm manner, using eye contact and communicating respect for your child.

Get some assistance. If you need to learn more about ADHD, are finding it hard to implement the above suggestions, or feel like you are losing your grip on your child or family, consult with a mental health professional who regularly works with ADHD children and get the help and support that you need.

 ## How Do I Put It All Together?

The case of distractible David. Mr. and Mrs. Eaton decided to find out more about ADHD. They contacted C.H.A.D.D. and found helpful and informative material there. After consulting with their pediatrician, they decided to take David to a child psychologist for an ADHD evaluation.

"David," explained Mr. Eaton, "we want to meet with a doctor to see how well you can pay attention and stay focused on your work. The doctor will help us figure out if there's anything we can do to help you do it better."

The psychologist carefully and thoroughly interviewed David's parents and reviewed David's past records and current school performance. She spoke with David's teacher on the telephone and had David's parents and teacher complete a set of behavioral checklists in order to get a more complete view of David's behavior at home and school. In David's case, additional psychological or academic testing was not required.

The evaluation indicated that David did meet the criteria for ADHD and the psychologist carefully reviewed these results with the Eatons. They set up a meeting with the school principal to share these results and it was decided that a team meeting would be held to develop a 504 plan that would include certain classroom modifications, such as using nonverbal signals, desk cards, an assignment notebook, modifying his homework assignments, and changing his seating assignment.

David was also placed on a small amount of medication by his pediatrician. He responded well to the medicine and it was agreed that he would take regular "medication vacations" in order to keep tabs on how well he could do without the medication as he got older.

David's parents met several times with the psychologist to learn how to effectively address David's challenging home and school behavior. The psychologist suggested putting together a behavioral contract to help David with his positive school behavior. They did, and used a daily behavior sheet to collect ratings from David's teacher for completing assigned work in class, the neatness of his work, and following classroom rules. The teacher rated David on a one-to-three scale for each target behavior twice a day; one rating in the morning and one in the afternoon. The daily behavior sheet was sent home with David each day and the teacher ratings translated into points with which he could obtain items from his reward menu.

Mr. and Mrs. Eaton also helped David settle into an after-school routine and incorporated timely homework completion (without arguing) into his Simple Contract as well. In addition to the rewards on David's menu, negative consequences were also given if David earned less than a certain number of points each day.

David responded positively to the combination of academic modifications, environmental structure, behavioral tools, and a low dose of medication. However, things were not a breeze for David and his family. David still forgot his class materials occasionally, drifted off-task when doing his chores, and did his share of arguing. The medication had also slightly reduced his appetite, and he took longer to get to sleep at night.

David and his parents continued to consult with their psychologist as additional issues arose. Later that year, David benefitted from therapy sessions to help him improve his problem-solving and anger-control skills and the whole family grew closer by learning to improve the way they communicated with each other. In their family devotions, they always thanked God for making everyone in their family special and for having great plans for each of them.

Mr. and Mrs. Eaton met other parents from their church with ADHD children and, over time, developed a helpful support network. They learned to know their own limits and pick their battles, accepting that things in their family would be different from families without ADHD children. While the challenges related to David's ADHD never went away completely, the Eaton family learned how to respond to these challenges, keep things in perspective, and view every member of their family as a wonderful gift from God.

Chapter 40

Poor Grades

The case of frustrated Frankie. Mr. and Mrs. Riggs noticed that their eight-year-old son, Frankie, had been spending a lot of time on homework this year. Frankie was in the third grade and his parents began to notice last year that some of the work, especially reading, was not coming easily for Frankie. This year, Frankie had become quite frustrated with his homework and was beginning to resist doing it. This was a new experience for Frankie's parents, because Frankie had always been a good listener and an easy child. They started to wonder if some of Frankie's work was actually beyond what he could do.

 ## Why Does This Happen?

Slow but normal development. Children do not always develop abilities at the same rate. It is perfectly normal for one child to develop skills and abilities somewhat faster or slower than another child. The fact that skills and abilities develop at different rates and times is part of the "ebb and flow" of childhood development. It is only when a child's development falls significantly below what is expected for his age that more serious concerns arise.

A learning disorder can be the cause of poor grades at school. This can only be confirmed by ability testing and achievement testing, which is usually completed by a school psychologist, a clinical psychologist, or an educational specialist. If a learning disorder is diagnosed, the next step is to develop a plan with the school for appropriate educational assistance.

It is also possible that a child may not have a formal learning disorder, but may still have weaknesses in certain academic or ability areas that have a notable impact on his school performance. In these cases, schools may be able to provide additional academic assistance and additional assistance can be obtained privately as well.

Attention problems can also contribute to poor grades. If a child has ADHD, it can make it much more difficult to stay focused during class lectures and discussions and to concentrate on homework for extended periods of time. In fact, undiagnosed ADHD often has a negative impact on a child's grades. This is why it is important to be working with a therapist who is very familiar with the many interventions for ADHD and can help you put together a comprehensive treatment plan for your child.

Other problems can be the culprit behind poor grades for some children. Physical problems, family difficulties, oppositional behavior, depression, anxiety, peer problems, and so on—all of these can influence your child's grades if they significantly affect your child's health, behavior, or school motivation. If one of these factors is affecting your child's school performance, consult with a professional right away.

 ## What Can I Do?

Check with the teacher. The first thing to do if you suspect that your child is having too much difficulty with his school work is to check with your child's teacher. Teachers are a great source of information and can provide valuable insight about your child's learning style and the problems he or she is having. The teacher's input should help you begin to determine whether your child's difficulty is due to academic problems or is the result of other factors.

Get an evaluation if need be. If you think a learning disorder, ADHD, or some other physical, educational, or psychological problem may be contributing to the academic difficulty, an evaluation may be advisable. Depending on what you suspect may be the problem, talk with your pediatrician, the school psychologist, or a qualified therapist. These professionals should be able to help you determine the nature of your child's difficulties and put together an effective treatment plan.

Improve study habits. It will probably not come as a surprise to you that problems with grades often coexist with poor study habits. You can really help your child by getting him settled into a routine for homework and studying. Provide a quiet place with adequate lighting and plenty of space for books and materials. Have a regular time for homework and figure out a way to insert breaks into the homework routine if needed. You may also need to help your child get into the habit of rechecking the instructions before starting an assignment, skipping difficult problems and coming back to them, doublechecking his work for accuracy, and taking brief notes to help with reading comprehension. If your child is working with a tutor, the tutor should be able to provide valuable assistance in this area. See "Homework" and "Not Paying Attention" for more ideas.

Academic assistance will be needed for some children. This is a must if your child has a learning disorder. It also can be very helpful if your child does not qualify for a learning disorder diagnosis but still struggles in certain academic areas. Talk with your school psychologist or principal to find out what resources are available in your school district and which will be most helpful for your child. You can also have your child work with a private tutor or receive help from an educational therapist if needed.

Reward positive effort. There are several ways that you can use rewards to encourage your child in his academic efforts and make doing homework a little more fun. Using the Pour-It-On Technique, make sure that you consistently provide your child with positive feedback when you see him making a reasonable effort on his school work. Let him know that you see his effort and are very proud of him for his hard work.

Once your child is receiving the classroom modifications and additional academic assistance that he needs, you can consider using a Simple Contract with your child, choosing from target behaviors such as nightly homework completion, reasonable grades (C's or better), and positive effort marks on report cards. Most children find this type of program to be fun and motivating.

Build self-esteem. A child with significant academic problems is at risk for falling into negative thinking traps. Lots of them. "I'm stupid," "I can't do it," and "Everyone will laugh at me" are phrases that I have heard children with poor grades say far too many times. Here are some ideas for helping these children to develop a balanced and accurate view of themselves:

Remind them that they are loved and valued. Make sure your children know how important they are to you and to God. Regularly tell them that you love them and emphasize the fact that God made them special, has great plans for them, and loves them very much. In spite of the frustration that you may feel at times, make sure to spend regular quality time together and find ways to keep your relationship strong.

Have realistic and positive expectations. Many people who have struggled with school have gone on to achieve great things in life. Some who struggled with reading now teach in college. Others are leaders of successful companies. While keeping your expectations realistic for your child, make sure that they are very positive as well. Send the unmistakable message that you *know* your child is a capable and talented person, that God has unbelievable plans for his life, and that success is not always defined by A's and B's.

Point out strengths and successes. Your child is likely to remember every question he missed, every spelling mistake he made, and every assignment that he had to do over. However, he likely has forgotten every question he answered correctly, every word spelled right, and every assignment turned in on time. By pointing out the things your child does right, you will help him learn to keep his perspective in balance and to avoid disqualifying the positives. Make sure to notice his strengths in non-academic endeavors as well, as his abilities may shine in unexpected places.

Teach them to respond to failure effectively. Life is full of failed experiences, mistakes, and disappointments for us all, and the child with academic struggles is no exception to the rule. Children will never learn to achieve success until they learn to handle failure. Use the ideas discussed in "Giving Up" to help you teach your child to turn failures into building blocks for success.

Gently correct negative thinking. Be on the lookout for negative thinking traps! When you see your child fall into one, such as "I'll never be able to do it" or "I'm so dumb," use the guiding questions in the Glossary to help him examine his thoughts and find a more accurate way to view the situation.

Help them find activities that they enjoy or are good at. Without pushing too hard, do your best to get your child involved in one or two clubs, sports, hobbies, or any activity that can help develop other areas of competence. It can be far easier for your child to deal with a difficult time at school if he can experience a sense of satisfaction and self-confidence in other areas of life.

Place a greater emphasis on effort and attitude than on performance. While performance does count, effort and attitude count even more! I would much rather have strong effort with a weaker performance than a strong performance with very little effort. It is often said that those who succeed in life are not the exceptionally gifted, but those who persevere and don't give up. Encourage your child to make his best effort (while keeping it reasonable) and let him know that in your eyes he has earned an A-plus!

How Do I Put It All Together?

The case of frustrated Frankie. Mr. and Mrs. Riggs had a meeting with Frankie's teacher who confirmed their concerns about his reading ability. They then spoke with the school psychologist who agreed that an evaluation would be helpful. As it turned out, Frankie did meet the criteria for a reading disorder and an Individualized Educational Plan was developed to modify his reading expectations and provide him with additional assistance in reading several times a week.

While Frankie's homework load was reduced, it was not eliminated. Mr. and Mrs. Riggs maintained their expectations about daily homework completion, which was easier now that his assignments had been modified. However, Frankie still found his reading homework to be difficult, even though it was now more manageable.

"I can't do it!" Frankie said in frustration, slamming his pencil on his workbook. "Hang in there, buddy," replied Mrs. Riggs, "we just want you to try your best." She squeezed him on the shoulder, and took a look at the word he was stuck on. "You know how to sound out that word," she said encouragingly, "just go slow. You'll get it."

Mr. and Mrs. Riggs made sure to provide plenty of specific verbal rewards and positive encouragement when they saw Frankie make a good effort. A homework routine was developed that required him to complete his homework prior to any television or computer time.

Mr. and Mrs. Riggs also made it a point to help Frankie learn to think about his reading disorder in an accurate way. They talked together about some of the comments they had heard him make, and helped him to realize that needing a little extra help with reading did not have anything to do with his intelligence.

"Frankie," Mr. Riggs said, "everybody has things that they are good at and things that they need a little help with. Some people are good at reading, but they have a hard time with math. Or they have a harder time with reading but are good at math and at hockey, like you. When I was a boy, reading was hard for me too, but I kept working at it and now, I do okay." That made an impact on Frankie, as his father was a teacher.

"It's like having a souped-up race car," Mr. Riggs continued, "with a really fast engine. Like Uncle Rod's Porsche, remember?" Frankie did.

"But what if one of the gauges got stuck sometimes?" Mr. Riggs asked. "The rest of the car would still work just like it is supposed to. We'd just have to work at fixing that one gauge, right?"

"Right," answered Frankie.

"Well, pal, you are like that race car, and your reading is like that gauge that gets stuck," explained Mr. Riggs. "Your engine works great and your car goes super fast. You just have a gauge that gets stuck sometimes, and all your hard work is helping that gauge to work better. Do you understand?"

"Yeah, I get it," said Frankie. "I want my race car to be bright red."

Frankie worked hard and profited from his extra reading help. He even spent some additional time working with a private tutor to help with reading and study skills. The effort that his parents made to encourage Frankie and help him learn to recognize his strengths and develop other areas of competence went a long way toward preventing his reading disorder from trampling his self-esteem into the ground. While Frankie and his parents continued to have their moments of frustration during the following years, Frankie's reading skills slowly improved and he learned that God had given him a pretty good race car after all.

Chapter 41

School Anxiety

The case of jittery Joann. "I don't want to go, Mommy," Joann said with tears in her eyes while finishing breakfast before school. This had been happening for the last couple of days and had caught Mrs. Reid entirely off guard.

Six-year-old Joann had loved kindergarten and had done well in her first three weeks of first grade. While Mrs. Reid was able to get Joann calmed down and into the car, Joann often turned on the tears again as soon as they entered the school parking lot. As Mrs. Reid walked her into class, Joann regained her composure once they entered the classroom. With a few nervous glances at her mom, Joann quietly watched some other children play a computer game until the teacher began the class day. Mrs. Reid was able to slip out and Joann would be fine for the rest of the day. However, Joann's anxious feelings really bothered Mrs. Reid and she felt confused and sad that her daughter was feeling this way about school.

Why Does This Happen?

An anxious predisposition. Some children are described by their parents as being "born worriers." A look at the family tree often reveals a history of worriers and suggests that this inclination has a hereditary component for some children. While these children are not doomed to a life of apprehension, they may have to work harder to learn how to cope with everyday stressors and challenges. See the related problems of "Learning To Make Friends," "Giving Up," and "Fears" for more ideas.

Anxious expectations are frequently at the root of anxious feelings and behavior. Children worry about specific negative outcomes or just "something bad happening." They may have difficulty identifying and verbalizing these fearful thoughts, which can make it harder to get at the source of the problem. Often, these anxious and negative expectations are exaggerated, but your child is not able to recognize this or formulate a better way of looking at things. As a result, anxious feelings sprout up and your child tries to avoid the situation.

A fear of new situations is common for anxious children. Almost everyone has had on occasion the experience of feeling a little shy or awkward, often in response to being in an unfamiliar social situation. Anxious children often experience this more intensely and more frequently than their peers. The fear of social rejection and a lack of social confidence team up to do a powerplay on the anxious child's desire to tackle new situations. The result is that the child turns down many new and fun opportunities and gravitates toward settings that feel comfortable and safe.

What Can I Do?

Talk with your child about what is worrying her. Worried feelings are the result of worried thoughts. Help your child uncover what she is afraid will happen. You can do this by pinpointing the situation that prompts the anxious behavior and then by helping your child identify what she thinks about when that situation happens.

You can ask, "When you start getting ready for school, what do you think about? What goes through your mind? Has anyone been mean to you or hurt you? What are you afraid might happen?" Perhaps your child has had a negative experience at school that you are not aware of. Gently explore the situation with your child, helping her to feel cared about but not pressured. With a little help, many children are able to tell you what they are worried about.

Talk to the teacher. If your child's anxiousness is notable, it may be helpful to have a talk with your child's teacher. He or she may be able to provide you with helpful information, insight, and observations that your child cannot provide. A good teacher will have genuine interest in your child and can be a valuable ally in helping your child learn to handle her anxiety.

Develop coping skills. As you explore your child's worried thoughts, you may find that she is anxious about a very real situation. Perhaps a peer has been mean to her on the playground or maybe she is struggling with an academic skill. If this is the case, the goal is to help her learn to handle the situation by thinking, saying, and doing the right things. For instance, if a child is bothering her on the playground, she can:

Think: "I don't have to let her bother me, I can just ignore her."
Say: Nothing (ignore).
Do: Walk away and find someone else to play with that is more friendly.

If a task at school has become difficult, she can:

Think: "This is hard right now, but if I keep on trying, God will help me do my best."
Say: Ask the teacher or a parent for help.
Do: Keep on trying her hardest.

Giving your child a concrete plan for how to handle the situation and then rehearsing it together is like throwing a strong rope to someone who has fallen into a big hole. They feel a sense of relief and hope because it gives them something practical and solid to hold onto that can help them begin to change their situation. You may have to modify various aspects of the plan as time goes by to fit your child's changing situation, but you will be teaching your child the powerful lesson that she has what it takes to handle a tough situation that previously she was trying to run away from.

Be on the lookout for negative thinking traps. You may find that your child's anxiety is fueled not so much by a real dilemma, but by an exaggerated or imagined one. Your child may have fallen into a negative thinking trap of overgeneralization, all or nothing thinking, mind reading, or some other variety. For instance, perhaps your child has jumped to the conclusion that no one likes her because two girls that she wanted to play with were off playing by themselves one day and she couldn't find anyone else to play with. As a result she was wandering around at lunch time by herself and felt awkward and left out. The problem here is that your child is viewing this isolated situation as proof that no one likes her, when it is nothing of the sort.

Instead of telling your child that her thinking may be mistaken, it is more helpful to let her discover this on her own. As your child describes the situation, ask her questions that will help her examine the validity of her conclusions. You can ask questions such as:

- "If two children are playing by themselves one day, does it mean that they don't like the other children in the class?"
- "When you wanted to play with Emily, did that mean that you didn't like Megan, or Abby, or Melissa, or did you still like them too?"
- "Did you ask the other girls if you could join in?"
- "Did you look for any other children to play with?"
- "What are the names of some children in your class who you think are nice?"
- "How would you say 'Hi' to another person, or ask them to play?"

Gently lead your child to the realization that there are other ways of looking at the situation. Then, crystallize your work together by devising a simple summary that is a much more accurate way to view the situation. In our example, a good summary would be:

"Allison and Carol wanted to play by themselves today and that's okay. Sometimes I like to do that too. I can always ask if I can join in or look for someone else to play with, like Kelsey or Jenna. The friendlier I am to others, the more friends I will make."

There may be many times when you will need to help your child correct her anxious thinking. As you do this in different situations, you may find that she falls prey to certain negative thinking traps repeatedly. You can point this out to her, using past examples to help her see how these negative thinking traps cause her to think things that are not true and worry about things that are not likely to happen. Be patient as your child learns the important skill of keeping her thoughts on track.

Get your child to school. If your parental instinct tells you that your child may be in an unsafe situation at school, then listen to your child and investigate the situation to make sure that your child is safe before sending her back to school. If you do not have any concerns about your child's safety in the school environment, then getting your child to school is an important part of the process. Blending a caring attitude with a firm dose of reality, tell your child that she *will* be going to school. Period. This type of approach helps to diminish your child's hopes of talking her way out of school and can reduce the motivation to argue. Let her know that you want to talk with her about her feelings and help her with whatever is bothering her. But not going to school is not an option.

Keep your child at school. For children who become anxious at school, allowing them to leave school can inadvertently reinforce their anxious behavior. Establish the precedent from the start that your child will stay at school when she feels anxious. If legitimately needed, she can take a short trip to the nurse's office, but will then be taken back to the classroom as soon as she is able.

Give attention for the right behavior. While you will genuinely listen to your child's feelings and help her correct her thinking, do not accidentally reward her anxious or avoidant behavior by providing too much attention. After you have responded to your child's feelings and have discussed helpful ideas for handling the situation, decrease the emotional intensity a couple notches by moving into "matter-of-fact mode." Communicate through your actions and words that your child is going to school and while she may feel a bit nervous, she can handle it. There is no emergency;

she will be okay. Reducing your immediate attention to overanxious behavior and responding with a calm demeanor can help your child to regain her composure as she follows your lead and takes confidence in your confidence that things will be all right.

Pray together. This is a wonderful opportunity for your child to learn that God is a very present help in times of trouble. Pray together that your child will feel God's comfort and will remember that he is always with her. Specifically ask God to help your child to be brave (just like David was brave when he beat Goliath, and Esther was brave when she talked to the king) and to learn how to handle the situation the best way. Thank God in advance for helping your child to get through this situation and for always being right there with us.

Get additional help if needed. If your child appears excessively anxious or does not respond readily to your efforts to help, consult with a child therapist who can further evaluate the situation and help your child learn how to conquer her anxiety.

 ## How Do I Put It All Together?

The case of jittery Joann. Joann's resistance to school in the mornings continued for a few weeks, with some days more intense than others. Eventually, Mrs. Reid uncovered that Joann was feeling left out because the one girl that she had made friends with the second week, Sarah, had suddenly paired off with another girl and they spent all their play time together. Mrs. Reid's heart went out to her little girl, who had always been a little shy, as she saw the sadness and hurt on her face. She also knew that this would not be the last time that something like this might happen, so she decided to help Joann learn how to handle this situation, rather than run from it.

After dinner one night, Mrs. Reid talked with Joann about what had happened with her friend. "Joann, I know you felt really sad about what happened with Sarah. Do you still feel that way?" Mrs. Reid asked.

"Nobody likes me there," Joann sulked. "All the girls already have all their friends. I don't ever want to go there again."

"Honey, I know that it can really hurt when you try to be friends and someone doesn't try back," Mrs. Reid empathized with her daughter. "What else do you think you can do, besides quitting school?" she asked. Joann could think of nothing.

With gentle questions, Mrs. Reid helped Joann to see that if Sarah is becoming really good friends with another girl, it doesn't mean that they still can't be friends or that Sarah doesn't like her. "Yeah, I guess Sarah could still be my friend," concluded Joann. They talked about how it is fun to have more than one friend and moved the conversation toward how Joann could get to know some of the other girls in the class.

With Mrs. Reid's prompting, Joann was able to name two other girls she thought were nice and they talked about how Joann could get to know those girls. They put together a simple plan for what Joann can say at recess or lunch times to join into games of tag or ask another girl if she wants to play (decide who she wants to talk to, decide what to say, say it in a friendly way).

When Joann complained about going to school in the mornings, Mrs. Reid matter-of-factly affirmed that Joann was going to school and reminded her that there were many nice children in her class and the more friendly she was to others, the more others would want to play with her. They reviewed Joann's plan for joining in and asking others to play and did a few quick mock rehearsals. Before they climbed in the car, they took time to pray together and thanked God for making Joann such a friendly and wonderful girl and for helping her to be friendly to everyone in her class.

While Joann continued to shed tears before school on occasion, these episodes began to decrease in intensity, and then in frequency. She began to come home with reports of playing tag or doing a fun activity with another girl and eventually got to know a couple girls that she had not played with before.

Occasionally, Mrs. Reid still had to help Joann find her way out of negative thinking traps. However, as Joann had more positive peer experiences, she found it easier put things in proper perspective, which began a positive chain of events. Her social confidence slowly increased and she became friends with a small group of girls.

Joann even had two of her friends stay at her house overnight one weekend. As Joann's school resistance faded out, Mrs. Reid made sure to let Joann know how proud she was that she had turned a tough situation into an opportunity to make some brand new friends, while keeping her old ones.

Appendix A

School Behavior Charts and Homework Log

Daily School Behavior Chart

Name: _____ Day: _____

Please rate the student with a G (Great!), F (Fair), or P (Poor) for the following target behaviors:

Target Behaviors	Subject				

As we have discussed, please send this sheet home with _____ each day.

Teacher Initial: _____.   Thanks, _____.

Daily School Behavior Chart

Name: _____ **Date:** _____

Dear Teacher, please rate the student's behavior in each of the following areas for each class period or subject: 4=Excellent, 3=Good, 2=Fair, 1=Poor, 0=Absolutely unacceptable.

Behavior	1st	2nd	3rd	4th	5th	6th	7th

Teacher Initial: ____ ____ ____ ____ ____ ____ ____

As we have discussed, please initial and send this sheet home with _____ on a daily basis.

Thanks, _____.

Homework Log

Name: _____

Dear _____, please review this homework log each day for accuracy, initial at the bottom and send home with _____. Thanks!

Subject	Monday	Tuesday	Wednesday	Thursday	Friday

Teacher Initial: ____   ____   ____   ____   ____

Appendix B

Your Child's Development

The work of developmental researchers Jean Piaget and Erik Erikson provides us with a foundational knowledge of how children develop. This knowledge can help us understand the thinking abilities and social challenges characteristic of different ages. In turn, we can then develop reasonable expectations and provide appropriate responses to help our children successfully move through each important stage of development. Keep in mind that the suggested ages below are approximate. Some children reach these stages on a slightly faster or slower timetable.

Birth to Eighteen Months

Thinking abilities. These children learn about the world through the senses and through repeated experience. Gradually, they will develop object permanence, which is the ability to view objects as being separate from themselves.

Social challenges. Erikson labeled this stage as basic trust versus mistrust. The goal is for each child to develop a sense of trust and to learn that the world is a safe place. This sense of trust forms the basis for later stages of development.

Things to do. Provide a stimulating environment with lots of brightly colored objects, room for exploration, and plenty of interaction. Promptly meet your child's physical and emotional needs, create a safe environment, and maintain appropriate behavioral limits.

Eighteen Months to Three Years

Thinking abilities. Children increase their ability to use language to communicate. However, they still see the world only from their own viewpoint and are not able to reason logically or consider the consequences of their actions.

Social challenges. With increasing abilities, toddlers are learning to do many things on their own that previously had to be done for them. They have an increased awareness of themselves as individuals and understandably want more independence. However, they cannot do all that they would like due to physical limitations, safety concerns, and time constraints. Their verbal skills and patience are still developing, and all of this is new to them, which explains their need for reassurance, tendency to cling, and penchant for throwing tantrums.

Things to do. This stage serves as a building block for the development of self-esteem and self-confidence. Whenever possible, let these children do as much as they're able to do, offer a predetermined set of choices, and provide gentle assistance with task completion. Both excessive parental control and a lack of opportunity for autonomy may delay skill-building and the development of confidence in their abilities.

Three to Five Years

Thinking abilities. Still seeing the world very much from their own viewpoint and not yet being able to reason logically, preschool-age children also experience what is known as "magical thinking." They believe that what they think is real. You guessed it: Santa Claus, the tooth fairy, and monsters are real to them. Not surprisingly, fears and nightmares appear more frequently during this stage of development.

Social challenges. At this age, children tend to show increased initiative, become self-motivated and active, and enjoy learning new things. They can now cooperatively interact with other children in creative play. The goal is to help the child develop the skills to succeed in and enjoy these new peer relationships and to develop a positive attitude toward learning and exploration.

Things to do. As these children are not yet logical thinkers, reasoning often fails to relieve their common fears. Concrete responses such as night-lights, examining the room together, and reassurance that you will protect them are often useful, as are simple coping statements, such as, "Mom and Dad will keep me safe," and "I can do it if I don't give up." Help them develop mastery over feared objects by incorporating them in a safe and friendly way into your play together. Create an environment that encourages and rewards learning and trying new things. Help your children to master basic social behaviors, such as taking turns, which will aide their interactions with peers. Criticism and parental overcontrol may inhibit self-confidence and contribute to the fear that they are doing something wrong or cannot succeed without parental direction.

Six to Twelve Years

Thinking abilities. Children now begin to understand the reasons for rules and can link consequences with behavior. They can take in different aspects of a situation and understand that there can be more than one possible solution to a problem. Their ability to understand a situation from another person's point of view also begins to develop at this time. The ability to engage in complex abstract reasoning, however, is still out of reach.

Social challenges. Children in this age range have now entered the world of school and peers. They must master academic tasks and learn important social skills that will lay the foundation for success both now and in later years. The goal is to help these children succeed in both of these areas, as their ability to have successful academic and social experiences and to respond effectively to challenging experiences will have a significant impact on their developing self-view.

Things to do. Without taking over, do what you can to help your children succeed in the areas of school and peer relationships by helping them develop good study habits, holding realistic and positive expectations, being consistent with reasonable behavioral limits, and obtaining additional help if needed. As always, keep your relationship with your children strong by spending one-on-one time as well as time together as a family. Teach your children to effectively handle failures and disappointments and to develop a balanced view of themselves.

Guide them in learning positive ways to relate with peers and effective methods for solving peer and family problems. Encourage them to consider other people's feelings and require them to treat others with respect. Make sure that your children know how valuable they are to God and how positively he thinks of them. Provide lots of positive feedback and encouragement, gradually helping them to develop the self-confidence and skills they will need to successfully manage the teenage years just around the corner.

You can contact Dr. Cartmell at

1761 S. Naperville Road
Suite 200
Wheaton, IL 60187
(630) 260–0606

For helpful parenting tips, articles, Q&A, and more, visit Dr. Cartmell's website at:
www.parentlifesaver.com